"A MUST FOR MYSTERY BUFFS."
Cleveland Plain Dealer

Mystery addicts: now you can get a good night's sleep.

With DETECTIONARY by your bedside, no need to toss and turn, trying to remember who played Charlie Chan in the movies before and after Warner Oland.

Never again will you lie awake, wondering if it's too late to phone a friend to ask whether Richard Stark wrote about Parker or vice versa, or if one of them is Donald E. Westlake, and which one of them has no first name. No more falling asleep at last and waking up bleary-eyed, trying to remember the question.

Never again. Think of it.

"WHODUNIT FANS, STORY EDITORS, ASPIRING WRITERS, GAME SHOW CONTESTANTS AND COLLECTORS OF ODD INFORMATION WILL FIND IT A USEFUL COMPENDIUM OF PLOTS AND CHARACTERS."
Los Angeles Times

DETECTIONARY

a biographical dictionary of leading characters
in detective and mystery fiction, including
famous and little-known sleuths, their helpers,
rogues both heroic and sinister, and some
of their most memorable adventures, as
recounted in novels, short stories, and films.

Compiled by Otto Penzler, Chris
Steinbrunner, Charles Shibuk,
Marvin Lachman, Francis M.
Nevins, Jr.

Edited by Otto Penzler, Chris
Steinbrunner & Marvin Lachman

Conceived and produced by
Mill Roseman

BALLANTINE BOOKS • NEW YORK

Library of Congress Catalog Card Number: 75-27326

ISBN 0-345-29086-0

This edition published by arrangement with
The Overlook Press

Originally published in a private, limited edition by
Hammermill Paper Company, Inc.

Manufactured in the United States of America

First Ballantine Books Edition: December 1980

PREFACE

Mystery fiction has a history almost as old as literature itself. Enthusiasts are known in every country and at every social level. A substantial part of each year's list of new books, films and television programs is devoted to meeting their interests.

Prior to the compilation of this book there had not, to our knowledge, ever been published a biographical dictionary listing the major characters of detective fiction. For the aficionado, and even the more casual reader, this appeared to be a distinct need, to which this volume sought to provide at least a partial answer.

The book you hold is not the first incarnation of the DETECTIONARY. It was published originally, in a private, limited, numbered edition, by Hammermill Paper Company, for its clients and colleagues in the world of book publishing. It was received with gratifying enthusiasm, and then a curious thing happened—a mystery not unlike some of those found in the book's pages. It kept disappearing from the shelves of the publishers to whom it had been sent, where it was intended to remain as a reference.

The vanished copies had made their way home, to the bookshelves and the night tables of the publishers and their families. Hammermill began receiving letters of praise, not for the papers which the book had been developed to demonstrate, but for the contents themselves.

Among these letters, a large proportion contained requests, often importunate, for additional copies, or at least for information as to where they could be purchased. Since the original edition, by intent, was small and soon exhausted, these requests could not be met. We learned that a number of copies had found their way into rare-book shops, where they were commanding a heady price.

Now, thanks to the insight and enterprise of The Overlook Press whose President, Peter Mayer, was one of the original volume's recipients, the evidenced interest in the book can be satisfied. Devotees of mystery and crime fiction can again meet their favorite heroes and villains, and perhaps make new acquaintances among characters they had not previously encountered.

As a first effort of its kind, this volume undoubtedly suffers from many of the disabilities that inevitably affect such undertakings. Some readers will find their favorites slighted. Others will quarrel with the judgments and emphases which reflect the enthusiasms of our contributors. To survey the vast body of detective literature, select the most representative and significant examples, compress them in this brief compass and yet retain something of the flavor of the originals, is a large and perhaps also a dangerous undertaking.

We were fortunate to find five dedicated armchair detectives, steeped in the genre, who were bold enough to take the case. Their collaboration in the compilation of this book and its subsequent revision for this edition, has at least laid the basis for the further scholarship in the field which their pioneering has already stimulated.

Otto Penzler, a Sherlock Holmes devotee, is a member of the Baker Street Irregulars and the Priory Scholars. A long-time bibliophile, he owns an extensive collection of rare and early detective fiction and memorabilia.

Chris Steinbrunner, an officer of the Mystery Writers of America, sold his first radio script—a mystery in the "Shadow" series—while he was still in high school. He has written and produced many television programs, including specials on James Bond and Sherlock Holmes.

Charles Shibuk is a member of the Mystery Writers, a founder of the Fantasy Film Club, a contributor to "The Armchair Detective," and a paperback mystery collector of almost 30 years' standing. Marvin Lachman, also a frequent contributor to "The Armchair

Detective," specializes in the study of regional mysteries. Francis M. Nevins is a lawyer who boasts a collection of more than 3,000 volumes of detective fiction, and has edited collections of stories in the field.

The shape of the hardcover book is the product of the considerable talents of the late Jerome Snyder, protean artist, illustrator, designer and author, and of his wife, Gertrude Snyder, who is responsible for the design of this revised and updated edition. In the compilation of the Index, we are indebted to her and to Marcy Yurmark.

For the interest, vision and encouragement which made possible the first appearance of this book, and laid the basis for this present edition, we and the readers to whom it brings pleasure owe a debt of gratitude to Hammermill Paper Company.

Mill Roseman

INTRODUCTION

It was a momentous day in April, 1841, when "Graham's," a now-forgotten magazine, published the first detective story: "The Murders in the Rue Morgue," by its own famous editor Edgar Allan Poe.

This short story, today more widely read than ever before, marked the first appearance of C. Auguste Dupin, the father of the modern detective as we know him today. In the 130 years which have passed, M. Dupin has accumulated a vast band of successors; their critical acclaim and popular success continue.

This DETECTIONARY has been created to serve as a guide and an introduction to M. Dupin and to such other long-celebrated detectives as Sherlock Holmes, Hercule Poirot, Sam Spade, and Ellery Queen, as well as to some much more recent members of the fraternity, detective heroes like Lew Archer and Rabbi David Small, whose current exploits are noted with increasing regularity on the best-seller lists.

Lesser-known sleuths, such as Roger Sheringham and the Doctors Thorndyke and Priestley, who were famous in their day but are now almost (happily, not quite) forgotten, are also counted in our survey, along with many of their even more obscure brethren. Many of our detectives never appeared between book covers, but had their exploits recorded in a wide range of magazines. These, too, are examined in this survey.

A selected list of celebrated, unusual or otherwise particularly noteworthy cases—usually from novels, but including many which appeared as short stories—is also cited here, primarily to illustrate and recall the milieu in which these detectives functioned.

As Sherlock Holmes had his faithful friend and assistant Dr. Watson, so too did many more of these detectives have their helpers. Their services may have ranged from bumbling to vital, but each served at least to illuminate the brilliance and ingenuity of a great detective; these, too, are included.

Since it is the detective's function to solve crimes—ranging from petty theft to the most gruesome of murders—it is obviously necessary that there be criminal adversaries to test the mettle of our great sleuths.

These, however, we have been reluctant to list, since the premature revelation of the identity of any of these hidden villains should be a punishable offense. We have limited our study to such far-from-secret professional criminals as Dr. Fu Manchu—whose very name is a synonym for indescribable evil—and to a few well-known ornaments of the criminal classes. It is, after all, notable that Sir Arthur Conan Doyle's brother-in-law, E. W. Hornung, created the master thief Raffles as a necessary obverse to the infallible detective of the Sherlock Holmes variety, and, furthermore, many of those rogues, emulating the real-life Vidocq, eventually joined the forces of law and order.

Finally, we have included a selected group of mystery and suspense films, many of which feature the same detectives, helpers and rogues listed in the literary sections. Mystery has been a part of the art of the motion picture from its beginnings: the very first film to attempt any sort of plot, "The Great Train Robbery," is the story of a crime and the apprehension of its perpetrators: a mystery film. Crime films and melodramas account for a healthy percentage of the motion pictures produced each year—so large a concentration, indeed, that the section on film included in this book can be no more than the beginning of a proper study. Many shuddery favorites—including films which have won the Edgar Award of the Mystery Writers of America as Best Mystery of the Year—are omitted here. What has been attempted, since this is essentially a guide to literary detectives, is a brief survey of some of the best detective work done in films, designed to stir memories of shadowy manor houses and dark pursuers—for the mystery story, in the images evoked by the printed page or those manifested on the screen, is a highly visual medium.

Said Sherlock Holmes to his most faithful chronicler, "I know, my dear Watson, that you share my love for all that is bizarre and outside the conventions and humdrum routine of everyday life." Not only Watson shared that love. And it is to this melodramatic, grotesque, excitement-filled corner outside the boundaries of the everyday that we hope the DETECTIONARY will be an entertaining guide.

Chris Steinbrunner / Charles Shibuk / Otto Penzler

CLUES TO THE DETECTIONARY

As noted, this dictionary of detective fiction is comprised of four sections—one on the detectives themselves, one on rogues and companions in crime or its detection, one on celebrated cases, and one on the detective and mystery motion picture—plus an alphabetical index to authors.

Since detectives and their quarry are notorious for crossing lines, many entries are found in more than one section. To facilitate cross-reference, we have worked out a system of clues.

Each section has its own symbol: ★ for detectives, ● for rogues and helpers, ■ for cases, and ▲ for movies.

In the text, a symbol next to a name or title indicates that it will also be found in the section indicated. Thus, the listing for Sam Spade, in the detectives section, also carries a ▲, and one among the titles will have a ■, indicating that Mr. Spade will be found under movies and cases.

Titles enclosed in quotation marks have been published in story form only; others appeared as books.

DETECTIVES

Sleuths courageous and timorous, ratiocinative, lucky and rambunctious, from Abbott, Pat and Jean to Zoom, Sidney.

ABBOTT, PAT and JEAN
creator FRANCES CRANE

The parents of pretty, dark-haired Jean Holly of Elm Hill, Illinois, were killed in an auto accident when she was 18. She moved to an artists' colony in Santa Maria, New Mexico, where she opened a store called "The Turquoise Shop." Here, she met Pat Abbott, a tough private detective from San Francisco who enjoys painting. A native of Wyoming, Pat has dark hair, green eyes.

Pat and Jean marry, but World War II soon separates them as Pat, a Marine Corps lieutenant, spends two years overseas doing intelligence work. When he returns, Jean joins him in New Orleans, where they take an apartment (and encounter murder) in an old Southern mansion. Pat does most of the team's detective work, while Jean frequently stumbles into danger.

ABNER, UNCLE
creator MELVILLE DAVISSON POST

Uncle Abner is the most famous detective in literature known only by his first name. He lives in the America of Millard Fillmore's Presidency in a mountain community of Virginia. He is grim, yet quite likable in a pioneer-rugged sort of way. There are no brilliant feats of deduction or exhaustive examination of scientific minutiae for the Virginia squire. Instead, he relies on his knowledge of people and his judgment of their souls to help him in his investigations. He has no official status and does not seek the job of crime-solving, but his strong moral convictions (strengthened by a deep knowledge of the Bible) compel him to act as the righter of wrongs and protector of the innocent in his community.

ADAMS, NURSE
see PINKERTON, MISS

ALCAZAR, DR.
creator PHILIP MAC DONALD

Ellery Queen★ once had described Dr. Alcazar as "a Sherlock Holmes★ and an Arsène Lupin● crammed simultaneously into

3

the same pair of pants." Although this self-styled clairvoyant functions as a detective, he is, nonetheless, also a charlatan. The Doctor (a title, incidentally, to which he has no right!) is first encountered on the midway of a small circus in California. He is giving readings into the future for as little as 50¢.

Alcazar's appearance is impressive: tall, graceful, lean. His face is of "extraordinary pallor; his dark eyes, large and lustrous and glowing. His black, well-tended hair, impressively gray at the temples, surmounted an Olympian brow. . . ." He uses his detective skills to make accurate guesses about the people who come to him for readings. This is far from lucrative, so he decides to turn his talents to solving a crime for which a reward has been offered. Success leads him to contemplate setting up business as a private investigator, aided by his weight-guesser friend, the loyal Avvie du Pois.

ALLEYN, CHIEF INSPECTOR RODERICK
creator NGAIO MARSH

Physically tough, Roderick Alleyn is a good man to have nearby in moments of danger. He is intelligent, perceptive, and cultured enough to appreciate and discuss the theatre, art, and music. He can move about quite easily in social circles with friends like Lord Robert "Bunchy" Gospell. The man who chronicles Alleyn's adventure is Nigel Bathgate●, a journalist.

Alleyn does not look like a typical policeman and would, in fact, "do" very nicely at any social gathering. This should be no surprise, since his mother, Lady Alleyn, is prominent in British social circles. He is tall and lean, has dark hair and gray eyes with corners that turn down. He is a serious man, not given to smiling easily. Nonetheless, he is handsome and his deep voice and lean, long-fingered hands impress women meeting their first policeman.

He remains detached in most of his cases, though he is decidedly human. He becomes emotionally involved when one of his friends is murdered. His involvement takes the form of love when, during one case, he meets the attractive and famous portrait painter, Agatha Troy, whom he later marries. The Alleyns are to be separated for more than 3½ years during World War II, due to Roderick's assignment to New Zealand. Their meeting, on his return, is poignant.

APPLEBY, JOHN
creator MICHAEL INNES, pseudonym of J. I. M. Stewart

John Appleby has had a liberal education but has also been through intensive training in a modern police college. His is clearly a schooled, but still free, intelligence. He also possesses the useful habits of contemplation, poise, and forcefulness. He even marries well, albeit for love, his bride being an attractive, talented sculptress named Judith Raven.

Appleby rises rapidly through the ranks, solving many difficult cases which garner him considerable publicity. He is appointed Assistant-Commissioner of Scotland Yard and is even knighted. When he retires after serving as Commissioner of Metropolitan Police for all of London, it is not to a life of inactivity. While Sir John and Lady Judith finally get to relax and do some traveling, they often find a murder which can only be solved by his special talents.

ARCHER, LEW
creator ROSS MACDONALD, pseudonym of Kenneth Millar

Lew Archer has succeeded both Sam Spade★ and Philip Marlowe★ as this country's outstanding private detective. He was born June 2, 1914, and joined the Long Beach, California, police in 1935; unfortunately, he was too honest to remain with that particular police department, leaving it to become an independent investigator, his career ever since, except for World War II experience in Military Intelligence.

Many of his early investigations involved divorce cases and, ironically, he was divorced, because his wife, Sue, did not like the people with whom his profession caused him to associate. He is painfully honest but practical. Until 1969, he avoided involvement with women he met on cases, though he was never indifferent to the charms of attractive females.

Although in a violent, sordid profession, Lew Archer remains a decent, sensitive man. He is especially sympathetic to the problems of the young in society. His tastes are catholic and he can appreciate a good book, a classical symphony, and a painting by Kuniyoshi. He hates Los Angeles smog but remains in the city because that is where the services of a private detective are most needed. He can readily identify many trees, flowers, and birds.

ARMISTON, OLIVER
see PARR, DEPUTY

ASHENDEN
creator W. SOMERSET MAUGHAM

Ashenden is the first important secret service man whose cases are presented in a truly realistic manner. He demonstrates that the life of a spy is no great game, filled with secret societies, beautiful women, and hairbreadth escapes. It is sometimes boring, sometimes confusing, and sometimes frightening. Ashenden is a writer, therefore unusually well-qualified to work as a spy. His profession gives him freedom to move.

He has an extensive knowledge of European languages. He admires goodness but can live with evil. He is generally detached in his relationships with people, being interested in even the dullest men but rarely feeling any more than a superficial interest. He has the ability to see the defects, as well as the merits, of those few with whom he is intimate. Everyone he meets becomes source material for another story—hardly the basis for a deep feeling of mutual affection.

Since he is a famous writer, he is perfectly willing to let his familiar name give him advantages he could not enjoy otherwise. He is never bored. It is his theory that only stupid people require the outside world to keep themselves amused—anyone of intellect can employ his own resources to prevent boredom.

Ashenden is based on the real life exploits of Maugham, who served in British Intelligence during World War I. Perhaps this explains why there is not a word of description of the hero.

AVENGER, THE
creator KENNETH ROBESON, pseudonym of Lester Dent

The underworld named Richard Henry Benson "The Avenger" in tribute to his dedication to the fight against crime. Relatively small (5'8", 160 pounds), he is nevertheless athletic. He has shiny black hair, a lean, square face, pale gray eyes. He is a multi-millionaire, of supernormal intelligence, skilled in more professions than any man on earth: medicine, surgery, dentistry, law, electrical engineering, aerodynamics.

"The Avenger" has six capable, loyal aides and he, himself carries two weapons, a pistol and a knife nicknamed, respectively, "Mike" and "Ike." Perhaps his friends and weapons substitute for his family. His wife, Alicia, and daughter, Alice, were killed by thugs.

BAILEY, STUART
creator ROY HUGGINS

Bailey is an honest, pipe-smoking private detective who started his career quite modestly after World War II. Not having an office of his own, he was content to rent desk space in a telephone-answering service on Broadway, not far from "Skid Row" in downtown Los Angeles. He drove an old, pre-war automobile and charged his clients modest rates. A decade later, spurred on by his success as a television hero, he has a much more posh business address on the world-famous Sunset Strip.

A sensitive man, Bailey, unlike many detectives, abhors unnecessary violence—especially hitting women. He has many books (which he has read) in his apartment near Westlake Park, and he also collects records, especially folk songs and ballads.

BARON, THE
creator ANTHONY MORTON, pseudonym of John Creasey

Early in his career, John Mannering led a double life—a respectable gentleman on one hand and, on the other, the flamboyant jewel thief known as The Baron. When he married Lorna, a lovely and talented artist, he turned over a new leaf; his Baronial adventures over the past 25 years have been on the side of the law. He is both a reputable antiques dealer and a consultant to Scotland Yard. His old rival, Superintendent Bristow, cannot purge doubts that The Baron has changed.

BATMAN▲
creator BOB KANE

Hooded, with a spined, bat's-wing cape, the muscular Batman was the perfect 1930's Depression personification of a crimefighter: anonymous, gymnastic, relentless. Yet, unlike most comic-book heroes, Batman often solved real mysteries. In nearly all his adventures, he demonstrated ratiocination—unmasking mystery villains or determining where a gang would strike next.

Batman is a vengeful, brooding man of mystery, identityless, with a driving hatred of crime. When young Bruce Wayne's parents are killed by a gunman, he vows war on the underworld, taking as his symbol a bat—the fearsome creature of darkness. Originally, Batman is a somber, sinister, dark hero. After a year he adopts a young orphan, Dick Grayson, whose circus acrobat parents have been killed in a fall. The two athletes form the team of Batman and Robin.

The setting of their adventure is Gotham City, a metropolis resembling New York in more than name. It is overrun by criminal gangs ruled by incredibly colorful plotters: the Penguin, perpetually in formal dress, with an obsession about umbrellas so great he uses them in all his crimes; and the clown-faced Joker, who starts each daring robbery with a bizarre pun. Just as Batman is a grotesque figure, so are his adversaries—Two-Face, the Cat Woman, etc. He often battles them against industrial exhibits where ordinary, everyday objects are reconstructed as giant replicas.

The team's personal lives are fantastic. Wayne is heir to a fortune, and lives in a suburban manor, under which lies a vast cave where Batman and Robin train for their athletic crimefighting, keep mementoes of their cases and house their vehicles of pursuit: The Bat-car, sleek and fast, and the Bat-plane, recently replaced by the Bat-jet. A traditional English butler, Alfred, is the only person who knows their identity. They are summoned by Gotham City officialdom when a searchlight flashes the gigantic outline of a bat against the night sky. Batman's relationship with his handsome young ward has been the subject of psychiatric speculation, most intensely in Dr. Frederic Wertham's "Seduction of the Innocent."

In recent years, there have been attempts to modernize Batman's traditionalist approach to mystery cases: he has given up most of his aristocratic trappings, including Alfred, and Robin has gone to college, hopefully to a calmer life. Largely inspired by the pulp hero, The Shadow, young cartoonist Bob Kane created Batman for the same publishing house that enjoyed such success with another crime-fighter, Superman.

BAYLISS, BERT
creator CAROLYN WELLS

Bert Bayliss, a New York private detective of the World War I era, was born to a wealthy family and great social position. He became a detective because "it pleased his sense of humor to pursue a calling so incongruous with his birth and station." He accepts a case only when it appeals to him by being especially difficult. He has created a Doctor Watson● in his own mind, "Harris," to whom he explains his theories. "Harris" must question those ideas but ultimately is forced to agree that Bayliss' theories are correct.

BEAUMONT, NED
creator DASHIELL HAMMETT

Ned Beaumont is a political hanger-on, a friend of Paul Madvig●, the city's political boss, in "The Glass Key"■. He is tall, lean, narrow-eyed and mustached, a cigar-smoking gambler whose hat always seems a bit too small. He has an acute fondness for money and pretty girls—not necessarily in that order. His foray into the detective field is as an amateur only.

BECK, MARTIN ....
creators MAJ SJÖWALL and PER WAHLÖÖ

For nearly half his life, Detective Superintendent Martin Beck has been a policeman, usually in Stockholm, Sweden. Although he is not ambitious, promotions have come regularly because of his intelligence, thoroughness and conscientiousness; if necessary, he will give up a vacation to undertake a new assignment.

Beck is in his mid-forties but his hair has not turned gray. He has a lean face with a broad forehead and a strong jaw. His mouth is thin and wide, his nose short and straight. If he smiled occasionally, one would see healthy, white teeth. He is thin, round-shouldered and always looks tired.

A few women might consider him attractive but most find him ordinary. His long marriage is no longer happy. His wife has become lazy, self-satisfied—no longer the lively girl he married. He, in turn, finds fault with her too quickly. They try vainly to preserve their marriage, largely for their teenage children, a boy and a girl.

BECK, PAUL
creator M. MC DONNELL BODKIN

Paul Beck describes his own ability, which is considerable, in the most off-hand way. "I have no more system than the hound that gets on the fox's scent and keeps on it," he says. "I just go by the rule of thumb, and muddle and puzzle out my cases the best I can." His best is quite good. He enjoys a reputation as one of the cleverest detectives in London—a man who had "puzzled out mysteries" where others had failed. He is stout, strongly built, and wears dark gray tweed, "suggesting the notion of a retired milkman" more than a detective. His face is bronzed and weatherbeaten, and he has light brown hair and reddish-brown side-whiskers. He has an innocent smile and his blue eyes are always wide, giving the appearance of being surprised.

BEEF, SERGEANT WILLIAM
creator LEO BRUCE, pseudonym of Rupert Croft-Cooke

The burly, red-faced Sergeant Beef is a lackadaisical but remarkably astute village policeman who solved a number of intriguing cases in the late 1930's. After several successes, he retired from the force to return as a private inquiry agent.

In his first case he matched wits with thinly-disguised versions of Father Brown★, Lord Peter Wimsey★, and Hercule Poirot★, and outwitted them all.

BEHRENS, SAMUEL and CALDER, DANIEL
creator MICHAEL GILBERT

Two middle-aged Britishers, Samuel Behrens and Daniel Calder, were recruited as spies in the 1930's and have had a long career, considering the risks in their profession. Mr. Behrens, the elder of the two, was born in 1910 and educated at London University and at Heidelberg, where he specialized in European languages. He taught in Germany from 1929 through 1939 but was a British spy during the last six years of this career. He remained in British espionage service after World War II, merely shifting his focus to accommodate a new enemy in a colder war. His hobbies are beekeeping and chess.

Mr. Calder was born in 1913 and educated at Salisbury and at the University of Perugia in Italy. He remained in Europe as a Reuters correspondent, assigned to such capitals as Athens, Budapest, Baghdad, and Bucharest from 1932 through 1939. However, from 1935, he, too, was in the service of MI 6, the British spy group. He has also continued in this organization, working smoothly with Mr. Behrens, who lives in nearby Lamperdown, Kent, when they are not traveling. Calder's hobbies are firing small arms and playing the cello whenever time permits.

BENCOLIN, HENRI
creator JOHN DICKSON CARR

The sardonic Henri Bencolin has been called the foremost police official and the most dangerous man in Europe. He resembles Mephistopheles; his black hair, parted in the middle, twirls up like horns. His eyes gaze inscrutably and the hooked eyebrows point downward. He has high cheek-bones, an aquiline nose, a small mustache and a pointed black beard. He has an official position with the Paris Police, juge d'instruction, but has accepted fees for solving cases in his spare time. His exploits are narrated by Jeff Marle●, a journalist.

There is a legend about Bencolin, believed throughout Paris, which says that when he habituates the more questionable cafes of the city, dressed in evening clothes, someone is in danger. When he wears an ordinary sack suit, he is out for pleasure alone. He likes to drink beer, smoke cigars, and listen to the loudest jazz, sitting obscurely in a gloom of colored lights under thick tobacco smoke. Proprietors and waiters effusively bow and offer champagne. However, when he wears the familiar cloak, top hat, and silver-headed walking stick, and when there is a slight bulge under his left arm—that means trouble and he is avoided. Bencolin knows Parisians like their detectives to be picturesque.

BENSON, RICHARD HENRY
see AVENGER, THE

BENT, JOHN
creator H. C. BRANSON

A non-practicing doctor, John Bent is a genial, compassionate, bearded intellectual. Formerly an employee of the United States Government in the Intelligence Department, he is now a private detective in New York. He smokes constantly and enjoys a quiet, relaxed life.

BERESFORD, TUPPENCE and TOMMY
creator AGATHA CHRISTIE

During World War I, Tommy Beresford is working for British Intelligence (though his detractors contend that no division of the government could be less appropriately named for his talents). Prudence "Tuppence" Cowley is a nurse (the same profession which her creator had).

When Tuppence is recruited for spy work, she falls in and out of danger; she also falls in love with Tommy. They marry after the war but, soon becoming bored with peace-time activities, they form the detective agency advertised as "Blunt's Brilliant Detectives." The firm is disbanded when Tuppence gives birth to twins but reactivates herself in World War II.

The question of the ages of the Beresfords is puzzling, since their twin son, Derek, though born in 1929, is an RAF lieutenant in the war years. Obviously a precocious child! Tuppence retains a tendency to wander alone into danger throughout their career. With them, as he has been for the last fifty years, is Albert, the Beresfords' domestic mainstay.

BISHOP, ROBIN
creator GEOFFREY HOMES, pseudonym of Daniel Mainwaring

The tall, handsome debonair Robin Bishop is an unusual newspaper reporter—he is neither hard-boiled nor wise-cracking.

BLAISE, MODESTY
creator PETER O'DONNELL

The young, beautiful, curvaceous Modesty Blaise is a female James Bond. She made her debut in a British comic strip and quickly became the heroine of a movie.

BONAPARTE, INSPECTOR NAPOLEON
creator ARTHUR W. UPFIELD

Found under a tree, next to his dead mother, the infant, who would grow into the detective called Napoleon Bonaparte, was taken to the nearest mission station. Shortly thereafter, he was observed trying to eat a biographical volume on the late French emperor. The matron who named him evidently had a whimsical sense of humor.

Bony (as he is known to his friends) did well at mission school, and went on to earn an M.A. at the Brisbane University in Australia. He joined the Queensland police department, where his prowess as a tracker led to rapid promotion, ultimately to the rank of Inspector.

Suave, slender, handsome, with blue eyes, black hair, and light brown coloring, Bony has the habit of rolling his own cigarettes. His inheritance from his mixed parentage provided an uncanny ability to read "The Book of the Bush," and the faculty of reason. While he possesses an enormous ego, Bony's claim is justified that he has never failed to finalize a case.

BOND, JAMES▲
creator IAN FLEMING

A legend in his lifetime is James Bond, also known as 007, the number, assigned to him by the British Secret Service, which indicates his license to kill on their behalf. The son of a Swiss mother and Scottish father, he had a public school education before being sent down from Eton. Bond is associated with the pre-World War II Bentley he drives, and the .25 Beretta automatic he conceals in his left arm holster when on assignment. A crack shot, 007 is also a superb athlete; if caught without a gun, he can destroy an opponent with judo or karate.

Women always have found the tall, dark, muscular Bond most attractive. He has had his pick of many, ranging from duchesses and countesses to spies and doxies. Many women who develop too close a relationship with 007 die violently. In addition to enjoying women, Bond also loves to gamble, drink fine cognac and champagne, and smoke heavily. Bond is also famous for the enemies he makes—including such arch villains as SMERSH, SPECTRE, Dr. No, Goldfinger● and Le Chiffre.

BONNER, THEODOLINDA ("DOL")
creator REX STOUT

One of the few female private eyes in literature is the attractive 24-year-old "Dol" Bonner. "Dol" is essentially independent, having been left on her own when her father suffered financial ruin and killed himself. She says she hates all men because she wa jilted by her fiancé. The one exception appears to be her younger brother, whom she supports—and spoils—with the proceeds from her private detective agency. Almost twenty years after her first case, she becomes involved in one of Nero Wolfe's★ adventures and appears to be one of the women he can tolerate.

BRADLEY, MRS. BEATRICE ADELA LESTRANGE
creator GLADYS MITCHELL

Dame Beatrice Bradley is in charge of a psychiatric clinic and is the psychiatric consultant to the British Home Office. She likes traveling, walking (generally at a brisk pace), and also is a devoted scholar of the Sherlock Holmes★ Canon, which involves her in a murder. She also engages in scholarly research in her family history, particularly one ancestor: Mary Toadfax, a reputed seventeenth-century witch.

Intelligence and perception are Mrs. Bradley's strong points; her looks fall a bit short. She is quite masculine and dresses in a decidedly old-fashioned manner (she uses a motor-veil when driving). Her hand has been described as claw-like. She has black hair and "black eyes as bright as a bird's."

BRADLEY, INSPECTOR LUKE
creator HUGH PENTECOST, pseudonym of Judson Philips

The soft-spoken, tough-minded Luke Bradley began his career as a detective with the Homicide Bureau of the New York City Police Department. During World War II, he solves mysteries as a lieutenant for Naval Intelligence, bringing to his tasks the experience of his former association.

BREDDER, FATHER JOSEPH
creator LEONARD HOLTON, pseudonym of Leonard Wibberley

A member of a Franciscan order, Father Bredder is chaplain at the Convent of the Holy Innocent in Los Angeles, Cal. Born and raised in Twin Oaks (a small Ohio town near Toledo), he joined the Marine Corps in World War II and saw service in Guadalcanal. He is an avid sailor and was once part of the crew of a boat which sailed from San Pedro, Cal., to Honolulu, Hawaii. His other hobby is gardening; he is seldom happier than when he is working with the soil. Father Bredder is a big man, in his early fifties.

BROWN, FATHER
creator G. K. CHESTERTON

Apparently a gentle, commonplace priest, Father Brown appears to be rather dull-witted in the presence of his adversary. He is inconspicuously short and, Chesterton tells us, has a face "as round and dull as a Norfolk dumpling; he had eyes as empty as the North Sea; he had several brown paper parcels which he was incapable of collecting; he had a large, shabby umbrella which constanty fell to the floor." He is even given the "harmless, human name of Brown."

However, despite these outward gaucheries, Father Brown possesses a sharp, subtle, sensitive mind. His unusual method of detection ignores the standard practice of collecting clues and making deductions. Instead, he employs his understanding of human nature and tries to think like a criminal. He says: "I try to get inside a man, moving his arms and legs; but I wait till I know I'm inside a murderer, thinking his thought, wrestling with his passions; till I have bent myself into the posture of his hunched and peering hatred. Till I am really a murderer. And when I am quite sure that I feel like the murderer, of course I know who he is."

For this kind, unobtrusive Roman Catholic priest, problems of crime are not problems of law so much as they are problems of character. He rarely concerns himself with the police and his sympathies are, more often than not, with the criminal. To him, a robber is not an enemy of society who must be brought to justice and punished. To Father Brown, the criminal is a soul who must be saved, an evil-doer whose sins must be brought to light for his own good.

His greatest success comes with Flambeau●, that colossus of crime who repents, reforms and becomes an extremely successful private detective. Father Brown is considered by Ellery Queen★ to be one of the three greatest detectives of all time (Sherlock Holmes★ and C. Auguste Dupin★ are the other two).

The author, G. K. Chesterton, was a devout Roman Catholic and patterned his good-hearted little Essex clergyman after a real-life priest of his acquaintance, Father John O'Connor.

BROWN, JANE and DAGOBERT
creator DELANO AMES

Dagobert Brown, a tall, red-headed amateur detective, will go to any lengths to avoid employment; he loves to connive invitations to be a house guest. His pretty wife, Jane Hamish Brown, is British and the author of mystery novels. She is working on a travelogue titled "My American Journal." The Browns drive a second-hand car and Jane seldom breaks Dagobert's rule about never talking to the driver.

BROWN, VEE
creator CARROLL JOHN DALY

Vee Brown leads a double life. By day, he is a tough, two-fisted, hard-boiled dick; by night, he writes popular, sentimental songs under his real name, Vivian Brown. His adventures appeared in American pulp magazines in the 1930's.

BRYCE, HENRY and EMILY
creator MARGARET SCHERF

Amateur detectives Emily and Henry Bryce are furniture finishers for interior decorators on Manhattan's wealthy East Side. Henry is proficient at this well-paid, highly skilled work. His scatter-brained wife spends an inordinate amount of time worrying about her weight.

BUCKET, INSPECTOR
creator CHARLES DICKENS

Inspector Bucket is the first English detective to appear in a novel. He is the official bloodhound of the law and appears to be the prototype—stolid, composed, confident, honest, thoughtful, hard-working, and chivalrous.

Bucket is certainly not the sharp-faced, awe-inspiring detective who brilliantly deduces the solution of a complex problem. He is stoutly built, middle-aged, with an engaging appearance of frankness. He wears a hat, carries a stick and generally stands with his hands behind his back, carefully and quietly listening. He wears a mourning ring on his little finger and a diamond brooch (with a tiny stone).

There is nothing noteworthy about his physical appearance and his most remarkable characteristics are his doggedness and his apparent ability to be omnipresent; no matter how quick the pace, Bucket always manages to "lurk and lounge." "Otherwise mildly studious in his observation of human nature, on the whole a benignant philosopher not disposed to be severe upon the follies of mankind, Mr. Bucket pervades a vast number of houses and strolls about an infinity of streets: to outward appearances rather languishing for want of an object." He is fond of his fellow man and will gladly share a drink with most of them; he'd rather have a bit of fine old sherry than anything.

Though he is among the kindest and most compassionate of men, Bucket is capable of sudden anger when thwarted—as are all men of character. In Bleak House, he tells Smallwood, "I am damned if I am going to have my case spoilt by any human being in creation. Do you see this hand, and do you think that I don't know the right time to stretch it out and put it on the arm that fired the shot?" When he is hard at work, his fat forefinger seems inspired. "He puts it to his ears, and it whispers information; he puts it to his lips, and it enjoins him to secrecy; he rubs it over his nose, and it sharpens his scent; he shakes it before a guilty man, and it charms him to his destruction."

Bucket is married to a lady who has a natural genius for detection and—though his determination and tireless efforts enable him to solve the crimes at Bleak House—it is with her valuable assistance that he is able to obtain sufficient evidence to successfully conclude his case.

BUELL, REVEREND MARTIN
creator MARGARET SCHERF

In Farrington, Montana, the Reverend Martin Buell presides over Christ Church and becomes involved in the unorthodox hobby of solving murder cases, incurring the stern disapproval of his housekeeper, Mrs. Beekman. To the criminal, only the dog Bascomb is less threatening.

CABOT, PHILIP
creator ROMAN MC DOUGALD

Something of an American Albert Campion★, Philip Cabot is an urbane, nimble-minded private detective who is on good terms with both the rich and the police.

CADEE, DON
creator SPENCER DEAN, pseudonym of Prentice Winchell

As Chief of Store Protection for Amblett's, an exclusive Fifth Avenue department store, Don Cadee has many opportunities to become involved in large-scale crimes, ranging from organized shoplifting to murder. A former Marine, he is tall, lean, and physically fit. He is unusually dedicated to his employer, putting in many unpaid overtime hours. He thinks nothing of prowling the large store after closing if he feels a potential thief may be hiding. His professional devotion extends to elements in his personal life; he is engaged to Sybil Forde, an operative in Amblett's Store Protection Department.

CALDER, DANIEL
see BEHRENS, SAMUEL

CALLAHAN, BROCK
creator WILLIAM CAMPBELL GAULT

Before becoming a detective, Brock "The Rock" Callahan was all-pro guard for the Los Angeles Rams when they were NFL champs. In one of his earliest cases, he trades upon his contacts in the football world to solve a murder involving the team and its rookie quarterback. Most of Callahan's cases, however, do not involve football; they involve his attempts to earn a living as a private detective and retain his honesty. As a result, he antagonizes potential clients who would like him to do shady things. Brock has no illusions that he is a brilliant detective. Persistence is his major weapon and he will stick with a case until things fall into place.

His girl friend, clothes designer Jan Bonnett, calls him "an economic idiot" and won't marry him because of his profession.

CAMPBELL, HUMPHREY
creator GEOFFREY HOMES, pseudonym of Daniel Mainwaring

Humphrey Campbell is a two-fisted, woman-chasing, hard-boiled private eye but he drinks nothing stronger than milk.

CAMPION, ALBERT
creator MARGERY ALLINGHAM

When he first came on the scene, Albert Campion was described as ". . . a lunatic . . . quite inoffensive . . . just a silly ass." At that time, he was a con-man who bragged that he lived by his wits and would do anything for money provided it wasn't vulgar or sordid, using such aliases as "Mornington Dodd" and "Tootles Ash." Perhaps the foolish expression in his eyes and the idiotic, high-pitched voice which he affected were merely attempts at disguise. It is likely that Campion really meant to be a serious detective all along. He was, after all, Cambridge-educated.

By the mid-1930's, Albert Campion no longer pursued a life of crime and was then described as mild-mannered, bespectacled and scholarly. At that time, he lived with his valet, ex-burglar Magersfontein Lugg, in a private flat above a police station off Piccadilly Lane. From this convenient location he functioned as Scotland Yard's expert on society matters and proved to be of great assistance to official detectives Stanislaus Oates and Charlie Luke.

As Campion grew older (he was born in 1900) he continued to grow more serious and responsible. He fell in love with, and married, airplane designer Amanda Fitton. As his hair whitened, more and more people came to him for advice and he was often described as a kind of "universal uncle." During World War II and afterwards, his investigative talents were used by the British Government in espionage work.

CARLISLE, KENNETH
creator CAROLYN WELLS

Young, handsome silent-film star Kenneth Carlisle gave up a lucrative Hollywood career when "talkies" became popular. Unlike many film idols, forced to quit because their voices were not good, Carlisle, who had a fine voice, retired because he was tired of public adulation, lack of privacy, and the world of show business. He believes he has a flair for investigation and pursues a career as a private investigator. He lives on Manhattan's East Side.

CARNACKI, THOMAS
creator WILLIAM HOPE HODGSON

Carnacki is a psychic detective, a ghost finder, who is called into a case to discover or explain certain phenomena. His cases generally have every appearance of being connected with the supernatural, although many times that appearance is deceptive. He is a skeptic concerning the truth or untruth of ghost-tales but is not given to believing or disbelieving them "on principle." He does not let "cheap laughter" blind him to the possible truth of a fantastic legend.

On a case, he employs the paraphernalia of his trade—garlic, jars of water, bebe ribbons, etc. When night descends and he is alone with his thoughts (and possibly some Thing from the Other World), he is scared half to death.

When he has a new story to recount, he sends a short note to his friends—Dodgson, Jessop, Arkright and Taylor—nestles into his big easy chair with a pipe and begins without preamble. When he has finished, he just says, "out you go" genially and the evening is concluded.   .

CARRADOS, MAX
creator ERNEST BRAMAH, pseudonym of
Ernest Bramah Smith

The greatest of all blind detectives, Max Carrados could read ordinary newspapers with a touch of his sensitive fingers and could recognize acquaintances he'd not encountered for 25 years, merely by hearing their voices. As a young man, when he "had to trust (his) poor misleading eyes," he had been named Max Wynn. The loss of his sight in no way impaired his good humor and overwhelming kindliness.

His knowledge is profound in countless fields, ranging from paleontology and prehistoric flints to electricity, to Greek tetradrachms (Carrados is a numismatist). He is wealthy and has the time and interest to help people in distress. A pure amateur, his only fee is the satisfaction of solving (or preventing) crime. He is generally introduced to a case by Louis Carlyle, a private inquiry agent who relies on him to provide solutions for his cases.

Though Carrados is blind, his disability has not reduced his interest in life or crippled his energies. His blindness has, according to the author, "impelled him to develop those senses which in most of us lie dormant and practically unused. Thus you will understand that while he may be at a disadvantage while you are at an advantage, he is at an advantage while you are at a disadvantage." Wise, witty, gentle Max Carrados is one of the most beloved detectives in literature.

The author, Ernest Bramah Smith, is one of the true mystery men of literature, preferring anonymity and reticence about his personal affairs. It was, in fact, once a strongly held belief that no such person existed and that "Ernest Bramah" was a literary hoax, perpetrated by a small group of English authors. Mr. Smith denied the rumor.

CARTER, NICK
creator NICHOLAS CARTER, pseudonym of
a series of authors

The hero of literally thousands of dime novels in turn-of-the century America, Nick Carter is probably the cleanest living detective (save perhaps Father Brown★) in literature. He never smoked cigarettes (though he enjoyed a quiet cigar in the comfort of his study) and was never seen to drink a glass of hard liquor (though a foamy mug of cold tap beer was downed on occasion; never, however, did he become intoxicated). He never swore, never doubted the powers of love.

He was a fine athlete, with broad shoulders and sturdy limbs. His chin was square, his eyes level, his skin clear and bronzed. It never occurred to him to tell a lie, unless he was engaged in a battle of wits with villains, when he would stop at nothing to see that justice was done.

Nick had been married to a bright little girl, Ethel, who was murdered tragically, and he always regretted that he had not been present to prevent her death. Nick's recent exploits as a secret service agent have also been recorded.

Many writers have authored the stories under the Nicholas Carter pseudonym but Frederick Van Rensselaer Dey wrote the greatest number.

CASEY, JACK "FLASHGUN"
creator GEORGE HARMON COXE

Jack "Flashgun" Casey is the highest paid photographer in Boston. His job at "The Express" leads him into the investigation of many murders. He is 6'1", 215 pounds—all bone and muscle—but he is declared 4-F because of a trick knee. He is about 35 years old. Casey's young assistant, Tom Wade, swears by him, but his editor, McGrath, and his frequent police opponents, Lieutenant Logan and Sergeant Manahan, often swear at him.

Though the names are changed, Casey bears a striking resemblance to another Coxe creation, the slightly more cultured photographer, Kent Murdock★, also of Boston.

CELLINI, EMMANUEL
creator KYLE HUNT, pseudonym of John Creasey

A good psychiatrist must be something of a detective, ferreting out clues from his patient's mind. He also relies on intuition, as does psychiatrist-detective Dr. Emmanuel Cellini. Currently Cellini has his office in London, though once he had a lucrative practice in New York.

The elderly Dr. Cellini is still quite handsome, his movements those of a much younger man. He is pale, white-haired and white-mustached. Neither tense situations nor hot weather can cause him to lose his coolness. His philosophy is modern but he remains faithful to his pre-World War II Morris, his ancient, weather-beaten trilby hat and his wife, Felisa. A one-time ballerina, Felisa is now a comfortably plump matron. She is a good listener and Cellini often discusses his cases with her, asking her help.

CHAFIK, CHAFIK J.
creator CHARLES B. CHILD

Dapper little Inspector Chafik J. Chafik is one of the more exotic but least known of detectives. He travels throughout Baghdad with his faithful companion, the tall, gaunt Sergeant Abdullah. Chafik, a religious man, takes his job so seriously that he can often be observed talking aloud to himself as he ponders a case. His only relaxation seems to be his stamp collection.

Chafik and his wife, Leila, are childless until they adopt an 8-year-old Baghdad waif named Faisal. It would, perhaps, be more accurate to say that Faisal adopted the Inspector, since the boy took to following him, even saving his life before the adoption was completed.

CHALLIS, BART
creator WILLIAM F. NOLAN

The office of Los Angeles private detective Bart Challis is in the smoggy, downtown section of the city. He has lived in Los Angeles only since 1966, when he got his private investigator's license. Challis makes no pretense of being perfect. His spotty career has only bordered on respectability and he drinks too much. However, he likes his new profession, feeling he is "doing (his) bit against the mugs who chop up society." His unorthodox manner of handling cases brings him into conflict with Lieutenant Lennie Krause, of the Los Angeles Police Department.

CHAMBERS, PETER
creator HENRY KANE

Young, handsome Peter Chambers is both a private detective and a gentleman. He enjoys entertaining pretty girls in his penthouse, which overlooks New York City's Central Park. He is an habitué of the city's most exclusive and expensive night clubs, where he indulges his taste for good jazz, food, and drink.

CHAMBRUN, PIERRE
creator HUGH PENTECOST, pseudonym of Judson Philips

As resident manager of the Beaumont, New York City's top luxury hotel, Pierre Chambrun frequently must find solutions to murders which, if left unsolved, would damage the hotel's reputation. The French-born manager came to the United States as a small boy but his training took him back to Europe. In World War II, he remained in his native land to join the Resistance.

After more than 30 years in the hotel business, he is regarded as being at the top of his profession. He can adopt a Continental manner but realizes that the Beaumont is an American institution and keeps its atmosphere strictly American. Small and dark, he is stocky, with heavy pouches under his dark eyes.

CHAN, CHARLIE▲
creator EARL DERR BIGGERS

The famous Hawaiian detective of Chinese origin, Charlie Chan, is quite fat but walks with light, graceful steps. His cheeks are as round as a baby's, his skin is ivory, his amber eyes are slanted, and his black hair is close-cropped. Charlie, his wife and eleven honorable children live on Honolulu's Punchbowl Hill.

His dress is Americanized but his speech retains many Oriental patterns. He is especially fond of appropriate aphorisms, such as, "Mind like parachute—only function when open;" "When money talks, few are deaf."

CHANDLER, CLIFF
creator BAYNARD KENDRICK

Cliff Chandler is a private detective hired by the luxurius ocean liner, S.S. Moriander, to forestall or, if necessary, investigate crime on the floating hotel. The slim, debonair sleuth with the crisp black hair enjoys the vacation-like atmosphere of the ship and mingling with the passengers.

CHARLES, NICK and NORA▲
creator DASHIELL HAMMETT

The former ace operative for the Trans-American Detective Agency, Nick Charles is a clever, witty dick in the best hard-boiled tradition. He is tough (when he gets shot by Shep Morelli, he dismisses the wound as a mere scratch) but can—like so many tough guys—act like a baby, as when he pleads with his pretty young wife, Nora, to let him have a drink before breakfast.

Nick is a Greek, tall and slim (but he is not The Thin Man, as has been frequently missupposed by many) and very attractive (and attracted) to ladies. Nora is a 26-year-old lanky brunette with "a wicked jaw" as her husband describes it. John Guild, the cop assigned to the case when Nick is shot, thinks Nora is the greatest and calls Nick a lucky man. He comes around simply to see Nora.

Nick and Nora Charles get along beautifully and seem to be the happiest married couple in the detective field. Like most detectives' wives, she likes to express her views, and, like most detectives, Nick tolerates her "help."

The author, Dashiell Hammett, worked as a Pinkerton detective for eight years and undoubtedly picked up a great deal of background information for his tale about Nick and Nora Charles, as well as for his other books about Sam Spade★, and Ned Beaumont★ and the Continental Op★. He was not the first practitioner of what has become known as the hardboiled school of detective fiction, but he was the first writer to try his hand at the uniquely American style, and influenced scores of authors.

CHITTERWICK, AMBROSE
creator ANTHONY BERKELEY, pseudonym of
Anthony Berkely Cox

One has heard of the least likely suspect; Ambrose Chitterwick is the least likely detective. Apart from an interest in criminology, Mr. Chitterwick is a blue-eyed, mild-mannered milquetoast of absolutely no physical or mental distinction. Somehow, he manages to solve crimes that baffle the professional police and his fellow amateur detectives, such as Roger Sheringham★, also a creation of Anthony Berkeley.

CLANCY, PETER
creator LEE THAYER

The smooth-talking, red-headed private investigator, Peter Clancy, travels to exotic locales and solves the murder problems of the very rich. His fees are considerable and he never lacks clients, although he eschews publicity. The tall detective with the keen, steel-blue eyes is a success at his profession and has been since his first investigation in 1919.

As he grew older, he began to have second thoughts about the time-consuming elements of his profession. He never took a longed-for hunting and fishing vacation because a case beckoned near his country home in New Jersey. Here, he met his valet and friend, Wiggar, the victim's servant who promptly "adopted" Clancy. Clancy regrets never having married. He says, " . . . all the girls I liked married somebody else."

CLANE, TERRY
creator ERLE STANLEY GARDNER

Formerly a lawyer in California and a member of the U.S. Diplomatic Service, suave adventurer Terry Clane gave up a promising career to undertake studies of culture and "concentration" in a Chinese monastery. His motives may not have been entirely scholarly, however, since he was probably after gold and gems hidden in the monastery. Unsuccessful, he returned to the United States, where he continued his involvement in crime and adventure, usually on the right side of the law. He is 29, is 5'11", 185 pounds, with dark, wavy hair, blue eyes and a smooth complexion.

CLEEK, HAMILTON
see under ROGUES & HELPERS

CLUNK, JOSHUA
creator H. C. BAILEY

Joshua Clunk, the psalm-spouting, hypocritical criminal lawyer is much hated by Scotland Yard, even though frequently he manages—for his own purposes—to solve their murders for them. His cases generally take him the length and breadth of the British country-side and moors.

COCKRILL, INSPECTOR
creator CHRISTIANNA BRAND

Cockrill is a shrewd and crotchety Detective Inspector of the Kent police. He wears a soft felt hat, set sideways on his head, and a disreputable old mackintosh, in the pockets of which he often fishes for either paper or tobacco. He is a little man who appears to be older than his actual age. He has deep-set eyes beneath a broad brow, an aquiline nose and a mop of fluffy white hair fringing a magnificent head. Widely noted for having a heart of gold beneath his irascible exterior, he is affectionately known as "Cockie."

COFFEE, DR. DANIEL
creator LAWRENCE G. BLOCHMAN

For many years, Dr. Daniel Webster Coffee has been the chief pathologist and director of laboratories at Pasteur Hospital in the busy midwestern town, Northbank. The tall doctor performed countless miracles with a microscope, enabling his friend, Max Ritter (the youngest, swarthiest, skinniest, and homeliest detective in Northbank), to compile an excellent arrest record.

Dr. Coffee's long-suffering wife is less fortunate. She has set an unofficial record for being awakened at ungodly hours when her husband has been summoned to perform autopsies on murder victims. Frequently at Dr. Coffee's side is a pudgy resident in pathology, Dr. Motilal Mookerji, formerly of Calcutta, India.

COLT, THATCHER
creator ANTHONY ABBOT, pseudonym of Fulton Oursler

Despite the many administrative burdens of his office of New York City Police Commissioner, Thatcher Colt enjoyed solving bizarre murder cases on his own. "Of the 19,000 policemen he commanded, Thatcher Colt was the best all-around athlete, the hardest worker, the most invincible crook hunter." He was also possibly the best dressed man in New York public life.

The black-haired, brown-eyed bachelor lived on Manhattan's West 70th Street in a five-story house which included a gymnasium, a library containing a collection of 15,000 crime books and, hidden in a wall, a choice stock of wine.

According to Tony Abbot, the chronicler of the Commissioner's adventures, Colt wanted to be a musician or poet, not a policeman. He wrote sonnets to the girls he loved. Looking at his poor romantic record, one must question the quality of his poetry. While fighting in France during World War I, Colt lost his red-haired girl to a duke; another sweetheart ran off with a contract bridge champion in 1937. Later that year, he married pretty Florence Dunbar, who may be credited with prolonging his successful career by talking him out of resigning.

In an era when most famous detectives were amateurs, Colt was a professional, solving his cases by careful, solid police procedure, rather than by esoteric psychological reasoning.

CONTINENTAL OP, THE
creator DASHIELL HAMMETT

The nameless operative of the Continental Detective Agency in San Francisco is one of the best private detectives in the country. In one case, he is described as "the toughest, hardest, strongest, fastest, sharpest, biggest, wisest, meanest man west of the Mississippi River." Making due allowance for exaggeration, that is considerable praise for a man who otherwise is described only as "fat and forty." He is single, and courageous enough to be willing to risk his life for a client. His boss at Continental, "The Old Man," has been a detective since 1875.

Hammett based The Continental Op on his one-time colleague at Pinkerton's Detective Agency, Assistant Superintendent James Wright.

COOL, BERTHA
creator A. A. FAIR, pseudonym of Erle Stanley Gardner

Bertha Cool, a mammoth woman, weighs more than 200 pounds. In her sixties, with gray hair and twinkling gray eyes, she has the benign appearance of a favorite grandmother. Her language, however, is less reminiscent of a grandmother than of a sailor. She doesn't believe in wearing confining clothing, so when she walks in her loose garments, she looks "like a cylinder of currant jelly on a plate." Her partner in a private detective agency, Donald Lam★, remarks "she flowed past like a river." Bertha's secretary is the shy, efficient, Elsie Brand.

CORDRY, JASON and PATRICIA
creator JAMES O'HANLON

An attractive couple in their mid-twenties, James Cordry and his wife, Patricia Preston Cordry, live in North Hollywood, California, where they work as extras in motion pictures. Between acting assignments, they become involved in murder cases. At São Paulo Racetrack, Jason is a suspect until he finds the murderer. On a trip to New York City, they witness a murder at Coney Island and, when Jason is hired to solve the case, Patricia is planted in a sideshow as an observer.

CORK, MONTAGUE
creator MAC DONALD HASTINGS

Mr. Cork, the General Manager of the Anchor Insurance Co. of London, has a very good nose for a false claim. Though he is an elderly man, he is well taken care of by his wife, Phoebe, who is solicitous of his health. As a result of this attention, he is more active than many younger men.

CORRIGAN, TIM
creator ELLERY QUEEN, pseudonym of Frederick Dannay and Manfred B. Lee

The suave, one-eyed Captain of the New York Police Department Main Office Squad, Tim Corrigan frequently gets involved in unorthodox cases with his Korean war buddy, Chuck Baer.

CRANE, BILL▲
creator JONATHAN LATIMER

Bill Crane is a private detective whose "beat" is Illinois, especially Chicago. A modest, quiet man of 34, he looks even younger, his face clear-skinned and tan. He is an alcoholic who will drink virtually anything and has been known to sleep off his drunken stupors in strange places.

CROOK, ARTHUR
creator ANTHONY GILBERT, pseudonym of Lucy Beatrice Malleson

Arthur Crook is a shrewd, scheming lawyer whose sharp-tongued speech often betrays his Cockney origin. He has lived most of his life in London's Brandon Street, a block that managed to survive the worst attacks of Hitler's Luftwaffe. His appearance has been compared unfavorably with Toad of Toad Hall. A burly man, he has a bright red face, bright red hair and a bright red car, which looks as if it had been manufactured from old tin cans, and which Crook drives at unreasonable speeds. The beer-drinking lawyer believes all his clients are guiltless. If he cannot convince the police of their innocence, he puts on his other hat and finds the criminal.

CROW, ANDERSON
creator GEORGE BARR MC CUTCHEON

Anderson Crow is a rustic sleuth who, as its first citizen, dominates the scene at Tinkletown, New York. He is dignified and as imposing and rugged as the tallest marble shaft in the little cemetery on the edge of town. As Town Marshall, Fire Chief, Chairman of the Board of Health, Commissioner of Streets, Truant Officer, Commander of the local G.A.R., member in good standing of three detective agencies (with a nickel-plated star to prove it), and turnkey of the Tinkletown hoosegow, Crow's position of absolute authority goes unchallenged. He has a system of governmental law all his own and no political inducement could have persuaded anyone to try to displace him. Crow's methods of law enforcement have proved so successful that no crimes have been perpetrated in Tinkletown for many years.

CROWDER, UNCLE GEORGE
creator HUGH PENTECOST, pseudonym of
Judson Pentecost Philips

George Crowder was once a famous criminal lawyer and a County Prosecutor with a great political future. However, when he prosecuted and sent to the electric chair a man who was later proven to be innocent, he blamed himself for the miscarriage of justice. He gave up his law practice and moved to a small house in the woods near Lakewood, Connecticut, where he spends his time hunting, fishing and walking through the woods. He tries to help his neighbors.

He spends a great deal of time with his twelve year old nephew, Joey Trimble, whose father, the Lakewood druggist, does not approve of his brother-in-law's "shiftless" existence. Joey, however, has learned a great deal about ethics from the man he calls "my dear Uncle Sherlock."

CRUMLISH, FATHER
creator ALICE SCANLON REACH

Forty-eight years a priest, Father Francis Xavier Crumlish now has his parish at St. Brigid's in Lake City, a large grain port near the Canadian border. It is not an easy assignment for him because of his arthritis, his heartburn, the bishop, and housekeeper with whom he must cope. He would like to relax in his old age, watch more baseball on television (he especially enjoys seeing Willie Mays) and play the church organ. Father Crumlish is a warmhearted man whose parishioners often become involved in crime, so there is no rest for him when the wicked commit murder or robbery and the priest's young friend, Lieutenant Tom Madigan, asks his help.

CUFF, SERGEANT
creator WILKIE COLLINS

Sergeant Cuff is a methodical, hard-working, dependable professional police officer. He is persevering and energetic, with the very human quality of fallibility. He even makes the unforgivable mistake of suspecting the heroine. When Superintendent Seegrave● has no success locating a stolen moonstone, Cuff appears, preceded by his reputation as the finest detective in

England. Frequently he requires the help of amateurs and sometimes is completely mystified, though ultimately he prevails and brings the case to a successful conclusion.

He looks like anything but a detective, despite the lean, hatchet-face and steely gray eyes of Sherlock Holmes★. Cuff is well advanced in years and extraordinarily thin; his skin is parched yellow and dry as dust. His voice and his tread are soft. His wizened old figure does not comfort the principals in the case, since he looks so little like their concept of a policeman.

Cuff's hobby and passion is roses; he even whistles "The Last Rose of Summer" when he is preoccupied. When he retired from the detective force, Cuff settled in a little cottage in a small town, where he kept a beautiful rose garden.

Sergeant Cuff is drawn from a real-life detective, Inspector Whicher of Scotland Yard, who solved the actual case of Constance Kent, which served as the model for The Moonstone■.

CZISSAR, DR. JAN
creator ERIC AMBLER

When Hitler took over Czechoslovakia, Dr. Czissar of the Prague Police was forced to flee to England as a refugee. Immediately he armed himself with a Chamberlain-type umbrella and a letter of introduction from someone high in the Home Office. The fussy little doctor plans to acquire a knowledge of London crime detection and has selected Assistant Commissioner Mercer of Scotland Yard as his mentor. The latter is a reluctant teacher but finds he can avoid neither the doctor nor his invariably correct solutions to currently unsolved crimes.

D.A., THE
creator ERLE STANLEY GARDNER

In a close vote, Doug Selby was elected District Attorney of Madison County, California, in 1936. The voters liked the handsome young man with curly hair, a devil-may-care look in his penetrating eyes, and a forceful mouth. He entered politics to reduce local corruption. Though his job is prosecuting criminals, Selby is equally interested in solving mysteries and identifying murderers. His job is a natural extension of his hobby, reading mystery stories.

DANE, TIMOTHY
creator WILLIAM ARD

Timothy Dane is an effective private eye with a good reputation for honesty. He is handsome and, when pretty girls show interest, he responds.

DANNING, DAVID
creator DON VON ELSNER

A former Colonel in the Office of Strategic Services, David Danning operates his own agency, specializing in complex, high-level corporate trouble-shooting. His cases frequently lead him to his beloved Hawaii, and into murder.

DARE, SUSAN
creator MIGNON G. EBERHART

Young Susan Dare is, like her creator, a female mystery writer. Susan is attractive, charming, romantic, gushily emotional, with a habit of stumbling into real-life murders.

DA SILVA, CAPTAIN JOSE
creator ROBERT L. FISH

The flamboyant liaison officer between the Brazilian police and Interpol, Captain José Da Silva, with his friend Wilson (the only American Interpol agent in the country) shows us the colorful sights of Rio, São Paulo, and the lush green Brazilian jungle.

Da Silva (Zé, as he is known to his friends) is 39 years old and has been a Rio policeman for about 15 years. He has a college degree in criminology. He is tall and dark, but his swarthy face is too hard-looking to be called handsome. A brave man who has often risked his life, nonetheless he has a deep-seated fear of flying. He is partial to Reserva San Juan cognac and United States cigarettes, which he mooches from Wilson (whose first name remains undisclosed).

Wilson purposely attempts to cultivate a nondescript appearance, to mask his identity as a detective. He is Ohio born and adept at karate, picking pockets, and piloting small boats.

DAWN, PAUL
creator JAMES YAFFE

Paul Dawn is a good-looking, intelligent young man with a far-away expression in his eyes. His idea of action is to sit in an easy chair, fondling a bottle and letting his mind wander. Somehow, he has been able to persuade the New York City Police Commissioner to put him in charge of the Department of Impossible Crimes, an obscure division attached to the Homicide Squad. This scheme does not exactly please his colleague, Inspector Fledge, and probably Dawn exacerbates the situation even more by calling Fledge a "middle-aged bloodhound."

DAX, SATURNIN
creator MARTEN CUMBERLAND

Saturnin Dax is Commissaire of the Police Judiciaire (First Mobile Brigade), a position once held by fellow Parisian, Inspector Maigret★. His huge appetite (he takes five lumps of sugar in his coffee) keeps him a very large man. He wears a bushy mustache. M. Dax is happily married, the father of five children. When working on a perplexing case, he goes about humming Schubert's Unfinished Symphony.

DEE, JUDGE JEN-DJIEH
creator ROBERT VAN GULIK

In his younger days, Judge Dee served as magistrate in various provincial cities where he achieved fame by solving many difficult criminal cases. He later became a minister at the Imperial Court and, by his wise counsel, was able to exercise a beneficial influence on the affairs of state. His trusted advisor was Hoong Liang●.

The character of Judge Dee is based on Ti Jen-chieh, one of the great ancient Chinese detectives. A person of historic importance and a well-known statesman of the T'ang dynasty, Ti lived from 630–700 A.D. Because of Dee's (or Ti's) wide reputation as a solver of crimes, later Chinese mystery fiction (predating Poe) incorporated him into a group of crime stories.

Robert Van Gulik, a noted Orientalist, has used this personage in a series of period detective novels, many of which were based ∅n records.

DENE, DORCAS
creator GEORGE R. SIMS

Dorcas Dene, née Lester, is a bit-part actress who left the stage to marry a young artist. Her husband went blind and, to pay the bills, the pretty Mrs. Dene took a client in a detective case. Her initial success leads her to a career as one of the best private detectives in the England of her day.

DENE, TREVOR
creator VALENTINE WILLIAMS

Bespectacled Trevor Dene is one of the bright young men of Scotland Yard. A Cambridge graduate, he is resented by some older colleagues because of his education and social polish. Dene is married to an American and spends as much time detecting in the United States as in England, solving crimes on a wealthy Long Island estate and in the Adirondacks.

DEPARTMENT OF DEAD ENDS
creator ROY VICKERS

An obscure branch of Scotland Yard, the Department of Dead Ends takes other departments' rejected cases. All clues, exhibits, and theories are carefully filed for future reference. Under the direction of Superintendent Karslake and Inspector Rason, they wait for new information which will stimulate a new train of thought.

Most of the actual investigatory work is done by Rason, who is considered lucky by most of his colleagues. Their view may be based on jealousy but it may also be due to the poor record he compiled when matched with the famous female thief, Fidelity Dove●. Rason, himself, is modest in describing his function as "a fool kept at Scotland Yard on the principle of setting a fool to catch a fool."

DEPARTMENT OF PATTERNS
creator VICTOR CANNING

The French equivalent of Scotland Yard's Department of Dead Ends is the Department of Patterns. Its headquarters is a shabby 18th century building on the Quai d'Orsay in Paris. In charge of the Department is the venerable M. Alphonse Grand. Papa Grand, as he is commonly known, is over sixty, has white hair, and bright, crystal-clear blue eyes. He always wears a high, old-fashioned, stiff collar.

His office is a little attic room with a tiny window overlooking the River Seine. He heads a small but dedicated group whose job is to "sift through masses of old criminal data, official records and photographs, newspaper reports and files, hoping that by arrangement and analysis, some pattern of significance may emerge." The Department's "raison d'être" is the pursuit of all unresolved murders, crimes and inexplicable accidents, files which the more traditional departments close after several months of unsuccessful investigation.

The "bible" used by the Department is a book written by Papa Grand called the *"Manual of Pattern Making";* only five copies of this remarkable volume exist. The tales of the Department of Patterns have been compiled by a young recruit named Renoblier.

DEPARTMENT Z
creator JOHN CREASEY

Department Z is the counter-espionage arm of British Intelligence, presided over by graying, balding, lantern-jawed Gordon

Craigie. His field agents come and go through many adventures, but the canny Scot stays at the helm throughout.

DE PUYSTER, REGINALD
creator RUFUS KING

Perhaps the wealthiest of all detectives, Reggie De Puyster inherited more than twenty million dollars from his father, old Warring De Puyster, "the bearcat of Wall Street." Reggie is a dandy: immaculately tailored, trim, elegant. He is also bright, witty, articulate. He is not, however, a detective who depends exclusively on his brains to solve a case. A superb athlete, well-muscled, with a devastating punch in either fist, he has been known to end a case with a hard left hook to the villain's jaw. Though generally he works as an amateur, Reggie has a connection with the O'Day Detective Agency on lower Broadway.

DEVEREAUX, JOHNNY
creator JOHN ROEBURT

Johnny Devereaux is a twenty-year police veteran. He is bone-crushingly tough, trading punches, shots, and heartaches with the opposition.

DIAVOLO, DON
creator STUART TOWNE, pseudonym of Clayton Rawson

Don Diavolo is a magician who perfects his tricks in a Greenwich Village basement, where he is frequently visited by the harried Inspector Church of Homicide, either to arrest the Don for an impossible crime or to ask him to solve it. Diavolo appears only in four pulp novelettes in 1940.

DIMARCO, JEFFERSON
creator DORIS MILES DISNEY

Jeff DiMarco, a product of the Boston tenements, is a claims adjustor for the Commonwealth Insurance Company of that city. He is not a heroic character but nevertheless is an admirable one. He is concerned about people, especially those he feels are being victimized. He is tenacious also and, once he suspects someone is trying to defraud Commonwealth, he will investigate as if he alone had to pay off on the policy.

DiMarco is a believable person with his share of both frailties and virtues. In early cases, he tended to get over-involved with suspects, especially with attractive women. Later, approaching middle age, he has the normal reaction of concern as his waistline expands and his hair grays.

DOVER, CHIEF INSPECTOR WILFRED
creator JOYCE PORTER

The pasty-faced, 240-pound Scotland Yard Inspector, Wilfred Dover, is one of the most incompetent (and laugh-provoking) sleuths in literature. He has been described as "irascible, boorish, rude and crude." He is less interested in clues than in food and drink—especially if someone else is paying the bill. A mass of gastro-intestinal symptoms, rumbles and belches seems to emanate continually from his body. All activity brings an alarming red to his face.

Two people are loyal to Dover. His assistant, Sergeant Mac-Gregor, loathing him, covers for him, supplies him with good ideas—and free cigarettes. Dover's long-suffering wife reminds him to put in his false teeth before leaving the house in the morning.

DRIFFIELD, SIR CLINTON
creator J. J. CONNINGTON, pseudonym of
Alfred Walter Stewart

Sir Clinton is a slight, almost ordinary-looking person with a shrewd and penetrating gaze. His face is tanned; a firm mouth is topped by a close-clipped moustache. He is a conventional dresser but his teeth and hands show considerable care. He is about 35 years old and has risen to the position of Chief Constable of his district.

DRUMMOND, BULLDOG▲
creator "SAPPER", pseudonym of H. C. McNeile

Captain Hugh Drummond, a demobilized officer who finds peace dull after the Great War, has the appearance of an English gentleman: a man who fights hard, plays hard and lives clean. He is slightly less than six feet tall and quite broad, without being inordinately heavy. His best friend would not call him good-looking but he possesses that cheerful type of ugliness which inspires immediate confidence. His nose has never fully recovered from the final year in the Public School Heavyweight boxing competition. His mouth is less than small. Only his eyes redeem his face. Deep-set and steady, with eyelashes that many women envy, they show him to be a sportsman and an adventurer. Drummond goes outside the law when he feels the ends justify the means.

When H. C. McNeile stopped recounting the exploits of Drummond, Gerard Fairlie continued the redoubtable detective's adventures.

DULUTH, PETER and IRIS
creator PATRICK QUENTIN, pseudonym of several authors and collaborations, primarily Hugh Wheeler and Richard Wilson Webb

Peter and Iris Duluth are not the usual frivolous husband and wife team—they have too many serious problems. They meet in a mental hospital, where theatrical producer Peter is trying to cure himself of alcoholism, and actress Iris is recovering from melancholia. Early in their career, they are helped with their cases by a psychiatrist, Dr. Lenz. The Duluth marriage is not always a happy one and, at times, is on the brink of divorce. Actually, the Duluth family history reminds one of Greek tragedy. Brother "Jake" Duluth, a book publisher, had a wife who died mysteriously and a son who hates him. Jake, in turn, has had reason to suspect the boy of murder.

DUPIN, C. AUGUSTE
creator EDGAR ALLAN POE

C. Auguste Dupin, the first detective in literature, was poor but of "illustrious parentage." He was young, romantic and eccentric. He would remain in his room for a month at a time without admitting a visitor. Living in his small back library at No. 33 Rue Dunot, Faubourg-St. Germain, with an anonymous chronicler, Dupin prefers to sit behind closed shutters, lighted only by "a couple of tapers which, strongly perfumed, threw out only the ghastliest and feeblest of rays." From this stronghold, he sometimes came out at night, "when the fit was upon him," to walk the streets and enjoy "the infinity of mental excitement" afforded by observation.

He read widely and once admitted writing "certain doggerel" suggestive of the limerick form. He was a heavy smoker, enjoying a quiet meerschaum with his friend. He wore green spectacles for his short-sightedness.

Dupin had an open contempt for the police of Paris and their methods. He enjoyed startling his friend by analyzing his personal thought processes. He is less human than most detectives —the personification of analysis and the mouthpiece of logical activity.

Poe is the father of the detective story as well as the creator of the short story form as we know it today. His morbid, brooding personality was reflected in his tales of terror, and his brilliant mathematical mind is reflected in his Dupin tales of ratiocination (a word he invented).

EGG, MONTAGUE
creator DOROTHY L. SAYERS

Less well-known than Lord Peter Wimsey● but an astute thinker in his own right, Montague Egg is a mild-mannered commercial traveler. He is always ready with a bit of doggerel from "The Salesman's Handbook," or with the solution to the crimes that come his way.

87TH PRECINCT SQUAD
creator ED MC BAIN, pseudonym of Evan Hunter

Located on the island of Isola (really Manhattan) is the 87th Precinct Squad, which deals with urban crime. Although Detective Steve Carella gets the most attention, all the policemen are interesting, from the Lieutenant who heads the squad down the ranks.

The Lieutenant is Peter Byrnes, a humane man who knows what it is to have family problems. In his absence, Sergeant Dave Murchison is in charge. Clerical chores are assigned to the squad's clerk, Alf Miscolo. The youngest squad member is Bert Kling who is in love with a college girl. Bert enjoys reading and is partial to Sherlock Holmes★.

Other members of the squad are Detective Brown and Detective "Cotton" Hawes, the big Southerner with the streak of white in his hair. The 87th's cross-to-bear is Andy Parker, a braggart with few saving graces. The object of many jokes is Meyer Meyer, whose father displayed a perverted humor when naming his son.

If Carella seems to be the most active detective in the 87th, it isn't because he volunteers for assignments; it is because a man named McBain prepares the duty roster. Carella has every reason for wanting to be off duty as much as possible. His wife, Teddy, is beautiful. She was born a deaf mute which, on several occasions, has made her vulnerable to the kind of trouble from which she must be rescued.

ELDON, SHERIFF BILL
creator ERLE STANLEY GARDNER

The genial, aging sheriff of Southern California's Rockville County, Bill Eldon is a shrewd, cautious man who is unpopular with local political leaders. They consider his methods dated, though even they admit he gets results. With the experience of hunting game animals and criminals for many years, the heavy-set sheriff has the ability to move with silent cat-like agility.

EVANS, HOMER
creator ELLIOT PAUL

Boston-born Homer Evans lived in Paris before World War II, surrounding himself with a joyous, undisciplined group of bohemian artists. A lover of all art forms, Evans is especially fond of music, and listening to Beethoven puts him into a near-trance. Miriam Leonard, an American girl studying music in Paris, is a close friend Homer loves more than the fine arts. He also has a deep attachment to drinking, chasing women, and brawling.

FALCON, GAY ■ ▲
creator MICHAEL ARLEN, pseudonym of Diran Kuyumjian

Gay Stanhope Falcon describes himself as hard-boiled and he is—though, like the best of us, he is susceptible to the charms of a pretty girl. He has other names, "equally improbable" (in his words) and possesses passports in the names of Falcon, a soldier called Colonel Rock and a Paris journalist named Spencer Pott.

Despite popular characterizations that were made into successful motion pictures, he is neither suave nor charming. He is tall, with a long, lean, dark, saturnine face, graying hair, and deep-set, penetrating eyes. He has been married twice to pretty women.

He is not a policeman and not a storyteller, but a man who earns his living by keeping his mouth shut and engaging in dangerous enterprises. He has had a hand at being a soldier, a gambler, a secret agent, an airplane salesman, a white hunter, a purser, a war correspondent, a long-distance swimmer, a professional dancer, and a good salmon-fisherman.

FALKENSTEIN, JESSE
creator LESLEY EGAN, pseudonym of Elizabeth Linington

A pleasant air of indecision surrounds Los Angeles attorney Jesse Falkenstein. He has trouble even making up his mind with regard to religion: formerly Jewish, he is now agnostic; his wife, Nell, is Christian. He would like to fire his secretary, Miss Miller, an inefficient spinster, but does not have the courage. He is unable also to rid himself of Athelstane, a gigantic mastiff which threatens the Falkensteins' financial position because of the food it consumes.

Jesse has trouble getting organized but is a good detective when necessary. He is so good, in fact, he rarely makes a court appearance, securing his client's freedom by finding the guilty person before the trial. He is aided by Sergeant Andrew Clock, who dates Jesse's sister, Fran. Falkenstein often quotes from the Talmud. He likes to relax with a drink and listen to Bach records on his stereo.

FATHOM, MR.
see VERITY, MR.

FELL, DR. GIDEON
creator JOHN DICKSON CARR

A lumbering giant, Dr. Gideon Fell weighs in excess of 250 pounds. His face is wondrous: bright red, with an enormous mustache and tiny, sharp eyes. His eyeglasses, clamped firmly on his small nose, are anchored by a broad, black ribbon. He wears a shovel hat and a tent-like cape, usually carries a large, red handkerchief and two crutch-handled walking sticks.

He formerly lived in the North of England, but is now in London, at 1 Adelphi Terrace.

Gideon Fell is partial to beer, tobacco, mystery stories, building houses of cards and telling jokes (he is surprised when people laugh). When he talks, he rumbles and wheezes loudly.

The only cases which interest him are those involving locked rooms and other apparent miracles. Fell appears to be based on John Dickson Carr's mentor, G. K. Chesterton.

FELLOWS, CHIEF FRED
creator HILLARY WAUGH

Fred Fellows, Chief of Police of the small town of Stockford, Connecticut, works out of a tiny headquarters in the basement of the town hall. His cases are resolved by thoroughness and attention to detail rather than by deductions.

FEN, GERVASE
creator EDMUND CRISPIN, pseudonym of
Robert Bruce Montgomery

Erudite Gervase Fen is Professor of English Language and Literature at Oxford University. He is tall, lanky, about 40, with a cheerful, ruddy, clean-shaven face. His dark hair is carefully plastered down with water, but manages to stick up in spikes at the crown of his head. Usually he wears an enormous raincoat, and his hats can be described only as extraordinary. Happily married to a plain and sensible little woman, Fen is the proud possessor of a disreputable red roadster, limited driving ability, much good will, and boundless enthusiasm.

FINNEY, DR. MARY
creator MATTHEW HEAD, pseudonym of John Canaday

One wouldn't think that a medical missionary working in the African jungle would run into many baffling murder cases, but tough-minded Mary Finney shows that one need not live in an urban metropolis to be a detective. Even in these surroundings, Mary is involved in murder.

FINCH, INSPECTOR SEPTIMUS
creator MARGARET ERSKINE, pseudonym of
Margaret Wetherby Williams

Inspector Finch, expert in murder and lover of beer, solves murders committed in isolated manor houses that are full of dark shadows, ancestral secrets and mysterious happenings.

FLICK, ROBERT W.
creator JACK EHRLICH

In addition to having learned to rope cattle in his native Wyoming, Flick was also once an excellent amateur boxer. At present, he is a Parole Officer for the State of New York, assigned mostly to Nassau County. He is dedicated to his job, even studying psychology at Columbia on Saturdays to improve his understanding of the people with whom he works. His job is difficult. On call around the clock, he must respond whenever one of his parolees gets into trouble.

He works with the local police, especially with his friend, Inspector Bowman, whose wife likes Flick and frequently invites the bachelor to a home-cooked dinner. Flick is not unhappy. He rents an attractive apartment over the garage of a Long Island estate and always has beautiful women nearby to prevent loneliness. His hobby is playing jazz on the piano.

FORTUNE, DAN
creator MICHAEL COLLINS, pseudonym of Dennis Lynds

Danny Fortune (ne Fortunowski) has had only one arm since his youth. He lost his left arm in an accident while looting a docked ship and was known as "Danny the Pirate" thereafter. He went "straight" after his mishap, traveling widely as a merchant seaman, then establishing a one-man private detective agency in the Chelsea and Greenwich Village sections of Manhattan.

While he cannot readily explain his motivations for entering the detective business, the well-read, self-educated Fortune is honest and effective in his profession. His adventures also tell the story of his mistress, New York showgirl Marty; his best friend, bartender Joe Harris; and policeman Gazzo, a captain in the Homicide Bureau of the metropolis.

FORTUNE, REGGIE
creator H. C. BAILEY

If one hears a man-sized cherub with a schoolboy complexion use the epithet "Oh My Aunt!" one is aware of being in the presence of Reggie Fortune. Mr. Fortune, as he is generally called, is actually a practising physician and surgeon, and adviser to Scotland Yard's C.I.D. on medical matters. His stated detective philosophy is "simple faith in facts and no imagination —I believe in evidence." However, more than most detectives, he relies on intuition to solve his cases. He reserves his greatest antipathy for criminals who prey upon the young.

As befits someone of his corpulence, Reggie Fortune is a gourmet; when imbibing, he prefers seltzer water. The pipe-smoking doctor dislikes cold weather, which is "unfortunate," since he lives in Great Britain. Despite his rotund figure, Fortune moves quickly—especially behind the wheel of a car, where he drives wildly, needlessly frightening his wife, Joan.

FOX, TECUMSEH
creator REX STOUT

Tecumseh Fox, a Westchester County-based private detective, denies he is part Indian. His full name is William Tecumseh Fox, and he has a brother named William McKinley Fox. His base of operations is a large farm where he keeps so many animals that his neighbors have dubbed it "The Zoo." He is not averse to breaking a few laws and defying the police when he feels his clients' interests are at stake. Tecumseh Fox is far more active physically than his brother in the human-animal-detective kingdom, Nero Wolfe★, another Stout character.

FRAME, REYNOLD
creator HERBERT BREAN

Young, pleasant Reynold Frame is a photographer-journalist for "Life" magazine. His assignments generally take him to New England and involve him in fields such as colonial Americana, germ warfare, disappearances, and murder.

FRENCH, INSPECTOR JOSEPH
creator FREEMAN WILLS CROFTS

More than 30 years of meritorious service at Scotland Yard result in promotions for Inspector Joseph French, first to Chief Inspector, finally to Superintendent. A patient, thorough sleuth and a formidable manhunter, French prefers to work out of his office, away from the dull routine of paperwork. His strength is breaking alibis.

He is suave, easy-going, with a leisurely air. Keen, dark blue eyes twinkle in a good-humored face. He is stout, less than middle-height, and usually dresses in tweeds. French is happily married and likes good food and traveling.

GALL, JOE
creator PHILIP ATLEE, pseudonym of James Atlee Philips

Joe Gall is a freelance American agent with an occupational speciality: "Nullifier," which means he kills people for money when America is best-served with a timely death. He lives well on the proceeds. He has no compunctions about his job, as most of his "contracts" need killing.

GAMADGE, HENRY
creator ELIZABETH DALY

Charming, genteel, and well-mannered, Henry Gamadge is blunt-featured, colorless, but amiable. He has intelligent green-gray eyes. He is in his thirties, tall, with a well-constructed figure that has been ruined by many hours spent poring over books in scholarly research. He is an author, bibliophile, and consulting expert on old books, manuscripts and autographs. A native New Yorker (like Elizabeth Daly), Gamadge lives and works in an old residence in Manhattan's East 60's, assisted by Harold Bantz•.

GAUNT, JOHN
creator CARR DICKSON, pseudonym of John Dickson Carr

The conservative Parliamentarian Joan Gaunt is a criminologist of the old school—polite, quiet, deadly. He looks like a burnt-out man, yet is ringed with danger. He is tall, lean, buttoned-up in an old-fashioned dinner coat and white shirt, down the front of which hangs an eye glass on a string. An elongated, thin head with high cheekbones, has long, silvery hair brushed straight back from a high forehead. Under black brows, his gray eyes appear drowsy, dull—almost kindly. He has a mustache and a tuft of whiskers in the middle of his chin. His wrinkles are those of a man who has seen vast amounts of villainy.

GENTLY, SUPERINTENDENT
creator ALAN HUNTER

Stolid but brilliant, almost a British Maigret★, Superintendent Gently is a Scotland Yard homicide expect who seems constantly to chew peppermint creams as he studies a case.

GETHRYN, COLONEL ANTHONY
creator PHILIP MAC DONALD

It was about 1885 that a son was born to an English squire and to a Spanish mother who had been a dancer, actress, and painter. Apparently the boy, Anthony, inherited his mother's versatility, for he excelled both in studies and sports at Oxford. Later, he painted and wrote.

In his younger days, Gethryn was a shade over six feet tall, weighed about 175 pounds, had black hair and a very dark complexion. He rose from private to colonel during his World War I career. He had been wounded but returned to duty in the Secret Service.

After the war, he went to the country to live quietly on an inheritance and to write a novel. He was called upon to solve a local murder and soon acquired a reputation with Scotland Yard, and an attractive wife named Lucia. He enjoys riding and traveling through the countryside.

GHOTE, INSPECTOR GANESH
creator H. R. F. KEATING

The henpecked, harassed, downtrodden Inspector Ganesh Ghote, is the homicide expert of the Bombay Criminal Investigation Department. He is called upon to solve baffling, bizarre cases.

GIDEON, COMMANDER GEORGE
creator J. J. MARRIC, pseudonym of John Creasey

Commander (formerly Superintendent) George Gideon of Scotland Yard is a man with two loves. One is his family: his wife, Kate, to whom he has been married for more than a quarter of a century, and his six children (three boys, three girls). Since their marriage, he and Kate have lived in the same house on Harrington Street, Fulham, London, S.W. Kate as Gideon's wife, is his first love; London, his second love, is his mistress. Gideon has served them both well for many contented years.

The Commander is massive (6'2"), slow-moving, with a soft voice and a pale face. His large, slate-blue eyes are covered by heavy, sleepy-looking lids. When he is angry, he becomes a wide-awake, red-faced, bellowing tyrant. His subordinates stay far away when "G.G. is on the warpath." It is difficult to anger Gideon but the guilty party has reason to fear if the case involves child-murder or abuse, desecration of a church or dishonesty by a policeman or colleague.

GILLINGHAM, ANTONY
creator A. A. MILNE

Antony Gillingham is a humorous, youngish (age 30) amateur sleuth who is described as having "a good mind." He did not, however, always put it to much use during his checkered career, which included such jobs as tobacconist, valet, reporter, and waiter. He lives in London, as does his friend and "Watson●," Bill Beverley. Gillingham has been nicknamed "Madman."

GOLDEN, SERGEANT SAMMY
see SHANLEY, FATHER JOSEPH

GOOD, CARL
creator ROBERT O. SABER, pseudonym of Milton K. Ozaki

Short, dough-faced and slightly paunchy, Carl Good is a human and credible private eye. His adventures are full of strippers and ganglords and gunmen and corrupt cops and other familiar elements of the pulp publications.

GRANDFATHER
creator LLOYD BIGGLE, JR.

Octogenarian Grandfather (Bill Rastin) of Borgville, Michigan is one of the geriatric wonders of mystery fiction. As described by his grandson, a teenage "Watson●," the hale old man retains a good memory and a sharp, inquisitive mind. He is also one of the most conceited detectives this side of Hercule Poirot★. This trait does not endear him to Sheriff Pilkins, whom he always proves wrong. However, the help he gives the sheriff in solving some cases does help compensate for Grandfather's I-told-you-so attitude.

Grandfather is sensitive about his baldness and resents it when he is called an "antique Yul Brynner." He tells people that he has been bald a long time, having lost his hair from driving in an open car in the cold winter of '28. Fortunately, Grandfather's solutions to mysteries are more plausible than are his fantasies.

GRANT, INSPECTOR ALAN
creator JOSEPHINE TEY, pseudonym of
Elizabeth MacKintosh

Inspector Grant is the brilliant Scotland Yard detective with the questionable nerves. In one case, Grant is confined to bed following an accident in which he fell through a trapdoor while chasing a criminal. He is rescued from boredom by the gift of an intriguing portrait, the donor being a glamorous London actress, Marta Hallard, the current love of bachelor Grant's life.

Grant recovers from his injury, but his nerves are worse than ever and, on doctor's advice, he leaves for a trip to the Scottish Highlands. This trip proves to be the proverbial busman's holiday as he becomes involved in a murder. Although he is able to solve mysteries through deductive reasoning, Grant is proudest of his almost unerring instinct for spotting the one dishonest face in a lineup of a dozen men.

GREEN, JEFF
creator CARLTON KEITH, pseudonym of Keith Robertson

A handwriting expert by profession, Jeff Green is a private investigator by avocation. Though he is a resident of New York City, his cases take him as far afield as Zurich and Madrid.

GRYCE, EBENEZER
creator ANNA KATHERINE GREEN

Ebenezer Gryce is the first detective to appear in a novel written by a woman. He is quiet, competent, hard-working—not brilliant or eccentric, but one who gets his man by sheer hard work. He is middle-aged and comfortably portly, a kindly, gentle, likeable man. His patience and imperturbability inspire confidence and affection, particularly among women. There is no weakness in his character, and no lack of dignity, but he feels his profession does not qualify him to be thought of as a gentleman.

In "The Leavenworth Case," Gryce enlists the aid of the gentlemanly Mr. Raymond to acquire information for him in certain social situations; he uses a subordinate, "Mr. Q.," to perform some of the less dignified and more menial detective work, such as climbing over roofs to peer through windows, listening at doors and collecting clues.

When Gryce runs out of new clues and ideas, he arranges dramatic surprises for the suspects, most of which prove informative. He is efficient and sagacious, able to speak knowledgeably about diverse topics such as the "science of probability," firearms, and various grades of writing paper and the type of ash each would make if burned.

The author, Anna Katherine Green, was the daughter of a well-known criminal laywer and one of the most popular writers in America for nearly half a century.

GUBB, PHILO
creator ELLIS PARKER BUTLER

Philo Gubb's office doubles as headquarters for his twin trades of paper-hanger and detective. He is tall and very thin, a modern-day Don Quixote: a human flamingo. He must have read the stories of Sherlock Holmes★ because he wears a cap and dressing gown, and smokes a calabash.

His small-town office boasts a diploma from the Rising Sun Detective Agency's Correspondence School on its wall. An enormous collection of disguises helps him on his cases. As soon as he steps into the street in one of his false mustaches and costumes, the popular Gubb is greeted, by name, by half a dozen of the citizens of Riverbank, who are as accustomed to seeing him in disguise as out of it. While a few children enjoy the sight of Gubb all decked out in a new character, the older citizens pay little attention, realizing that Gubb is on another case. The citizens considered it merely a business custom, like the butcher tying on his apron before stepping behind the counter. On every case Gubb commits murder—on the English language.

HAMBLEDON, TOMMY
creator MANNING COLES, pseudonym of Cyril Henry Coles and Adelaide Manning

Thomas Elphinston Hambledon is a high-ranking member of the famous Intelligence Service of England. He teaches modern languages at Chappell's School and spends his holidays abroad, usually in Germany. Though he is a parson's son, his tastes are cheerful and expensive, quite beyond his ostensible means. He is easy-going, has a marvelous sense of humor, is friendly and has scored most of his notable successes simply because he is so easy to talk to and apparently trustworthy. He is deeply patriotic, saying, "If a country is worth living in, it is worth fighting for."

Though he has been in love, he has never married because of a total dedication to his job. His dedication pays off with spectacular successes. He researches his case thoroughly, and leaves little to chance.

HAMMER, MIKE▲
creator MICKEY SPILLANE, pseudonym of
Frank Morrison Spillane

The groin-kicking, shoot-first-ask-questions-later private eye, Mike Hammer, has been called everything from a paranoid to a fascist to a latent homosexual. He is tough and vulgar, a wise guy who uses vulgarity and crudities more than necessary, perhaps, but is, nevertheless, most attractive to women. He wears a stereotyped tan trench coat and a hat drawn low on his fore-head, and always carries a .38 revolver in the speed rig at his side.

HANAUD, INSPECTOR GABRIEL
creator A. E. W. MASON

A professional French policeman, Inspector Hanaud is a burly man of middle age. He has thick black hair and a pair of remarkably light eyes with heavy lids. He is comfortable and coaxing—not a fear-inspiring personage. He combines a respect for the law with a just kindliness. His sense of humor is as elephantine as his girth. In a moment of solemnity, Hanaud says, "For my soul's sake, I who live amongst crimes and squalor must laugh when I have friends to laugh with . . . even though there is little to laugh at."

The Inspector has no special equipment beyond that which any astute policeman might naturally acquire. His major ability, he claims, is to seize the skirts of chance and hang tightly to them. Celia Harland, a member of the cast of "At the Villa Rose"■, provided the best description of Hanaud when she told him, "I feel as if I had a big Newfoundland dog with me."

HANDY, SAUL
creator CORNELIUS HIRSCHBERG

Unhappy as a Chicago police detective, Saul Handy decides to move to New York City and become a jewelry salesman, taking a job on the "Diamond Block" (47th Street between Fifth and Sixth Avenues) where scores of jewelry shops are found. Saul's biggest problems are learning to appraise diamonds, selling jewels, and finding good delicatessen sandwiches.

Cornelius Hirschberg is a jewelry salesman and the authen-ticity of his book was a factor in earning it the Mystery Writers of America "Edgar" as the best first mystery of its year.

HANVEY, JIM
creator OCTAVUS ROY COHEN

Jim Hanvey is a gargantuan figure of a man, with lots of huge chins, and short, fat legs. He is ponderous in his movements, waddling when he walks. His cheap clothes barely fit around his enormous body. His bovine expression rarely changes and his eyes are fish-like, almost inhuman, seemingly incapable of vision, and reflecting absolutely no intelligence.

He smokes vile, black cigars that befoul the air. He plays for hours on end with a gold toothpick that hangs from a chain extending across his chest. It is one of his major physical efforts. Usually, he just sits with his shoes off and rests. He is, for all his uncouth appearance and actions, a sentimentalist who goes to the movies where he suffers and weeps with the actors.

Hanvey is a highly regarded private detective who has more friends in the criminal world than out of it. He befriends all law-breakers who go straight, though he is "the terror of crooks from coast to coast." His gold toothpick was the present of an internationally famous criminal, who gave it to him as a token of sincere regard.

HARDIN, BART
creator DAVID ALEXANDER

Ex-Marine Korean War hero Bart Hardin is editor of "The Broadway Times," a theatrical and horse-racing newspaper. He occupies an apartment above a Times Square flea circus. No one knows Broadway better than he. He is well-known for his generosity, his love of gambling and his brightly-flowered vests. His friendly rival on many cases is the ulcer-ridden Lieutenant Romano.

HARRINGTON
creator MEL ARRIGHI

Manhattan attorney Harrington is a born loser. He is being evicted for non-payment of rent, he cannot establish a regular clientele since he lost his last 10 cases, and his girl friend, who writes pornography for a living, spurns his advances. He is more successful as detective than as lawyer. He takes the case, without fee, of a young man who apparently committed murder while on an LSD trip, and solves the case without having to make a court appearance.

The 37-year-old Harrington is an army veteran and a New York University Law School graduate (class of 1954). A lifelong resident of Greenwich Village, he is a keen observer of its residents.

HATCH, CYRUS
creator FREDERICK C. DAVIS

The young professor of criminology, Cyrus Hatch, is involved in non-academic murders and other crimes. Assisted by his wife, Jane, and his cocky little bodyguard, Danny Delevan, Cyrus' deductions would be worthy of his father, the Police Commissioner of New York City.

HAWKS, JOAQUIN
creator BILL S. BALLINGER

Half Spanish and half Nez Percé Indian, Joaquin Hawks is a linguist and lover and smooth killer who undertakes a number of perilous assignments in Southeast Asia for the Central Intelligence Agency of the United States.

HAZELRIGG, CHIEF INSPECTOR
creator MICHAEL GILBERT

Red-faced, Bulky Chief Inspector Hazelrigg has an even disposition but, once in a while, his gray eyes freeze in fury. Rising in the ranks from constable, Hazelrigg has more than 30 years of experience, ranging from cases involving fascist organizations attempting to subvert the British government in the late 1930's to cases in his post-World War II specialty—black market crime. No matter what his assignment, Hazelrigg is dedicated. A cat in his office sometimes lies at his feet while Hazelrigg naps.

HEIMRICH, MERTON
creators RICHARD and FRANCES LOCKRIDGE

Heimrich is promoted from Lieutenant to Captain and later to Inspector in the New York State Police during the course of the series of books about him. There is also an improvement in his marital status, since he leaves the lonely life of the police barracks near Van Brunt in Putnam County, N.Y., to marry attractive widow Susan Faye, a local interior decorator. The marriage brings Heimrich much happiness, a ten-year-old stepson named Michael, and a wife with the habit of witnessing murders. Heimrich is a kindly, but dour, man with the annoying habit of beginning many of his sentences, "Now, . . ."

HELM, MATT
creator DONALD HAMILTON

World War II service taught Matt Helm the fine art of spying and trained him to kill. When he is asked to take another mission a decade later, he accepts, despite many doubts. Helm's doubts are well-founded, since resuming the life of a spy-killer (albeit in the service of his country) is enough to ruin his marriage.

Although he remains friendly with his ex-wife, he makes no attempt at reconciliation, realizing that the life of a spy is really for him. It is a life which takes him to Scandinavia, Hawaii, Mexico, the Canadian woods and Scotland. Occasionally (usually when recovering from a wound or injury) he finds the time to pursue his hobbies (hunting and fishing) and his peacetime occupation (photography).

HEWITT, MARTIN
creator ARTHUR MORRISON

The tales of Martin Hewitt, as related by Brett, his journalist friend, are more like those of Sherlock Holmes★ than adventures of any other sleuth. He is not as colorful or as eccentric as Holmes, however, nor as omnipotent.

As similar as his cases are to those of Holmes, his physical appearance is as far-removed. Hewitt is of ordinary height, stoutish, clean-shaven, with a round, smiling face and a pleasant, companionable nature. A gentleman, Hewitt was a lawyer's clerk and "some of the dust of his legal surroundings seems always to cling to him." He had been so skillful in collecting evidence for his employer's clients that he decided to enter business for himself as a private consultant.

He lives with Brett and has his office in an old building near the Strand. A plain ground-glass door bears the single word, "Hewitt." His methods of detection and the cases in which he is involved are unspectacular and he "has no system beyond a judicious use of ordinary faculties."

Like those of Holmes, Hewitt's adventures first appeared in the pages of the Strand magazines and were illustrated by Sydney Paget.

HILDRETH, BARNABAS
creator VINCENT CORNIER

Barnabas Hildreth is a detective who deals with scientific material much more romantically than does his English colleague, Dr. Thorndyke★. Employed by British Intelligence, Hildreth has a distinct love of the bizarre and is as at home talking to a gypsy in her own language as he is dealing with spies. The chronicler of his adventures, a journalist, leads the reader to believe that Barnabas has had an exotic past, though he gives few details about how his subject acquired the name, "The Black Monk."

HITE, QUINNY
creator RICHARD BURKE

Once a member of the official police force, Quinny Hite is a private investigator with one goal in life: marriage to his best girl, Joan. To date, he has been unsuccessful, his efforts hampered by murders or bureaucratic snarls. Hite wears a derby hat.

HOLMES, SHERLOCK▲
creator SIR ARTHUR CONAN DOYLE

Beyond question, Sherlock Holmes is the greatest and most famous detective in history. At the mention of his name, an image springs to life: a tall, slender, hawk-nosed detective, wearing a deer-stalker cap and Inverness cape, a calabash pipe clenched in his teeth, seeking clues with the aid of a magnifying glass. Even the people with whom he associates are better-known than are most historical characters: Doctor Watson●, his trusted roommate and chronicler of the adventures; Professor Moriarty●, the "Napoleon of Crime," the master criminal who rules the Victorian underworld; Mycroft Holmes●, Sherlock's older, larger, wiser brother; Irene Adler●, who will always be the woman to Holmes; Mrs. Hudson●, his long-suffering landlady; and Inspector Lestrade●, the inept Scotland Yard official.

Sherlock Holmes, the world's first consulting detective, wanted a roommate to share the expenses of his rooms at 221B Baker Street when a mutual acquaintance introduced him to John H. Watson, M.D., recently returned from army service in the East. When they meet, Watson is impressed by Holmes' appearance. His height, which exceeds six feet, seems even greater because he is so thin, his eyes are sharp and piercing, and the thin, hooked nose gives his whole expression an air of alertness and precision. His chin, too, has the prominence and squareness which mark the man of determination.

Before agreeing to share rooms, Holmes and Watson confess their shortcomings. Holmes says: "I get in the dumps at times, and don't open my mouth for days on end." He also smokes strong tobacco and keeps chemicals about, occasionally conducting experiments. He plays the violin; Watson soon learns that Holmes is nothing less than a virtuoso. Watson confesses to keeping a bull pup, objects to arguments because his nerves can't stand them, gets up "at all sorts of ungodly hours, and," he says, "I am extremely lazy. I have another set of vices when I'm well, but those are the principal ones at present." What Holmes has failed to mention is his addiction to cocaine.

The two friends are quite content in their new quarters, Holmes solving the most bizarre crimes of the day and Watson helping him, then, much to the detective's disgust chronicling the adventures. Holmes feels that, if they are to be told at all, they should be straightforward accounts of exercises in logic and deduction, not the sensationalized narratives penned by Watson.

Holmes possesses a remarkable intellect and has precise, minute knowledge in some areas, yet, astonishingly, is totally ignorant in others. Watson tells us Holmes' knowledge of literature, philosophy and astronomy are nil; of politics, feeble; of geology, practical but limited; of botany, variable (he is well up on poisons but knows nothing of practical gardening); of chemistry, profound; of anatomy, accurate but unsystematic; of sensational literature, immense (he appears to know every detail of every horror perpetrated in the century), and Holmes has a good practical knowledge of British law. He is also a fine athlete, being an expert singlestick player, boxer, and swordsman. On one occasion, Dr. Grimesby Roylott, a giant of a man, threatens Holmes, bending a poker into a horseshoe shape, to Watson's amazement. When Roylott leaves, Holmes straightens it with his hands.

Holmes explains his educational shortcomings: "I consider that a man's brain originally is like a little empty attic, and you have to stock it with such furniture as you choose. A fool takes in all the lumber of every sort that he comes across, so that the knowledge which might be useful to him gets crowded out, or at best is jumbled up with a lot of other things, so that he has a difficulty in laying his hands upon it. . . . It is a mistake to think that that little room has elastic walls and can distend to any extent. Depend upon it there comes a time when for every addition of knowledge you forget something you knew before." Holmes maintains a small but carefully selected library to supply him with the facts he requires in his investigations; several large scrapbooks are carefully maintained.

His relentless pursuit of criminals, especially Moriarty, has endangered Holmes' life on more than one occasion. The evil professor, in a rage of frustration, once had a face-to-face meeting with Holmes above the Reichenbach Falls in Switzerland. The adversaries grappled and, it was reported, both fell to their deaths. The world was stunned by the news and went into mourning for the great detective. After three years, however, Holmes returned. He had not died in the fall but had taken the opportunity to allow his enemies to think him dead. He had gone to Tibet, adopting the identity of Sigerson, a Danish explorer, and engaged in research. Except in the criminal world, there is universal rejoicing at Holmes' return to London and poor Dr. Watson nearly succumbs at the sight of his friend.

Although remote and aloof, Holmes inspires deep affection in those who know him well, such as Watson and the little band of street ragamuffins who eagerly track down clues at his command. In contrast to the police "regulars," Holmes calls his urchins the "Baker Street Irregulars"—a name later appropriated by a group of Sherlock Holmes scholars.

His life began on Friday, January 6, 1854, at the farmstead of Mycroft in the North Riding of Yorkshire. While at Oxford, he solved his first mystery (1874), a case later recorded as "The Gloria Scott." Three years later, he took rooms in Montague Street, beginning the private consultative practice that was to last for 23 years. In January, 1881, he met Dr. Watson and removed to Baker Street. Five years later, Holmes was involved in the most important international case of his career. Says Holmes: "It is a case, my dear Watson, where the law is as dangerous to us as the criminals are. Every man's hand is against us, and yet the interests at stake are colossal. Should I bring it to a successful conclusion it will certainly represent the crowning glory of my career." This adventure was published as "The Adventure of the Second Stain."

In 1891, Holmes and Moriarty engaged in their first physical encounter, resulting in the death of one and the near-death of the other. After a three-year hiatus, during which Holmes is believed to have had an affair with the lovely Miss Adler, he returned to resume his practice. When Miss Adler died, in 1903, Holmes retired to keep bees on the southern slopes of the Sussex Downs. Having learned the secret of long life from Tibetan lamas, Holmes still lives.

HORNE, CHARLES
creator WILSON TUCKER

Charles Horne is a thin, soft-spoken insurance investigator who lives and works in the Midwest in the years just after World War II. He needs knowledge in diverse fields, such as rural railroading and science fiction to solve his riddles.

HUNT, ELSIE MAE
see MULLIGAN, TIM

HUNTER, ED and AM
creator FREDRIC BROWN

The Hunter and Hunter Detective Agency in Chicago consists of handsome, brash young Ed Hunter and his wily Uncle Am (Ambrose), most of whose life has been spent as a carnival pitchman. When no one seems interested in finding the murderer of his brother—Ed's father—Am leaves his job and comes to the Windy City, which he describes as a "fabulous clipjoint."

Am is middle-aged, with the cheerful round face of a cherub (if a cherub were to wear a scraggly brown mustache). His only known vice is an enthusiasm for poker that keeps him up to odd hours of the morning. His nephew, 18-year-old Ed Hunter, has plans for their detective agency that will make it the biggest, best and most successful in the Middle West.

JACKSON, KANE
creator WILLIAM ARDEN, pseudonym of Dennis Lynds

The embittered but supremely competent industrial spy Kane Jackson hires out as a mercenary in the wars of high-level capitalism. His battle-hardened humanity and understanding of trapped people are more valuable to him than mechanical aids such as bugging devices.

JAMES, MICHAEL DANE
creator JAMES M. ULLMAN

Mike James is the head of a New York investigation firm which specializes in preventing industrial espionage and stock manipulation. A former professional football player, he is now in middle age, still broad-shouldered but slightly potbellied. He is square-faced, wears horn-rimmed glasses and in the days when men wore their hair shorter, he sported a crew cut.

JERICHO, JOHN
creator HUGH PENTECOST, pseudonym of Judson Philips

Huge, red-bearded Greenwich Village painter John Jericho is about 40 years old, 6'6", 240 pounds—suggesting a Viking warrior who has come through the centuries unmarred by time. Despite his prepossessing appearance, he is gentle, sensitive, and happiest when quietly painting in his Jefferson Mews studio. He cannot help getting involved with other people, always taking the side of the underdog.

JOHNSON, DR. SAM:
creator LILLIAN DE LA TORRE, pseudonym of Lillian Bueno McCue

One of the few men in history capable of being a worthy precursor of Sherlock Holmes★ is the noted Sage of Fleet Street, Dr. Sam: Johnson. And who is better to select as the forerunner of Dr. Watson● than James Boswell? Already well known are Dr. Johnson's famous friendship with the Thrales, his sympathy for the American Revolution, and the influence he exerted on London's literary tastes. In the volumes listed below, the reader is finally made aware of the many crimes he solved. Dr. Johnson is middle-aged, fat, and has a stubborn, choleric, pockmarked face. Although he bears a strong physical resemblance to Nero Wolfe★, he is more active than the famous New York detective, many of Johnson's cases ending with the renowned essayist grappling with the criminal.

JONAS, JONAS P.
creator E. X. FERRARS, pseudonym of Morna Davis MacTaggart Brown

Mr. Jonas is a garrulous old curmudgeon who is certain he can make a fortune if only he can get someone to set his memoirs to paper. He claims to have had an exciting, albeit discreet, career as a private detective. He specialized in being "invisible," wearing drab clothes and behaving in a drab manner so no one would remember him. Since retiring, he has tried, with some success, to get his niece to record his past triumphs.

JONES, AVERAGE
creator SAMUEL HOPKINS ADAMS

Adrian Van Reypen Egerton Jones, better known as Average Jones, is an advertising advisor living in the Cosmic Club—a club with a variety of members from every profession imaginable. He is young, good-looking without being overly conscious of it, well built, and impeccably dressed at all times. The Advisor has a wonderful sense of humor and an insatiable curiosity.

JONES, CAREFUL
creator PAT HAND, pseudonym of Thomas Costain

The fat old man named Careful Jones is the Robin Hood of the poker table. His philosophy: "Trim the rich to help the poor." At the same time, he does pretty well for himself. He epitomizes the poker face, seemingly impassive, almost apathetic about the game. He appears clumsy when dealing the cards, apologizing and pointing out that perhaps he is getting a little old. If his opponents in these high-stake card games feel sorry for him, they are sorrier for themselves afterward.

KEATE, NURSE SARAH
creator MIGNON G. EBERHART

Sarah Keate is an adventurous nurse whose medical assignments bring her face-to-face with murder. Her partner in detection is an enterprising young private investigator, Lance O'Leary.

KELLY, SLOT-MACHINE
creator DENNIS LYNDS

He got his nickname because those he deals with consider Slot-Machine Kelly a one-armed bandit. His physical handicap makes him, if anything, tougher. Many of his cases are set in the Chelsea district of New York City. Kelly has never appeared in a novel, but his creator put another one-armed Chelsea man between hard covers when he related the adventures of Dan Fortune★ who runs his own agency.

KENNEDY, CRAIG▲
creator ARTHUR B. REEVE

"The American Sherlock Holmes"★, the title that once applied to Craig Kennedy, a Columbia University professor. Kennedy, like Holmes, was a chemist, and many of his solutions to mysteries resulted from his scientific work. Kennedy was involved in cases in which the use of a lie detector, gyroscope, and a portable seismograph (which can differentiate footsteps) are important factors. The use of these scientific "miracles" was prophetic since the stories appeared more than half a century ago.

Kennedy was quite active, a master of disguise, and not averse to carrying a gun when danger threatened. In addition to teaching, he was a consulting detective, accepting large fees, and was an unofficial advisor to Inspector Barney O'Connor of the New York Police.

Kennedy's roommate was Walter Jameson, a newspaper reporter who chronicled his friend's adventures and attempted to solve cases on his own occasionally with indifferent success. Holmes' love for playing the violin is famous. Less well known is Kennedy's love for opera.

KERRIGAN, LIEUTENANT FRANCIS X.
creator JOSEPH HARRINGTON

Frank Kerrigan is an honest, conscientious, tireless policeman. He is not brilliant or intellectual, but has been rewarded with a promotion. Kerrigan is, basically, a doorbell-ringer. He persistently asks questions of everyone connected with a case until the information makes sense. His specialized knowledge of New York City life helps him on some cases. He is unfailingly courteous to the public, generous to everyone. It would be unfair to ascribe selfish motives when he gives up his vacation to help colleague Detective Jane Boardman.

KERRY, DETECTIVE-INSPECTOR DONALD
creator JEFFREY ASHFORD, pseudonym of Roderic G. Jeffries

Conscientious Detective-Inspector Kerry is the epitome of the hard-working, under-paid English policeman. Don Kerry has difficulty supporting his wife and young daughter on his salary. He must live near the police station, saving transportation costs. He is dedicated to and loves his job, though he finds some of the policemen with whom he works—Chief Inspector Clarke, a constant user of stomach pills, and Inspector Brendon, a religious fanatic—are difficult to get along with. Don is able to overlook their idiosyncrasies.

KILBY, MARK
creator ROBERT CAINE FRAZER, pseudonym of
John Creasey

A tall, lean man with silver-gray eyes in an eaglelike face, Mark Kilby is British by birth and a holder of the O.B.E., but he works as chief troubleshooter for a high-bracket American investment security corporation.

KILGERRIN, PAUL
creator CHARLES L. LEONARD, pseudonym of
Mary Violet Heberden

The hardboiled Paul Kilgerrin was seriously wounded in World War I but recovered sufficiently to handle assignments for U.S. Army intelligence. He and his friend, attractive widow Gerry Cordent, free-lance for the government.

After seeing Kilgerrin once, it is impossible to fail to recognize him in the future. His face is gaunt and swarthy, his black hair graying at the temples, his remarkable eyes seem hooded, like a falcon's. Well into his forties, his slim, 5'11" body is still youthful.

"KING, LEROY"
creator JAMES HOLDING

Just as Ellery Queen★ is really two men (Frederic Dannay and Manfred B. Lee), so is the parody counterpart, "LeRoy King," really two men (mystery writers King Danforth and Martin LeRoy). The writers are with their wives on an around-the-world cruise on the luxury ship, "Valhalla." The fact that they come across murder every time the ship puts into port (and sometimes at sea, too), doesn't spoil their vacation. Such happenings merely give them ideas for future stories, as well as an opportunity to practice what they write.

KLAW, MORIS
creator SAX ROHMER, pseudonym of Arthur Sarsfield Ward

Moris Klaw, the Dream Detective, describes himself as "an old fool who sometimes has wise dreams." He is able to absorb the atmosphere of the criminal act by lying down and sleeping at the scene of a crime. He carries an odically sterilized red silk cushion.

From the lining of his archaic brown bowler, he takes a scent spray and plays its contents on his high, bald brow, an odor of verbena filling the air. His skin has the color of dirty vellum and his hair, eyebrows, and beard are so toneless as to be virtually without color. He wears gold-rimmed pince-nez, a silk muffler, and a long black cloak. He is an antiques dealer and has a gray parrot that announces a visitor with, "The Devil has come for you, Moris Klaw."

A bit of a charlatan, Klaw has frequently been accused of being an insane theorist, yet he has never failed to point his finger at the guilty party. He is assisted by his beautiful brunette daughter, the graceful Isis.

LAM, DONALD
creator A. A. FAIR, pseudonym of Erle Stanley Gardner

Pint-sized physically but a superb thinker and tactician, Donald Lam is a disbarred attorney who entered the employ of tough-talking female private eye Bertha Cool. Despite his frequent brushes with the police, he quickly worked himself up to a full partnership in the firm.

LANE, DRURY
creator BARNABY ROSS, pseudonym of Frederic Dannay and Manfred B. Lee

A Shakespearean actor forced by deafness to leave the stage, Drury Lane retires to the Elizabethan manor house he has built on the Hudson. He proceeds to intervene in the dramas of real life as unofficial consultant on the tougher murder cases of New York City's Inspector Thumm.

LATHAM, GRACE
see PRIMROSE, COLONEL

LAVENDER, JIMMIE
creator VINCENT STARRETT

The ironic, whimsical, sentimental Chicago detective, Jimmie Lavender, "looks more like an actor or an army officer." A lock of white hair amid a mass of dark curls distinguishes his appearance. The brilliant amateur generally functions in the Chicago of the gangster era but his adventures have taken him to all parts of the nation and several foreign countries.

LEAMAS, ALEC
creator JOHN LE CARRÉ, pseudonym of David John Moore Cornwall

Alec Leamas is a secret service agent whose self-disgust, dehumanization, and degradation slowly, inexorably, become complete. He is doomed to be a martyr to a cause in which he does not believe, for he believes in nothing but satisfying himself with the most common pleasures. He is a masochist, despising himself, his associates, and his job. His ultimate act of depression is falling into a bored, boring love.

LECOQ, MONSIEUR
creator EMILE GABORIAU

M. Lecoq began as a minor detective who had a criminal record before joining the Sûreté. Later, he had to choose between a life of crime or one of police work, choosing the latter. The career of the earlier Lecoq bore a striking resemblance to that of a real Frenchman, François Eugène Vidocq (1775–1857) who joined the Sûreté after a life of crime, then wrote his memoirs in four volumes. These books influenced Gaboriau.

Lecoq was born, in approximately 1844, to a rich and respectable Normandy family. When his father died, financially ruined, Lecoq's law studies were interrupted. For a number of years he scraped out a menial existence, causing his contemplation of illegal means of becoming wealthy. An energetic man, he was rather small but well-proportioned. His eyes sparkled brilliantly or grew dull according to his mood.

As a detective, Lecoq had many strong points and certainly did not deserve being described as "a miserable bungler" by Sherlock Holmes★. He was a master at the use of disguise and developed tests to judge when a bed had been slept in and when the hands of a clock had been set back. He was capable of professional jealousy toward his chief, Gevrol, of the Detective Police, a courageous but careless sleuth.

LEITH, LESTER
creator ERLE STANLEY GARDNER

Lester Leith is one of Perry Mason's★ blood (or ink) brothers in the legal profession and one of the great con men on the American scene. It was once estimated that he "earned" 7¼ million dollars during his career and donated it to charity—

except for the 20% he kept for what he considered reasonable expenses. Most of his money was secured from baser crooks, whom he ultimately turned over to the police. Nonetheless, Leith's nemesis, police Sergeant Ackley, never stopped trying to incriminate him. Ackley placed a police undercover man as Leith's valet.

LEROUX, ROLF
creator PETER GODFREY

One of the few South African detectives in literature is Rolf LeRoux of Capetown, whose creator also hailed from that city. LeRoux has been appropriately described as avuncular; the man whom he helps solve crimes is his nephew, Inspector Joubert of the Capetown Police.

Behind LeRoux's smiling face and soft brown eyes is a razor-sharp mind, able to get to the heart of any problem in deduction. While his benign appearance may be a smoke screen for his intellect, he also provides a literal smoke screen from a malodorous pipe which he is seldom seen without. One other distinctive feature is a fine set of bushy chin whiskers.

LINDSEY, RALPH
creator BEN BENSON

Baby-faced Ralph Lindsey joined the Massachusetts State Police at the age of 21. He retained his youthful looks throughout his career, frequently being used as a "plant" to help secure evidence in juvenile crime cases. There is considerable pressure on Ralph to succeed with the State Police. His father, a trooper for 20 years, was shot in the line of duty and is paralyzed from the waist down. Officers who had served with the older Lindsey expect his son to carry on the family tradition of skill and courage.

LITTLEJOHN, INSPECTOR
creator GEORGE BELLAIRS, pseudonym of Harold Blundell

Famous as Inspector Littlejohn, this Scotland Yard sleuth received a promotion to Superintendent late in his career. Littlejohn is very conscious of his age and fears he is being "kicked upstairs." He also fears that he is patronized by the younger men with whom he works, and that they consider his methods dated. He has, however, lost none of his ability to sift through clues to arrive at a correct solution.

LOVE, PHAROAH
creator GEORGE BAXT

Pharoah Love is not a typical policeman. He is black, a homo-sexual, and frequently uses the seamy side of the law to solve a mystery. The tales of this cop abound in black humor.

LUPIN, ARSÈNE
see under "ROGUES"

LYNCH, BERTRAM
creator JOHN W. VANDERCOOK

In the 1930's, Bertram Lynch was an investigator for the Permanent Central Board of the League of Nations. His adventures, chronicled by Robert Deane, a professor of medi-eval history, take him to such exotic locales as Fiji, Trinidad, and Haiti.

"MAC"
creator THOMAS B. DEWEY

The private detective now known only as "Mac" was born in 1909 and had joined the Chicago police at the age of 23. He learned his job under the tutelage of Donovan, an honest veteran cop. Perhaps he learned it too well, for he solved a crime which "The Mob" did not want solved, and he was dis-missed from the police force. He became a private detective with a combination office and apartment near Chicago's North Side. This proved a comfortable arrangement for him.

In 1947, he described himself as "38 years old, a fairly good shot with small arms, slow thinking, but thorough, very dirty in a clinch." His early work was mostly in the Chicago area but later cases took him throughout Illinois, the Midwest, and finally to California, where he enjoyed the Los Angeles climate. He is especially concerned with the problems of the young.

MACDONALD, CHIEF INSPECTOR ROBERT
creator E. C. R. LORAC, pseudonym of Edith Caroline Rivett

The quiet, virtually faceless Chief Inspector Macdonald is a supremely competent Scotland Yard man. He is generally as-signed to assist the authorities of the provincial counties in unravelling baffling local murders.

MACLAIN, CAPTAIN DUNCAN
creator BAYNARD KENDRICK

Young, wealthy, and handsome, Captain Duncan Maclain was blinded while serving as an intelligence officer in World War I. With willpower and persistence, he mastered his disability by developing his remaining senses to serve in place of his lost eyesight. He turned to the challenges of the unlikely profession of private investigator. He is aided by his dogs (Schnuke, a seeing-eye dog, and the more lethal Dreist) and his partner, "Spud" Savage●, who married their secretary, Rena●. Maclain married Sybella Ford, the lovely owner of a decorating shop.

Maclain has cultivated the ability to shoot at sounds. His chief recreations are reading his collection of Braille books, listening to his Capehart, and assembling giant jigsaw puzzles.

MacWHORTER, ANGUS
creator HARRY STEPHEN KEELER

MacWhorter's Mammoth Motorized Show, the Biggest Little Circus on Earth, roars across the landscape—trouble never far behind. Whether MacW's trouble is a gruesome murder, a truckful of vanishing bank robbers, a lovers' quarrel or a plot to steal the entire circus, two things are certain: detective MacWhorter will do absolutely nothing and the problem will be resolved through a fireworks display of flabbergasting coincidences.

MADDEN, DAVID
creator DORIS MILES DISNEY

Postal Inspector David Madden, stationed in Dunston, Conn., investigates crimes involving the U.S. Mails. He does not fit the general stereotype of government employee, since he works long hours, often beginning before dawn and continuing late into the night. When he does get time to relax, he drinks beer and indulges in his only hobby, a stamp collection.

This 5'11", thin-faced Inspector has been a lonely man since his wife, Estelle, died of cancer in 1951. However, in a 1956 case, Madden, who is still young, showed considerable interest in an attractive widow, even though she was a suspect in one of his cases.

MADDOX, IVOR
creator ELIZABETH LININGTON

The story of Sergeant Ivor Maddox is really the story of the detective squad at the Wilcox Ave. police station in Hollywood, California. Maddox is a dedicated policeman with an unusual cross to bear: most women fall in love with him as soon as they see him. There are nights when he would rather curl up with a good mystery story. In fact, he is such an advocate of the values of mystery fiction that he converts policeman Rodriguez.

Other noteworthy members of the squad are Policewoman Sue Carstairs and Detective Drogo D'Arcy, who, with some justification, is sensitive about his first name. The squad operates under the relaxed supervision of Lieutenant Eden, functioning realistically in the unrealistic world that is Hollywood.

MAGRUDER, INSPECTOR JOHN B.
creators JEROME and HAROLD PRINCE

Inspector John B. Magruder has been a New York City policeman for more than 40 years, wearing old brown suits that have probably not been pressed since he bought them. He has a powerful neck and tightly pressed lips which look as if they have been "laid on each other like bricks." His eyes are watchful and wary. To anyone he suspects of a crime, he is definitely bad news; he is "the moment you come home late at night and see the yellow envelope of a telegram sticking out from under your door." Magruder is a "metropolitan manhunter," the one character to emerge solidly from the Joycean stream-of-consciousness fiction of the Princes.

MAIGRET, COMMISSAIRE JULES
creator GEORGES SIMENON

The patient Commissaire Jules Maigret, great-hearted investigator of the Police Judiciare, does not believe in physical clues or elaborate deductions; he solves his cases by quieter and simpler means. He will wander the streets, ask irrelevant questions, sit down at a sidewalk café to smoke his pipe and have a beer or a calvados, trudge bearlike back to his overheated little office on the Quai des Orfevres and look at reports. In short, he will absorb the essence of the milieu and probe the good and evil in the hearts of men and women until the person he is seeking reveals himself. In this respect, the patience of Commissaire Maigret is infinite.

For an English-speaking reader, dependent on tangible clues and chains of empirical reasoning, the Maigret stories may at first seem intellectually weak and insubstantial; on closer acquaintance they will be seen to have a strange and compelling fascination all their own, and the humanity of the characters and the sights and smells and sounds of France come alive on every page to be savored.

MAITLAND, ANTHONY
creator SARA WOODS, pseudonym of
Sara Hutton Bowen-Judd

The young British barrister Anthony Maitland specializes in spectacular murder trials and adroit exposure of the real killer. His quiet wife, Jenny, and his uncle and legal mentor, Sir Nicholas Harding, Q.C., provide moral and mental support in moments of crisis.

MALONE, JOHN J.
creator CRAIG RICE, pseudonym of Georgiana Ann Randolph
[Mrs. Laurence Lipton]

The appearances in court of this little Chicago lawyer are far fewer than his visits to the City Hall Bar of Joe the Angel. Malone is a hard-living, hard-drinking man. In his law offices, his frequent companion is a bottle of rye cached in the filing cabinet marked "Personal." Playing second fiddle to the whiskey is the unfortunate lot of his pretty black-haired secretary, Maggie Cassidy. Maggie is tremendously loyal to her employer, although he is generally months behind in paying her salary. Malone, who seems to have the "luck of the Irish," gets considerable devotion as well as assistance from Captain Daniel von Flannagan of the Homicide Squad.

MANNERING, JOHN
see BARON, THE

MARCH, COLONEL
creator CARTER DICKSON, pseudonym of John Dickson Carr

When Scotland Yard receives a complaint that does not seem reasonable, it is sent to Room D-3, Department of Queer Complaints, presided over by Colonel March. He is a large, amiable, sandy-mustached pipe-smoker who specializes in solving the impossible.

MARLOWE, PHILIP▲
creator RAYMOND CHANDLER

Philip Marlowe is a modern-day knight, heading down the "mean streets" of Los Angeles as he follows his profession: private detective. Marlowe is a man with a college background in a profession with no specific educational requirement. However, his interests are those of culture and sensibility. He can (and does) quote from Browning, Eliot, Shakespeare, and Flaubert. He likes the paintings of Rembrandt but has little taste for abstract art or atonal music. He plays chess and will relax by solving problems alone at the chess board. He is a man of principles, adhered to regardless of the consequences. Following these principles has caused him to take beatings and even to land in jail on several occasions.

Marlowe knows Los Angeles as do few other people. His ability to speak some Spanish helps in certain parts of town. He has been everywhere in the area, from the San Fernando Valley to the changing neighborhoods of downtown Los Angeles, from Hollywood to the beach at Santa Monica and the corrupt Bay City (patterned after Long Beach). Marlowe has grown disenchanted with his city, especially as the 1940's brought gangsters from the East and from Las Vegas.

Money and sex have never been unduly important to Philip Marlowe. In "The Long Goodbye" he meets 36-year-old Linda Loring, who offers both; she is the only woman with whom he has been known to fall in love. She proposes marriage but one has the impression that the independent Marlowe, now aged 42, is not ready to be tied down. However, evidence from an unfinished Marlowe story indicates that he does marry Linda Loring, lives in Palm Springs with her, but will not live on her fortune.

It is perhaps best to summarize Philip Marlowe by using the words of Raymond Chandler in his famous essay: "The Simple Art of Murder" (1944), "If there were enough like him, I think the world would be a very safe place to live in, and yet not too dull to be worth living in."

MARPLE, MISS JANE
creator AGATHA CHRISTIE

When Miss Marple first appeared, in 1930, she was described as a tall old lady with a wrinkled face and china blue eyes. She has changed very little in appearance, though there are indications she has grown more frail. She should be more than one hundred years of age by now (despite her recent attempts to convince us differently) and she still lives alone.

Miss Marple is an unashamed advocate of gossip as a means of obtaining the information she needs to solve her cases. Early in her career, she used bird glasses as a subterfuge for spying on fellow inhabitants of St. Mary Mead. Now she uses more subtle means.

Finances have been a problem for Jane Marple, as she has had to live on a small, fixed income. She has always been helped by her nephew, novelist Raymond West. In recent years, as he has gained fame, he has grown more generous to his aunt, even sending her on a vacation.

The last Jane Marple mystery, planned for publication after

the death of her creator, Agatha Christie, has the announced title of "Sleeping Murder."

MARQUIS, LIEUTENANT MARTY
creator JOHN LAWRENCE

Lieutenant Marty Marquis, the ruthless, totally amoral head of the Broadway Squad, keeps a Gestapo-like brand of law and order on the Main Stem during the Depression years. He is as hateful as he is effective; he thinks nothing of framing or assassinating people he wants out of the way. His mind is steel-trap keen and he believes his actions are justifiable for the overall good.

MARTINEAU, CHIEF INSPECTOR HARRY
creator MAURICE PROCTER

In the British town of Granchester, Chief Inspector Harry Martineau has had long years of police service. Criminals and careless subordinates have come to fear the eyes of "clouded steel" and the forbidding look on Martineau's handsome face. However, his wife and close colleagues know him to be a fair and dedicated person. Though Martineau meets many criminals, one, racketeer Dixie Costello, crops up often in the tales of the Granchester Police.

His own years as a Yorkshire policeman provide excellent background and qualifications for Procter to write what Anthony Boucher called "among the finest police novels written."

MASON, PERRY▲
creator ERLE STANLEY GARDNER

America's most famous criminal attorney, Perry Mason, was born in 1891. Though it is not possible to establish the exact place of birth, there is considerable evidence pointing to Fayette County, Pennsylvania. We know little of Mason's early career in Los Angeles. Mason is thought of as the unbeaten and unbeatable attorney, and this is generally borne out in his 85 cases. However, it should be noted that, in "The Case of the Terrified Typist," Mason hears the jury find his client guilty.

There is also conflicting evidence regarding his record in other, unrecorded, cases. In 1933, as an example, Della Street●, his secretary, is quoted as saying to him, "Some of your clients got hung; others got free." Later that year, during another case, Mason takes pains to contradict the impression which might have resulted from Della's remark, saying, "I haven't had a client hung so far."

In any case, Perry Mason has had great success and has established a lucrative law practice (he has collected a minimum of $600,000). Early in his career, Mason gave the impression that his practice was almost entirely criminal. However, he later admits that his office carries on a general practice. Though Mason does not advertise the location of his office, it can be found in Los Angeles, near 7th Street and Broadway.

Mason is a big man with long legs, broad shoulders and a rugged face. He has thick, wavy hair, an unlined face and he speaks in a well-modulated voice. He has little or no time for sports or exercise, yet he seems to be in good condition and acquits himself well in a fight. Perry Mason has never married, though there has been endless speculation regarding the degree of his intimacy with Della Street. He lives alone at a residential hotel.

Not only has Mason's name become a synonym for the skillful courtroom strategist but he, his secretary, Della Street, his investigator, Paul Drake●, and his adversaries, Hamilton Burger● and Lieutenant Tragg, have become part of the common consciousness of millions.

The earliest Mason novels (1933-36) were masterpieces of hardboiled pulp realism combined with staggeringly complex plotting. About 1937, under the influence of the slick magazines, the Mason tales became smoother, had more "love interest," but were as complex and fast-paced as ever. Serializations in the "Saturday Evening Post," a hugely popular Mason radio show during the 1940's and a television series begun in the late 1950s, added millions to the fans of the courtroom wizard. No Mason novel has ever gone out of print in this country.

MASTERS, CHIEF-INSPECTOR GEORGE
creator DOUGLAS CLARK

Masters is a tall, athletic Scotland Yard Chief-Inspector whose subordinate, Inspector Green, dislikes him intensely, undoubtedly because of jealousy. Masters, a bachelor, is handsome, well-dressed, and distinguished. He is also wealthy, supplementing his police salary to buy expensive clothes, food, and drink. He is fond of beautiful women and they, in turn, are attracted to the pipe-smoking gentleman Chief-Inspector.

MAYO, ASEY
creator PHOEBE ATWOOD TAYLOR

The "Codfish Sherlock," as Asey Mayo is called, has never been far from the sea throughout his life. He made his first voyage on one of the last of the clipper ships. Subsequently, he sailed as steward, cook, or ordinary seaman before retiring to Wellfleet on the Cape Cod peninsula of Massachusetts. He is now man Friday for the town's wealthiest tycoon. Apparently, the job gives him enough time to drive cars at top speeds and to solve many local murders.

In appearance, Asey Mayo is not impressive, since he is usually bedecked in old, worn clothing and walks with his tall, lean frame hunched over. His head is thrust forward, and his mouth often contains a wad of chewing tobacco. His appearance is deceptive; he is a detective with a profound knowledge of human nature and a remarkable record of deductive success.

McBRIDE, REX
creator CLEVE F. ADAMS

A hard-drinking, hard-boiled private detective, Rex McBride runs into much trouble with gamblers, ganglords, gunmen, corrupt cops, and easy women in the California-Nevada-Montana area during the World War II era.

McGEE, TRAVIS
creator JOHN D. MAC DONALD

Boat bum, lover, and philosopher, disgusted and saddened by all but a handful of people, Travis McGee is deeply concerned with whether or not honest relationships are possible. McGee is also the Simon Templar★ of the Sixties. He makes his living by recovering stolen property and keeping half the proceeds. Living on his Florida-based boat, the Busted Flush, and assisted by his maverick economist friend, Meyer, McGee goes forth to slay dragons.

McKEE, INSPECTOR CHRISTOPHER
creator HELEN REILLY

Inspector Christopher McKee is a tall, dour New York policeman of Scottish origin with a deep hatred for some of the criminals he encounters—especially the blackmailers and murderers. He is notable for his powerful, gaunt head and his long legs. He has a sardonic mouth and penetrating eyes, but is capable of real warmth and humor.

McKee was head of the entire Manhattan Homicide Squad before reorganization divided it into two geographical areas. He has, however, never been one to limit himself geographically. To solve New York mysteries, he has journeyed (or sent his assistant, Inspector Todhunter) to Canada and New Mexico.

McKINNON, TODD
creator LENORE GLEN OFFORD

Todd McKinnon is a pulp-magazine mystery writer, tall and slim with a sandy mustache above his lips and, frequently, a harmonica between them. He lives in Berkeley, California, with his wife and their daughter, Barby. Because Barby is an aspiring young actress, the McKinnons in one adventure attend the Shakespeare Festival in Ashland, Oregon, where they become involved in a mystery.

McNEILL, ANNE and JEFFREY
creator THEODORA DU BOIS

Jeffrey McNeill is a physician, but he and his wife, Anne, who generally narrates their cases, are better known among their acquaintances as amateur detectives. Their adventures lean toward the "Had-I-But-Known" and Gothic, with a respectable amount of brainwork added.

McPHERSON, MARK
creator VERA CASPARY

Mark McPherson is a tough, experienced New York City Police Lieutenant of Scottish ancestry who becomes emotionally involved in the search for the murderer of beautiful Laura Hunt. Epicene newspaper columnist Waldo Lydecker describes Mark as "a veritable Cassius who emphasized the lean and hungry look by clothing himself darkly in blue, double-breasted worsted, unadorned white shirt and dull tie. His hands were long and tense, his face slender, his eyes watchful. He carried his shoulders high and walked with a taut erectness."

MENDOZA, LIEUTENANT LUIS
creator DELL SHANNON, pseudonym of
Elizabeth Linington

Luis Mendoza was raised by his Mexican grandparents in the Los Angeles slums. The temptations of crime are never far away for children growing up there, and a life "on the wrong side of the law" was a distinct possibility for Luis who, as a teen-ager, ran an illegal Spanish Monte game in the back of a restaurant. However, under his grandmother's influence he joined the Los Angeles Police Department in 1942, the year of his 21st birthday. Shortly thereafter, when his grandfather died, it was learned that the miserly old man had been sitting on great wealth, acquired through shrewd real estate speculation. Though Luis inherited a fortune he decided to remain a policeman. A passion for bringing order and reason to a chaotic urban society and the pleasure he derived from solving hopeless cases influenced him to retain his job. He was successful and worked his way up through the ranks to lieutenant.

A slender frame makes him appear shorter than his 5'10" height. His thin, straight face has a long chin, a narrow black mustache above a delicate mouth, a long thin noise, black eyes and heavily arched eyebrows.

His wealth and build allow him to indulge his taste for custom-made, perfectly-fitting clothes. Because Mendoza is often bedecked in foulard ties, Homburg hats and pigskin shoes, his detractors say he looks like a gigolo. However, he is remarkably fit and can acquit himself well when faced with physical danger. Having disposed of a threatening criminal, Luis will then assess and bemoan the damages which fighting has done to his previously immaculate appearance.

Mendoza's interests included his expensive foreign cars, his frequent poker games, the cats who shared his apartment, and the women who temporarily shared his life. Then he met a red-headed divorcée, Alison Weir, and fell in love for the first time. The courtship of these two independent people was stormy, but they married after a case in which Luis rescued her from a crazed rapist-killer. They settled into a comfortable small apartment until they moved to a roomy, luxurious home in the Hollywood Hills, where they reside with their twin children, John Luis and Teresa Ann.

MERLINI, THE GREAT
creator CLAYTON RAWSON

One of the few magician-detectives in literature, The Great Merlini is a man of many likes and dislikes. His chronicler, free-lance writer Ross Harte, notes that Merlini hates the New York City subway system, beer, inactivity, opera, golf, and sleep. He is, on the other hand, highly partial to surf bathing, table tennis, puzzles, circuses, and Times Square, where he operates a magic shop. Merlini's friendly rival is Inspector Homer Gavigan of Homicide, an intelligent man who is, nonetheless, amazed by the magician's feats.

MERRION, DESMOND
creator MILES BURTON, pseudonyn of
Cecil John Charles Street

Restless, whimsically light-hearted Desmond Merrion served in British Intelligence during World War I. Thanks to his good friend, Inspector Arnold of the Criminal Investigation Division, he is permitted to gratify a passion for investigative work, acquired during the war. His cases are thorough and methodical.

MERRIVALE, SIR HENRY
creator CARTER DICKSON, pseudonym of John Dickson Carr

Bald-headed, cigar-chomping, evilly-scowling Sir Henry Merrivale has a rare genius (shared only by Dr. Gideon Fell★) for getting involved in locked-room murders or otherwise impossible situations. Elbowing aside the inadequate Inspector Humphrey Masters of the Yard, H.M. never fails to explain how the crime was committed, while providing generous portions of low comedy and intellectual excitement.

MINERVA CLUB
creator VICTOR CANNING

In London, city of exclusive clubs, stands the Minerva Club, one with the most unusual requirements for membership. Only those who have served at least two years in one of Her Majesty's prisons need apply. Dues are 50 pounds annually, and no one asks how the money is obtained. The members are the English equivalent of the memorable Broadway characters created by Damon Runyon, including such interesting antisocial types as "Milky" Waye, who is club secretary, Solly Badrubal, Jim O'Leary, and Flint Morrish, who once bought a prison.

MOM
creator JAMES YAFFE

Mom, a true armchair detective, operates from a dining room chair, where she dishes out chicken soup and solutions to mysteries to her policeman son, David. The time is always Friday night when the son and his wife come for dinner at his widowed mother's Bronx apartment. Occasionally, he will bring along his superior, the elderly but eligible Inspector Milner.

While dinner is being served, the facts of a mystery perplexing the New York Police Department are recounted. Mom uses her keen mind, and the skepticism which has thwarted many a heavy-thumbed butcher over the years, to arrive at the solution by the time she is ready to serve the Nesselrode pie. Though her view of human nature is quite jaundiced she can be romantic. She is also a great lover of grand opera. Mom's cases have been collected in hard covers.

MOORE, TOUSSAINT
creator ED LACY, pseudonym of Leonard Zinberg

"Touie" Moore, a black private detective, lives on 147th Street in Harlem in one room of an old-fashioned railroad flat that doubles as his office. He had done "skip-tracing" work for larger detective agencies before starting his own business. His one-man operation is not successful, however, and the pipe-smoking private detective often contemplates giving it up for steady employment as a Post Office letter carrier. His father was a student of Negro history, naming him for Toussaint L'Ouverture, the Haitian patriot. "Touie" served in the army during the Korean War and in World War II, earning the Bronze and Silver Stars for his actions.

MORAN, JIGGER
creator JOHN ROEBURT

Disbarred attorney, wheeler-dealer, and sometime cab driver, Jigger Moran is the man to see when one doesn't dare go to a lawyer or a private detective—and doesn't dare act himself. His fees are piratical (for he loves the crap tables) but he gets the job done and makes Homicide Captain Ahearn like the results.

MORAN, P.
creator PERCIVAL WILDE

New England handyman by day and defective detective deluxe by night, P. Moran is an assiduous student of the Acme International Detective Correspondence School. With the help of the pearls of wisdom contained in the School's lessons, P. blunders into all sorts of evildoings. If matters are resolved, it is no thanks to P.

MOTO, MR. I. O.▲
creator JOHN P. MARQUAND

Japan's top secret agent, Mr. Moto is a small, delicate man— almost fragile. His patent leather shoes squeak a bit when he walks. His black hair is carefully brushed in the Prussian style. When his mouth is open, he shows a row of shiny, gold-filled teeth and, as he smiles, he draws in his breath with a soft, polite, sibilant sound. His English is perfect, his voice low and well modulated.

He says of himself, "I can do many, many things. I can mix drinks and wait on tables and I am a very good valet. I can navigate and manage small boats. I have studied at two foreign universities. I also know carpentry and surveying and five Chinese dialects. So very many things come in useful. . . ."

Despite his modest stature, he is physically powerful and a master of the art of judo. His perfect manners and immaculate dress do not alter the fact that he will kill a man without turning a hair.

MULLIGAN, TIM
creator AARON MARC STEIN

Tim Mulligan and fellow archeologist Elsie Mae Hunt roam exotic locales (usually Central and South America) in search of rare, ancient relics. Instead of prehistoric artifacts, frequently they find murder, which they solve by using tolerant understanding of diverse cultures.

MURDOCK, KENT
creator GEORGE HARMON COXE

Kent Murdock, the Picture Chief for the "Boston Courier-Herald," is more educated and subtle than his cross-town rival, "Flashgun" Casey★. His salary is greater than any ever before earned by a Boston news photographer; it supports a comfortable apartment on Marlborough Street. In World War II, Kent served as Museum Monument officer in the Fine Arts Division of the Military Government. Previously he had earned a Purple Heart.

The tall, handsome Murdock (once played by Lew Ayres in a movie) is equally at home in a bar or in a drawing room. His ability to get along with people does not extend to his frequent rivals in the Boston Police Department, Lieutenant Bacon and Sergeant Keogh.

MURDOCK, RACHEL
creator D. B. Olsen, pseudonym of Dolores Hitchens

Against the wishes of her sister, Jennifer, spinsterish and cat-fancier Miss Rachel Murdock loves to interfere in the lives of others. When the problems she encounters include a pleasant bit of murder, Miss Rachel is just the maiden lady who can outwit those nice but conventional-minded policemen, as well as the criminal.

MURPHY, ADDISON FRANCIS
see RAMBLER, THE

MYCROFT, MR.
creator H. F. HEARD

Mr. Mycroft is an elderly gentleman who has retired to keep bees. He is tall and erect, though there is no hint of the military about him. His hair is white and he wears a short, sharp beard. He is extremely distinguished and there is an unmistakable arrogance and vanity in him; he would have made a splendid actor. His face is cold and serene—"a sort of unpolitical Dante" —a face "which might care little for public opinion but much for its opinion of itself." He seldom shows emotion, but when he is truly angry his eyes frighten the beholder.

Mycroft has displayed rare courage on more than one occasion. He is both loquacious and opinionated, hence a bit of a bore. It is believed by some that Sherlock Holmes★ took the name "Mr. Mycroft" upon his retirement to ensure anonymity and privacy.

NELSON, GRIDLEY
creator RUTH FENISONG

Captain (formerly Lieutenant) Gridley Nelson studied criminology, then joined the New York City Police Department, because he enjoyed the work and as a service to society. Of aristocratic background and heir to a fortune, the sharp-witted Nelson solves crimes with thorough, hard work, combined with intelligence.

NOBLE, NICK
creator ANTHONY BOUCHER, pseudonym of
William Anthony Parker White

On Los Angeles' "Skid Row" there is a thin, pale man who spends most of his time in the third booth on the left in Main Street's Chula Negra Cafe. This "wino" is Nick Noble, once the most honest and effective police lieutenant on the force, who was framed and dismissed from the department. After his wife died, as an indirect result of his disgrace, Noble does nothing now but drink sherry and shoo an imaginary fly from his nose. He has been virtually ignored by most of his former colleagues. However, young Lieutenant MacDonald of the Los Angeles Police Department is humble enough to consult Noble on difficult cases, and he finds that alcohol has not dulled the incisive mind.

NOON, ED
creator MICHAEL AVALLONE

On the surface, Ed Noon is just another private eye (later, private spy). A little deeper is a sad and confused little guy with three great loves—baseball, old movies, and atrocious puns— who continually runs into bizarre perversities.

NORTH, HUGH
creator VAN WYCK MASON

Hugh North made his debut as a Captain in Military Intelligence in 1930, rose to Major late in the 1930's and, apparently skipping the rank of Lieutenant Colonel, has been a full Colonel for more than two decades. North's philosophy has always been to live life to the limit, whether at work or play. He has never refused an assignment, no matter how dangerous. While he has been too busy to marry, he has not been too busy to know many beautiful women. The lean, pipe-smoking intelligence agent is dashing and handsome. Behind his contemplative countenance is a keen mind with remarkable powers of observation and retention.

NORTH, PAMELA and JERRY
creators FRANCES and RICHARD LOCKRIDGE

Pam and Jerry North are probably the most popular husband and wife detective team of all time. Pam is a dizzy, trouble-prone housewife; her book publisher husband, Jerry, proves a perfect foil. Unlike most detectives, they were born in mainstream fiction, the subjects of a series of sketches in "The New Yorker." Murder first confronted them in "The Norths Meet Murder," when they rented a vacant studio above their Greenwich Village apartment in order to hold a party. To their chagrin, a corpse came with the rented apartment. Lieutenant Bill Weigand and Sergeant Mullins have been friendly, albeit perplexed, companions of the Norths.

The Norths' exploits have had the distinction of being adapted for the stage, screen, radio, and television, with a variety of performers appearing as Pam and Jerry North.

OAKES, BOYSIE
creator JOHN GARDNER

Perhaps the most improbable spy in fiction is Boysie Oakes of Britain's Department of Special Security. He is handsome, cultivated, a devil with women; he is also afraid of airplanes and can't stand the sight of blood.

O'BREEN, FERGUS
creator ANTHONY BOUCHER, pseudonym of
William Anthony Parker White

The O'Breen, as he calls himself, is a wild, red-haired Irishman —a one-man detective agency in Los Angeles. He never knew his mother, and his father had many problems, including alcoholism. Fergus, however, grew up healthy and wise—if never wealthy—perhaps due to the influence of his sister Maureen, Head of Publicity at Metropolis Pictures. If O'Breen does have a problem, it is his allergy to cats. He sneezes seven times in their presence.

Born about 1910, O'Breen is highly catholic in his interests (and apparently Catholic in his religion). He is well-read, an eager cook, a great football fan, and a lover of classical music, especially Beethoven. These interests parallel those of his creator, Anthony Boucher.

OLD MAN IN THE CORNER, THE
creator BARONESS EMMUSKA ORCZY

The nameless Old Man in the Corner is the first true armchair detective in literature. He sits in a London tea shop and solves the mysteries of the day for Polly Burton, a young reporter for the Evening Observer. The Old Man never visits the scene of a crime, never questions the suspects, never examines clues, although he does enjoy attending inquests, deriving pleasure from the perplexity and discomfiture of the police. He just sits at his corner table and listens to Miss Burton's narrative, tying a piece of string into complicated knots and untying it. Somehow, he produces pertinent photographs and clippings from his pockets when discussing a case.

He is elderly, his clothes are shabby. He is pale and thin and his sparse, light-colored hair is brushed smoothly across the top of an otherwise bald crown. The Old Man is unlike most detectives in that his sympathies usually seem to be with the criminal, and he considers the police stupid and ineffectual. He bothers to solve mysteries only as an intellectual exercise. Crime interests him "when it resembles a clever game of chess, with many intricate moves which all tend to one solution." He believes his brain so superior to those of the criminal and the police that he states, categorically, "There is no such thing as a mystery in connection with any crime, provided intelligence is brought to bear upon its investigation."

The creator of this enigmatic, anonymous unraveller of mysteries also created the swash-buckling Scarlet Pimpernel.

OPARA, CHRISTIE
creator DOROTHY UHNAK

The widow of a New York City Policeman killed in the line of duty, Christie Opara is a policewoman. It is a strange occupation for a 26-year-old blonde who weighs less than one hundred pounds. However, her slender frame harbors great dedication to her job as a detective working for the District Attorney's office. Christie is interested in her boss, Casey Reardon, but he is married, so she continues to live as a widow with her son, Mickey, and her mother-in-law, Nora Opara, in a quiet house in Queens.

Christie is a one-woman United Nations: her father was Greek; her mother, Swedish. Her husband was Irish-Czech and the family name is of the latter nationality; therefore, Christie warns, pronounce it O-per-uh; not O'Para. The author was for many years a policewoman.

OWEN, BOBBY
creator E. R. PUNSHON

In 1930, when Bobby Owen joined the London Police as a constable, it was a most unusual profession for an Oxford University graduate. However, England had been hit by the "economic blizzard" of 1929, and career opportunities were limited. Although bored by the routine elements of his job, Owen does not feel being a policeman is "beneath" him. In fact, he works hard to succeed, pursuing difficult cases even during his off-duty hours.

Owen is regarded as a pushy youngster by some of his superiors, but not by Superintendent Mitchell. The talkative Mitchell, one of the most famous detectives at Scotland Yard, is impressed by Owen and teaches him a great deal. Mitchell is responsible for Owen's eventual transfer from the uniformed force to the Criminal Investigation Department.

Curly-haired, athletic Bobby Owen is a tall young man with a soldierly carriage who is said to be so good-looking that waitresses always serve him first. Besides having the tenacity of a bulldog in difficult cases, Owen has considerable skill as a sketch artist and can do a recognizable rough pencil portrait of a suspect.

PALFREY, DR. STANISLAUS ALEXANDER
creator JOHN CREASEY

Dr. Palfrey and his underground organization, Z5, spent the World War II years combatting Nazi plots. Since then, the brilliant doctor and his band have dedicated themselves to challenging supra-national conspiracies, especially mad scientists seeking world conquest.

"PALMER, HARRY"
creator LEN DEIGHTON

The reluctant, iconoclastic British agent who remains nameless in Len Deighton's novels was brought to life on the screen by Michael Caine with the name "Harry Palmer." He is lazy, cynical, ironic, and likes only one thing more than girls—sleeping, or "flaking out."

PARIS, WADE
creator BEN BENSON

Not all men who work for Wade Paris like him. He has no apparent weaknesses. He is all business and that business is preventing and detecting crime. This singleness of purpose is largely responsible for his rapid advancement from Detective-Inspector to Acting Chief of Detectives with the Massachusetts State Police. His subordinates call him "Old Icewater" because of his coolness under pressure, whether encountering an armed killer or a prison break.

PARR, DEPUTY and ARMISTON, OLIVER
creator FREDERICK IRVING ANDERSON

Deputy Police Commissioner Parr, the manhunter of Center Street, is fortunate in his choice of friends. When a case becomes too difficult for him, he can always count on the assistance of detective story writer Oliver Armiston. In the past, Armiston's mystery stories had contained such ingenious criminal devices that they had been used to good advantage by the underworld. Now, in a unique arrangement, the police pay Armiston *not* to write mysteries. Instead, Parr goes to see Armiston, describes the suspects, gives him the clues, and invariably leaves with the solution to what had seemed insoluble.

PECK, JUDGE EPHRAIM
creator AUGUST DERLETH

Wily old Judge Ephraim Peck dispenses justice and wisdom to the little Wisconsin village of Sac Prairie. Peck is honest, wise, kind, and possesses a fine sense of humor.

PEDLEY, BEN
creator STEWART STERLING, pseudonym of Prentice Winchell

The Chief Fire Marshall of New York City, Ben Pedley turns to detection when crime intersects his job, as it does in the hunt for a pyromaniac or for a killer who seeks to cover his murders by arson. The intelligent, resourceful Pedley is tough, athletic, and unusually young for his job.

PENNYFEATHER, PROFESSOR
creator D. B. OLSEN, pseudonym of Dolores Hitchens

The bookish Professor Pennyfeather is an unassuming literature teacher and also, as he frankly admits, is a born meddler who would rather dabble in murder than annotate a sonnet.

PERKINS, WILLIS
creator PHILIP WYLIE

In the Chelsea section of Manhattan lives a retired bank clerk, Willis Perkins, who is small, pale, mild—in short, the world's least likely detective. This middle-aged bachelor had led a Spartan existence until his retirement, spending all his spare time and money studying criminology, scientific detection and the art of disguise. He is now ready to launch a career as a consulting detective.

PETTIGREW, FRANCIS "FRANK"
creator CYRIL HARE, pseudonym of
Alfred Alexander Gordon Clark

In his early years, Frank Pettigrew, equipped with academic honors, showed great promise in the legal profession. Through a combination of personal difficulties and sheer misfortune, however, he became an aging, unsuccessful lawyer who must struggle to make ends meet. Dame Fortune eventually smiles on Pettigrew, who has an extraordinary ability to solve crime problems. In the course of one of his cases, he meets Eleanor Brown, a young lady half his age, with whom he achieves a happy marriage.

PHANTOM DETECTIVE, THE
creator ROBERT WALLACE, pseudonym of D. L. CHAMPION

Publicly, he is Richard Curtis Van Loan, a young, wealthy, frivolous playboy; privately, he is "The Phantom Detective," a masked (or disguised) crime-fighter identifiable only by a small, jewelled emblem. His goal: the preservation of law and order.

Equipped with an assortment of firearms and a makeup kit, he tangles with several large criminal organizations. He is a genius of disguise, a human chameleon. He is quick to use his gun but, being "a physical marvel, a mental phenomenon," he does not have to rely solely on firearms to vanquish criminals.

"The Phantom Detective's" crime-fighting associates are Steve Huston, a newspaper reporter; Chip Dorlan, who joined him as a mere ragamuffin and grew up to become a military intelligence officer; and his girl friend, Muriel Havens, who doesn't learn his true identity until nearly the end of his career.

PHIPPS, MISS MARIAN
creator PHYLLIS BENTLEY

Miss Marian Phipps is a detective in the class of Miss Marple★ when it comes to inner toughness, curiosity and perceptive intellect. She is more mobile than Miss Marple, driving her little car through the English countryside and visiting old churches, inns and the Shakespearean Festival at Stratford-on-Avon. She finds and solves murders wherever she goes. A famous mystery novelist, Miss Phipps goes on lecture tours.

For pleasure, she visits with Inspector Tarrant (of the Southshire police) and his wife. The modest Tarrant is not above accepting good deductive advice from Miss Phipps, who is described as having a "chubby pink face and untidy white hair." Her generous philosophy, in trying to solve crime, is: "The truth is the best gift one can wish for anyone."

PINKERTON, EVAN
creator DAVID FROME, pseudonym of
Mrs. Zenith Jones Brown

When she was still alive, the miserly wife of the timid little Welshman, Evan Pinkerton, insisted on taking boarders. One room was occupied by a young police rookie, J. Humphrey Bull, who later became a Scotland Yard Inspector. On the death of his domineering wife, Mr. Pinkerton inherited 75,000 pounds, giving him the chance to do things he had wanted to do.

Old habits die slowly, however, and Pinkerton still wears his old-fashioned celluloid collar, string tie, and brown bowler hat. The wistful expression on his gray face and gray lips remains, as does the shy timidity. He does go to the movies three times a week now and has the time to help his friend, Bull, solve mysteries.

"PINKERTON, MISS"
creator MARY ROBERTS RINEHART

Nurse Adams has been dubbed "Miss Pinkerton" by the police, with whom she works closely. She has all the skills of a competent Registered Nurse with the additional abilities of a brave and, occasionally, perceptive detective. Had she but known it was to be a steady thing when Inspector Patton first asked her to help solve a mystery while a nurse in a private home, she might have refused. She accepted, however, and became quite good at both aspects of her work.

In the book which bears her nickname, Nurse Adams has just completed a real nursing assignment and is trying to get some much-needed sleep when Patton awakens her to make some unreasonable demands. It seems there is a house in which evil lurks in every dark shadow. Will she take the assignment? Of course!

POGGIOLI, PROF. HENRY
creator T. S. STRIBLING

Henry Poggioli was born in Boston in 1888. Educated at Cornell, he earned an M.A. and Ph.D. in psychology. After a brief career as an anti-spiritualist lecturer, Poggioli joined the faculty of Ohio State University. He specialized in the criminal mind and was called upon to solve many bizarre cases. His method—trial and error deduction—led to occasional errors. In one case he was falsely accused of committing a murder as part of a psychological experiment.

After being out of the public eye for many years, Poggioli reappeared in semi-retirement in Florida. Though attracted to beautiful women, Poggioli never married; he believed men and women wanted different things from marriage.

POIROT, HERCULE
creator AGATHA CHRISTIE

Hercule Poirot is five feet four inches tall, has an egg-shaped head generally tilted slightly to the left. His eyes appear green when he is excited. Vanity compels him to squeeze his feet into black patent leather shoes which are too small. His enormous mustache is waxed and twirled into points at the ends. Considering his age, his hair is suspiciously dark.

Originally Poirot was a mainstay of the Belgian police and one of the leading detectives on the European continent. He was wounded in the leg during the German invasion of his homeland in 1914. As a refugee in England, he renews his acquaintance with Captain Hastings•, who also had been wounded. Poirot is staying with some other Belgian refugees near the mansion at Styles where Hastings is a guest. When murder occurs, Poirot repays English hospitality by agreeing to solve the crime.

Deciding to remain in England, he becomes a private inquiry agent in London. He shares a flat with Hastings, who recounts Poirot's adventures. The ménage includes two efficient aides: Poirot's valet, Georges, and his secretary, Miss Lemon.

In his first appearance, which takes place in approximately 1915, Poirot is described as elderly. It is clear that even if he were only 50 then, he is now well over one hundred years old. Fortunately, time has not dulled the sharp brain which he describes as his "little grey cells." He still insists on "order and method," and deprecates reliance on physical clues alone as a means of solving cases. His energy has seldom flagged and, though he has retired many times (once to raise pumpkins), an interesting case will always bring him back to action. Perhaps it is his tremendous confidence in his own abilities which makes him believe only he can solve the case.

Death must come as the end, even to Poirot. Ironically, it finds him at Styles, the scene of his first triumph in England. Though crippled by arthritis (he spends most of his day in a wheel chair) and subject to angina pectoris, Poirot has not lost his mental faculties to the ravages of time. His last case is a splendid achievement, a unique tour-de-force.

Poirot, at his death, became the only fictional detective to have his obituary printed on Page One of the New York Times.

PONS, SOLAR
creator AUGUST DERLETH

Dr. Lyndon Parker●, sitting in a pub near Paddington Station, is struck by the unusual looks of a man he later learns to be Solar Pons—who is called "The Sherlock Holmes of Praed Street" by the waiter. Pons is tall and slender, wears an Inverness cape and a hat with a visor. His face is long and thin, as is his nose, and he has a thin-lipped mouth. His eyes are dark and penetrating, surmounted by thick, dark brows. The Doctor and Pons become friends and Parker goes to share Pons' lodgings.

Pons is an advocate of the old-fashioned methods of detection, using his skills of deduction and ratiocination to solve many outstanding crimes. His interests and expertise are varied, ranging from chess, to music, to occult lore, to scientific treatises. When Sherlock Holmes stopped his activities in 1903, a void was felt in London. Solar Pons attempted to fill it, beginning his practice in 1907. He is not Holmes, of course, and he knows he isn't and he knows we know it, but he is a charming and effective impersonator.

August Derleth, the creator of Solar Pons, is a devout Sherlockian who was upset when Sir Arthur Conan Doyle failed to bring new adventures of The Master before the public. He wrote to him and asked his permission to write pastiches of Holmes and, meeting no opposition, did so. Derleth was then 19 years old.

POOLE, INSPECTOR JOHN
creator HENRY WADE, pseudonym of
Sir Henry Lancelot Aubrey-Fletcher

In his time, John Poole was a fine example of the new breed of policemen, college educated and police-school trained. He rose from the ranks to become the youngest inspector in the Criminal Investigation Department of New Scotland Yard. After a series of successful investigations (1929-53), Poole was promoted to Chief Inspector.

POTTER, HIRAM
creator RAE FOLEY, pseudonym of Elinore Denniston

Hiram Potter has been described as an American Albert Campion★. This denizen of Gramercy Park is a dispenser of truth in the murder problems of New York's upper crust. He looks like the White Rabbit but has the reputation of a Jonah. Many bodies have dropped in his vicinity but no murderer escapes.

PRIESTLEY, DR. LANCELOT
creator JOHN RHODE, pseudonym of
Cecil John Charles Street

Professor of applied mathematics at a famed British university, Lancelot Priestley was forced to resign after a heated dispute with the university authorities. He is quite wealthy, however, and now devotes his time to the solving of problems by mathematical means. His chief delight is in the debunking of widely-held theories through strict exercises of logic. His only recreation is to solve crime problems—sometimes brought to him by Superintendent Hanslet●—as exercises in logic. He is completely indifferent to the human elements and to questions of justice. The aging mathematician is dry and academic, with little humor, but is a genial host.

PRIKE, INSPECTOR LEONIDAS
creator LAWRENCE G. BLOCHMAN

When India was still part of the British Commonwealth, little Inspector Leonidas Prike was a dynamic investigator for the Criminal Investigation Department in India. His adventures usually appear as short stories.

PRIMROSE, COLONEL and LATHAM, GRACE
creator LESLIE FORD, pseudonym of Mrs. Zenith Jones Brown

Colonel Primrose is a short, plump, keen-eyed former West Pointer who became a consulting detective after having been wounded in World War I. He resides in a bachelor flat in the Georgetown section of Washington, D.C., where his interests and comforts are looked after by Sergeant Buck, his aide through war and peace for 28 years. Buck is very protective, especially when he feels the Colonel's bachelor status is threatened by designing females.

This description does not extend to Mrs. Grace Latham, who becomes the Colonel's inseparable (albeit platonic) friend. She is 38 years old at their first meeting, a widow whose lawyer-husband was killed in a plane crash, leaving her with two young sons. Her bad fortune is exemplified by the frequency with which she encounters corpses. Her good fortune is that the Colonel is seldom far away.

PRY, PAUL
creator ERLE STANLEY GARDNER

Paul Pry is a suave adventurer found only in pulp magazines of the 1930's. He is an American Simon Templar★, and a professional opportunist who lifts stolen goods from other criminals before the police pick them up. His partner, Mugs Magoo, is a one-armed ex-cop with a photographic memory for faces.

PRYE, DR. PAUL
creator MARGARET MILLAR

Whimsical, distinguished Dr. Paul Prye is a tall (6′ 5″), 35-year-old psychiatrist in Illinois. He finds unsolved murders at home, at Canada's Lake Rousseau, where he spends his summers, and at his own wedding, which was almost postponed because his bride and other members of the wedding party were suspects. It is possible that Dr. Prye discovered the generation gap a quarter of a century before anyone else. In 1942, he asked a particularly obnoxious teenager: "Could there be a new Youth Movement for the suppression of everyone over 30?"

PUMA, JOE
creator WILLIAM CAMPBELL GAULT

Private detective Joe Puma is a thoroughly modern man whom a client has called "a space age Sherlock Holmes." Though Puma considers himself a man of action, not a philosopher, he clearly is a detective who thinks about morality. Though he no longer believes in organized religion, he occasionally regrets having given up the Roman Catholic faith in which he was raised in Fresno, Calif.

His work in Los Angeles provides him with many temptations, but he is too honest to give in to these. Though he has occasionally questioned his own principles ("I would be a happy man if I had either more or less ethics"), his case record is one of scrupulous honesty. It is also that of a man who sticks to his ideals. "I am what I am . . . I don't intend to change my character for day wages . . . I don't take back talk from thieves at any economic level . . . If there is one thing I can't stomach it is the thought of a murderer breathing free air."

Work is not Puma's only interest. He enjoys reading good novels and seeing good drama on television. He also has a hearty appetite for good food and imported beer. Though a big man (240 lbs.), he has never been interested in athletics. A confirmed bachelor, Joe appears to be saving his energy for the many women in his life. He says: "Sex is THE big game."

PYM, MRS.
creator NIGEL MORLAND

Physically tough and badly dressed, Mrs. Palmyra Pym is still quite feminine. Born before the turn of the century, she was widowed after a short marriage. She began her crime-fighting career as a policewoman in Shanghai in 1935 and, 16 years later, long after her return to England, she was an Assistant Commissioner, Criminal Investigation Department—the highest-ranking woman in the history of Scotland Yard.

PYNE, PARKER
creator AGATHA CHRISTIE

For 35 years, Parker Pyne compiled statistics in a government office. When he retired, he wanted to employ this experience in a useful, enjoyable way. He placed an advertisement in the Personal column of the daily newspaper which read: "Are You Happy? If Not Consult Parker Pyne . . ." In this novel fashion, he enjoys his advanced years, helping to make others happy for fees they can afford. His look of British solidity immediately inspires reassurance in his unhappy clients. He is large, though not quite fat, has a bald head of noble proportions, and a pair of strong glasses that do not conceal his little twinkling eyes. He exudes benevolence, making it easy for one to confide in him.

QUADE, OLIVER
creator FRANK GRUBER

Oliver Quade, the Human Encyclopedia, and his straight man Charlie Boston fend off bill collectors by hawking a one-volume Compendium of Human Knowledge. Quade's skill as a book salesman and his memory for obscure facts are most impressive, but do not compare with his facility for running into murders in odd places.

QUARLES, FRANCIS
creator JULIAN SYMONS

Large, slightly dandyish and deceptively languorous, Francis Quarles sets up practice as a private detective shortly after World War II.

QUEEN, ELLERY▲
creator ELLERY QUEEN, pseudonym of
Frederic Dannay and Manfred B. Lee

In his early years, Ellery Queen was a supercilious aristocrat who condescendingly assisted his long-suffering father, Inspector Richard Queen of the New York Police Department. Young Ellery was a sartorial cliché, dressed in tweeds, wearing pince-nez, and carrying a walking stick. Tall and slender, he was a handsome gentleman, and one girl told him he had "devastatingly" silvery eyes. Later in his career, he dropped both the arrogance and the affected eyeglasses. He acquired a sense of humor and is, consequently, more attractive to girls. He is also more interested in them.

Ellery possesses an acute faculty of observation and, while he has sloppy habits, he is neat mentally, bringing many mysteries to an end by deductive reasoning. Because of his father's official connection with the police, Ellery enjoys the best of the professional and private detective's world: he is welcome at the scene of a crime and, with official sanction, has access to witnesses and clues; he also has the freedom to choose those cases which interest him.

The "author" has the distinction of being one of the most important personalities in the history of detective fiction. Not only is Ellery Queen, the detective, one of the most famous characters in literature, but the magazine which bears that name is the most important and successful of its type. As an anthologist, Ellery Queen is without peer, his taste unequalled. As a bibliographer and a collector of the detective short story, Queen is, again, an historical personage. Indeed, Ellery Queen clearly is, after Poe, the most important American of mystery fiction.

QUILLER
creator ADAM HALL, pseudonym of Elleston Trevor

Enigmatic, bitter, alienated, amoral, and ruthless, Quiller is, nonetheless, one of the most impressive of the British cold-war spies.

RAMBLER, THE
(Addison Francis Murphy)
creator FRED MAC ISAAC

Known as The Rambler, Addison Francis Murphy is an itinerant newspaperman who wanders the length and breadth of the United States during the Depression years. He earns subsistence money by working for small local papers for short periods, running into crime and adventure wherever he goes. His tales were recounted in the pulp magazines of the 30's.

RAND, JEFFREY
creator EDWARD D. HOCH

Though only in his mid-thirties, Rand is head of that branch of British Intelligence known as the Department of Concealed Communications. His unit has the responsibility of maintaining the security of Britain's codes, and decoding those of foreign powers. While his functions force him to deal more with words than with people, all is not simple in the world of the spy. Rand frequently travels around the world and is pleased with the opportunity, since the dampness of London depresses him and causes annual sinus attacks. He has had several dramatic meetings with his Russian counterpart, known as Taz.

RANKIN, TOMMY
creator MILTON M. PROPPER

A detective in Philadelphia's Homicide Bureau, Tommy Rankin has risen in police ranks at an early age. He is not brilliant, but he does possess a logical mind and has great determination and perseverance. His reputation as a detective is built on the foundation of solid achievement.

RASTIN, BILL
see GRANDFATHER

REEDER, J. G.
creator EDGAR WALLACE

John G. Reeder of the Public Prosecutor's office, London, was once connected with Scotland Yard and served for many years with Bankers Trust. He is an expert in solving bank robberies and the Yard calls him whenever they are troubled by a case. He is an authority also on forgery and can tell a counterfeit bill merely by feeling a corner of it. His extraordinary memory for faces has been invaluable in his career. He is introspective and looks like the benign, gentle man he is, but he carries a well-oiled revolver concealed in an inner pocket.

He is small and timid, a middle-aged man with sandy gray hair, mutton-chop whiskers and a pair of steel-rimmed pince-nez over which he looks owlishly. He wears an old-fashioned, flat-topped derby and carries a tightly-rolled umbrella hooked on his arm, rain or shine. No one has ever seen that umbrella unfurled, even in a driving rainstorm. A knife blade is hidden in the handle.

When he is home, Reeder likes to sit in his library (which

deals extensively with the many peculiarities of mankind) and meditate, playing an occasional game of patience while thinking intensely. The more philosophical he becomes, the more dangerous he becomes.

Because of his mild manner and gentle air of helplessness, he sometimes seems at a loss. He describes himself as malicious and says he sees wrong in everything. He credits his success in detection to his "criminal mind."

RETURN, DAVID
creator MANLY WADE WELLMAN

A full-blooded American Indian, David Return is a young brave of the Tsichah, a tribe combining features of the Cheyenne and Pawnee. To reincarnate the picturesque portrait of an ancient warrior, David needs only a feather in his black hair. He has broad shoulders, a narrow waist and a lithe, brown body.

Despite his appearance, David is a modern American. He is a government-trained Indian Agency policeman who works on a reservation. With his grandfather and mentor, Tough Feather, the senior Lieutenant of the Agency police, David serves the United States government "to make things better for all Indians." He uses modern implements of detection and drives a Plymouth sedan but his deductions are based on a deep understanding of Indian character and tradition.

RIGGS, BINGO
creator CRAIG RICE, pseudonym of Georgiana Ann Randolph
(Mrs. Lawrence Lipton)

Bony Bingo and his partner, Handsome Kusak, are the sole proprietors and sole employees of the International Foto, Motion Picture and Television Corporation of America. Their quest for the elusive buck leads them into murderous escapades in New York City, Iowa, and Hollywood.

RICE, STAN
creator BAYNARD KENDRICK

Miles Standish "Stan" Rice is one of the great eaters of mystery fiction. He calls himself "Rice, the hungry," and he eats enough to put Nero Wolfe★ to shame. Nonetheless, Stan remains thin and physically fit. Living in Florida for his health, he is a Deputy Game and Fresh Water Fish Commissioner and a Deputy Sheriff.

RIPLEY, JOHN
creators THE GORDONS (MILDRED and GORDON)

Special Agent John Ripley of the Federal Bureau of Investigation has the physique (six feet, 192 pounds) of the football quarterback he was in his school days. "Rip" grew up on a chicken ranch outside Tucson, Arizona. After attending the F.B.I. school in Quantico, Virginia, he was assigned to the New York office for three years, followed by several years in Chicago. Homesick for the desert, Ripley asks for a transfer to El Paso and is finally sent west—to Los Angeles.

Ripley treats people with great courtesy, not merely to carry out official F.B.I. policy but because he is a decent human being. Acutely aware of the dangers of his profession, Ripley has seen fellow agents killed in the line of duty. After one agent is killed on a routine raid, Ripley says: "You never know what's behind any door."

RIVERS, CHIEF INSPECTOR JULIAN
creator CAROL CARNAC, pseudonym of Edith Caroline Rivett

The long-limbed, deceptively lazy-looking Scotland Yard man, Chief Inspector Julian Rivers, is much like Inspector Macdonald★, who performs the same function in the same author's other books (under the E. C. R. Lorac pseudonym). Both sleuths are dogged, unspectacular, and sharp-witted, and both always learn the truth.

RODEN, JESS
creator A. B. CUNNINGHAM

The shrewd sheriff of Deer Lick, Kentucky, Jess Roden, uses sharp observation, common-sense, and his pack of beloved, keen-nosed hunting dogs to solve murders in his home region and as far away as Texas and New York City. These far-flung activities have given Jess nation-wide fame, resented by his jealous neighbors.

A bachelor, Jess lives in a small house "down below the pawpaw patch" not far from the Deer Lick depot. He is attracted to the charms of the pretty girls he meets on his cases —the more buxom they are, the better he likes them. He remains single, however, as his sloppy home, piled high with unwashed dishes, can attest. His house is not empty: there are five well-trained hunting dogs on the premises and Jess is always willing to acquire others. When not working on a case, Jess arises at six o'clock in the morning, walks down to the river and, if lucky, catches dinner for himself and the dogs.

ROLLISON, RICHARD
see TOFF, THE

ROME, TONY
creator ANTHONY ROME, pseudonym of Marvin H. Albert

Ex-commando Tony Rome is a hard-living, hard-loving private detective who works out of his Florida houseboat. In his adventures, he trades punches, bullets and wise-cracks with cops, gangsters, and women.

ROOK, HOWARD
creator STUART PALMER

Howard Rook is a former newspaperman, forced into retirement, who continues his love-hate relationship with the local Homicide Squad. He feuds with them continuously, co-operating only when there is no alternative.

RUSSELL, COLONEL CHARLES
creator WILLIAM HAGGARD, pseudonym of Richard Clayton

Nearing retirement after nearly half a lifetime of service in his country's interests, Colonel Charles Russell is an erect, urbane, and elegant figure who retains a seemingly infinite reservoir of patience. He is head of the Security Executive—a military intelligence organization operating on the highest levels of political diplomacy. In times of crisis, with the political fate of nations in the balance, the Colonel makes his decisions.

SACKLER, REX
creator D. I. CHAMPION

Just as Nero Wolfe★ has his literary forebear in Sherlock Holmes★, so Rex Sackler is the literary progeny of Wolfe himself. Unlike Wolfe, who is fat and, at times, extravagant, Sackler is painfully thin and a compulsive tightwad. Sackler has, as does Wolfe, a Roman first name, an erudite vocabulary, and has a bright, breezy chronicler of his adventures, Joey Graham being quite reminiscent of Archie Goodwin●.

SAINT, THE▲
creator LESLIE CHARTERIS, pseudonym of
Leslie Charles Bowyer Yin

Simon Templar (The Saint) isn't really a detective, meaning he was never officially a policeman. He was, however, once associated with Scotland Yard and did solve one of its toughest cases. He isn't really a criminal either, though he did more than his share of law-breaking, generally reaping a handsome profit. He is an adventurer, a 20th-century Robin Hood, whose ill-gotten gains are more often than not used to good purpose.

"I'm mad enough to believe in romance," he says. "And I was sick and tired of this age—tired of the miserable little mildewed things that people racked their brains about, and wrote books about, and called life. I wanted something more elementary and honest—battle, murder, sudden death, with plenty of good beer and damsels in distress and a complete callousness about blipping the ungodly over the beezer. It mayn't be life as we know it, but it ought to be."

He is tall, lean, broad-shouldered; his face is clean-cut, with deep-set blue eyes. His dark hair is patent-leather smooth and his bronzed skin gives him a healthy, ruddy look. His voice—a low, gentle drawl—conveys cavalier insolence. He is, indisputably, the most immaculate and elegant adventurer in London.

The Saint's first amour seems to be Patricia Holm, who bobs up in his adventures whenever he needs a feminine accomplice.

SANDS, INSPECTOR
creator MARGARET MILLAR

There have been very few recorded cases involving Sands, the colorless Inspector of the Toronto Police. He is middle-aged, middle-sized, with a "face that looked as if he had slept in it." He is a good listener and is adept at cross examination. He is equally effective talking to a hard-boiled gambler or to a neurotic young girl. After his retirement, bachelor Sands has moved to southern California. Most of his time is spent playing gin rummy or scrabble, and telling his neighbors anecdotes of his police days.

SARGEANT, PETER
creator EDGAR BOX, pseudonym of Gore Vidal

The "pleasantly piggish"-looking young press agent, Peter Cutler Sargeant III, is about 30 years old. He is a veteran of three years in the army, four at Harvard and three as drama critic with the "New York Globe." He never had a byline with the "Globe," ghost-writing the column for the regular critic, Milton Haddock, a confirmed alcoholic—when Peter asked for a raise, the "Globe" informed him he was now a free-lance writer, no longer with their staff.

He opened a one-man public relations firm in a one-room office with one filing cabinet on Madison Avenue, where a middle-aged lady, Miss Flynn, types his press releases. Murder appears in the most unusual circumstances, as when he takes as clients a ballet company or an ultra-right-wing U.S. Senator, and when he accepts an invitation to a posh Long Island estate.

SCHMIDT, INSPECTOR
creator GEORGE BAGBY, pseudonym of Aaron Marc Stein

A member of the New York City Homicide Bureau, Inspector Schmidt is accompanied on his investigations by Bagby, who chronicles the colorful adventures. Schmitty is thorough, at times brilliant, and complains about his aching feet continuously to anyone who will listen.

SCHOFIELD, PETE
creator THOMAS B. DEWEY

One of the few married private detectives, Pete Schofield has a gorgeous red-headed wife who enjoys "helping" her husband on cases. Schofield, who is quite handsome, meets many beautiful women, all of whom seem anxious to seduce him, despite his marital status. He is tough, but not over-anxious to get into a brawl.

SCOTT, SHELL
creator RICHARD S. PRATHER

Shell Scott has an eye for dames and a nose for trouble. He has appeared in paperback originals since 1950, distinguished by a self-mocking, sardonic humor, the Scott trademark.

SEETON, MISS EMILY
creator HERON CARVIC

Miss Seeton, a frail, elderly art teacher, carries a "brolly" (umbrella) for protection as she strolls the streets of London. She is fond of the theater, opera, and ballet. In walking home from Covent Garden, she has become involved in several crimes. A recently-inherited country home at Plummergen provides her with no relaxation but with further opportunity to encounter danger. Her amateur detective work has been aided by Superintendent Delphick (inevitably nick-named "The Oracle") and Detective Sergeant Ranger.

SELBY, DOUG
see D.A., THE

SHANE, PROFESSOR PETER UTLEY
creator FRANCIS BONNAMY, pseudonym of Audrey Walz

Professor Peter Utley Shane is "the man in gray": he has gray hair, a gray mustache, gray eyes, and wears gray clothes. He remains calm in the face of disaster and is infuriatingly omniscient. Francis Bonnamy, who narrates the professor's detective cases, was Shane's assistant at the University of Chicago, where they taught sociology and criminology from 1928 to the start of World War II. During the War, they work in Washingston, D.C. Bonnamy is a civilian assistant to the Signal Corps; Shane a Major in Military Intelligence (when he wears it, his khaki uniform looks gray).

SHANLEY, FATHER JOSEPH
creator JACK WEBB

An unusual detective team combines an amateur, Father Joseph Shanley, with a tough professional policeman, Sergeant Sammy Golden. Shanley is a handsome young Roman Catholic priest with a ghetto background. When not performing his religious duties or solving murders, Father Shanley may be found in the garden; he especially loves roses. Golden, his Jewish friend, is with the Los Angeles Police Department.

SHANNON, DESMOND
creator M. V. HEBERDEN (MARY VIOLET HEBERDEN)

The red-haired Irishman, husky Desmond Shannon, is reputed to be the highest-paid private detective in New York City. Basically a man of action, physically agile and tough, he is also well-read, and is especially interested in philosophy. He is idealistic and strongly antipathetic towards communism, once foregoing his usual fee to help a young veteran accused of murder, who, he believes, was framed by communists who had infiltrated the local government of Detten (a small town in New York.)

SHAPIRO, LIEUTENANT NATHAN
creators FRANCES and RICHARD LOCKRIDGE

Convinced that he should still be pounding a beat, Lieutenant Nathan Shapiro is probably the least self-confident homicide investigator in the annals of detective fiction. However, ably assisted by his boss, Captain William Weigand (who also assists Mr. and Mrs. North★), Shapiro shows that actions speak louder than doubts.

SHAYNE, MICHAEL▲
creator BRETT HALLIDAY, pseudonym of David Dresser

One of the most durable of private detectives is Mike Shayne, the tough, two-fisted, cognac-swigging redhead from Miami. He is tall, handsome, and almost as fond of beautiful girls as they are of him. Keeping him company on his cases are his patient, pretty secretary, Lucy Hamilton, and the Chief of Police, Will Gentry.

SHERINGHAM, ROGER
creator ANTHONY BERKELEY, pseudonym of
Anthony Berkeley Cox

Roger Sheringham, born in 1891, is a bit below average height, stocky and round-faced. He smokes a short-stemmed pipe with an over-large bowl, drinks beer and talks a lot—usually nonsense. An Oxford graduate, Sheringham makes his living as the author of best-selling novels (with frequent forays into crime journalism) but is aware of his literary shortcomings and cheerfully sneers at his reading public.

He is rude, vain, verbose, and offensive—he is also extremely fallible. His creator says Sheringham was "founded on an offensive person I once knew because, in my original innocence, I thought it would be amusing to have an offensive detective. Since he has been taken in all seriousness, I have had to tone his offensiveness down and pretend he never was."

Early in his career, it seemed only inspector Moresby● could tolerate him. As Sheringham becomes more popular, Berkeley's approach becomes more serious and an effort is made to fit the amateur sleuth into the more conventional concept of a great detective.

SHOMAR, LIEUTENANT SHOMRI
creator HENRY KLINGER

A debonair Israeli-born police detective with the Vandyke beard, Shomri Shomar is on loan to the New York City Police Department. He is as quick with a rabbinical proverb as able Charlie Chan★ is with a Confucian aphorism.

SILK, DORIAN
creator SIMON HARVESTER, pseudonym of Henry Gibbs

Rough-hewn, laconic, lonely, and sardonic, British agent Dorian Silk is the antithesis of the superman-cum-spy. His creator's knowledge of the Middle East and Far East is as considerable as his skill at realistic story-telling.

SILVER, MISS MAUD
creator PATRICIA WENTWORTH, pseudonym of
Dora Amy Dillon Turnbull

The elderly Miss Maud Silver had been a governess before retiring on a small, fixed income. She is rather shabby, dependent on her niece, Ethel Burkett, for gifts of clothing. When she decides to become a private detective to supplement her income, she soon earns enough to live in greater comfort. Money, however, has never been important to Miss Silver and she has always been willing to assist—without fee—Scotland Yard Inspectors Lamb and Abbott. Her strong moral principles, passion for justice and knack for reading clues (as well as the heart) enable her to compile a phenomenal record of success and earns her the respect of the Yard.

SLOAN, DETECTIVE INSPECTOR C. D.
creator CATHERINE AIRD, pseudonym of
Kinn Hamilton McIntosh

Detective Inspector C. D. Sloan is head of the Criminal Investigation Department in Berebury, a small market town in West Calleshire. Because of his understanding wife, Margaret, the fortyish Sloan has a happy home life. He enjoys pottering about in the little garden behind his house. He is fond of literary allusions and has a fine sense of humor—a necessity in dealing with his stodgy supervisor, Superintendent Leyes, and his callow assistant, Detective Constable Crosby.

SMALL, RABBI DAVID
creator HARRY KEMELMAN

An unlikely but effective detective is David Small, the young rabbi of the suburban Massachusetts town of Barnard's Crossing. He has almost as much trouble with his congregation as he does with murderers. He is regarded as too honest, too absentminded, and lacking in some of the social niceties. However, behind that surface appearance is a sharp deductive mind honed by the hair-splitting rigors of the Talmudic method.

In his very first case, he is suspected of the murder but, not only does he prove himself innocent, he becomes a friend of Barnard's Crossing's Chief of Police, Hugh Lanigan. The two friends often discuss religion over a cup of tea. Rabbi Small's involvements in crime do not keep him from being a devoted husband to his wife, Miriam, and a loving father to Jonathan.

SMILEY, GEORGE
creator JOHN LE CARRE, pseudonym of
David John Moore Cornwall

The short, fat, toad-like George Smiley is a deadly secret service agent. He is quiet, bespectacled, spends a great deal of money on poorly-fitting clothes and is described by his wife, Lady Ann Sercomb, as "breathtakingly ordinary." A scholar in obscure German poets, he left Oxford to join the secret service. Always withdrawn, his new career guaranteed the death of natural pleasure, and he regrets it. A sentimental man, he deeply loves England.

SMITH, SIR DENIS NAYLAND
creator SAX ROHMER, pseudonym of Arthur Sarsfield Ward

Nayland Smith and his companion, Doctor Petrie●, represent England and, indeed, what they see as the white race, in a battle for survival against the supernatural powers of the would-be Emperor of the World, the evil Fu Manchu●.

Smith is a hard-working, sometimes inept adversary, who has been described as more nuisance than threat to the super-human powers of Fu Manchu. He has worked, at various times, as a Scotland Yard Inspector, a Criminal Investigation Department Commissioner, and as a free agent on detached duty. He has a zest for adventure and never gives up in his battle with the evil Oriental doctor, though luck saves his life on more than one occasion. He has been knighted for his successful efforts to thwart Fu.

SPADE, SAM▲
creator DASHIELL HAMMETT

A hardboiled private detective from San Francisco, Sam Spade looks like a pleasant blond Satan with a V-for-Victory face. His jaw is long and bony, his chin a jutting V under the more flexible V of his mouth. His nostrils curve back to make another, smaller V. His yellow-green eyes are nearly horizontal. The V motif is picked up again by thick eyebrows rising outward from twin creases above a hooked nose; his pale brown hair grows down—from high, flat temples—to a point on his forehead. When he smiles, keeping his lips together, all the V's in his face grow longer.

He is six feet tall but the severely rounded slope of his shoulders make his body seem as broad as it is thick. The Fat Man, Casper Gutman●, calls Spade "wild, astonishing, unpredictable, amazing." Spade is headstrong, not afraid of trouble—a man of resources and judgment. When he speaks, he gets to the heart of the matter quickly, minces no words. He is not above taking a bribe. Though he hated his partner, Miles Archer, he tracks Archer's killers.

Spade's adventures were most memorably chronicled on film in the 1941 version of the story. A radio series also was popular.

SPIDER, THE▲
creator R. T. M. SCOTT

"The Spider" is, actually, wealthy New Yorker Richard Wentworth, a tireless warrior in the age-long battle against crime. Assisting the secret crime-fighter are Ram Singh, his Indian servant; painter Nita Van Sloan, his girl friend; and Apollo, Nita's Great Dane.

Not only must "The Spider" cope with several master criminals, but he must avoid the efforts of Stanley Kirkpatrick, the society-bred Police Commissioner of New York City, to learn "The Spider's" true identity. Kirkpatrick mistakenly believes the pseudonymous hero to be a criminal and wants to unmask him.

Wentworth employs a drawing of a spider as his symbol because "it strikes terror into the heart of his enemies." "The Spider" dangerously, courageously, suavely, uses his cigarette lighter, concealing the symbol, to light the Commissioner's cigarettes at social gatherings.

STARR, DR. COLIN
creator RUFUS KING

Young Colin Starr of Laurel Falls, Ohio, has inherited his father's small-town medical practice. A gentle, kindly doctor, Colin has "a heart as big as Lincoln's," and his strong, homely features have a therapeutic effect on his patients. His electric vitality and charisma combine with profound medical knowledge and sharp deductive reasoning ability to make him a successful doctor and a fine detective. In a case where most doctors would sign a certificate of death from natural causes, Starr detects murder.

STEVENS, GAVIN
creator WILLIAM FAULKNER

The shrewd attorney of Yoknapatawpha County, Mississippi, is an excellent detective in the tradition of the famous Uncle Abner★; the exploits of both avuncular detectives are recounted by admiring young nephews. Although he smokes a rustic corncob pipe, Stevens has the sophistication befitting a Phi Beta Kappa graduate of Harvard. After college, he returned to his native region in the back country of the deep South. Now the county attorney, he will not talk down to his less well-educated constituents. He has a wild shock of prematurely white hair and a lively, quick, thin face. He is an excellent chess player, able to plot his moves well in advance.

STONE, FLEMING
creator CAROLYN WELLS

Fleming Stone is "a quiet, rather scholarly looking man, with a sympathetic face and correct manners," all of which inspire confidence. People see him as a deep thinker and quick reasoner. He is a lover of books. When working on a case in his home city, New York, Stone sits at the desk in his library to ponder the clues and evidence until a solution develops in his mind.

STORM, CHRISTOPHER
creators WILLETTA ANN BARBER and R. F. SCHABELITZ

Successful illustrator Christopher "Kit" Storm has become unofficial artist at New York City Police Headquarters at the request of Detective Tony Shand of the Homicide Bureau. Kit sketches the people, clue, and locales of murder cases; when no solution to a case is found, he carefully restudies his sketches for new evidence.

In his thirties, Storm is tall, lean, brown-eyed, and handsome, with a slow, crooked smile that his wife loves. The Storms live in an East Side apartment building in Manhattan. During World War II, Kit was air raid warden for the building; when the Federal Bureau of Investigation discovered his special talents, they asked his aid.

STRANGEWAYS, NIGEL
creator NICHOLAS BLAKE, pseudonym of Cecil Day-Lewis

Nigel Strangeways is a young private investigator with sandy colored hair which droops over his forehead, causing him to resemble an overgrown prep school boy. He is six feet tall and has short-sighted blue eyes. He spots and falls in love with the attractive explorer, Georgia Cavendish. After their marriage, the Strangeways live in London, in a comfortable flat facing a 17th century square. When war clouds gather over Europe, the couple purchase a house in rural Devonshire.

Georgia is killed during World War II, and Nigel is understandably depressed. His eventual recovery is hastened by a romance with sculptress Clare Massinger.

STYLES, PETER
creator JUDSON PHILIPS

Peter Styles fought in Korea and came back to the United States in one piece, only to lose a leg in a car accident in Vermont, an accident caused by two hoodlums out to "get" Styles. In the accident, Styles' father lost his life.

Long a crusader against violence, Styles encounters it wherever he goes. He writes a column for "Newsday" magazine and believes in doing personal research, which often brings him to the scene of the crime. Even his home in Manhattan is in a high crime area. Although he walks with the aid of a wooden leg, Styles can move with surprising speed. He keeps in superb condition.

TAYLOR, MITCH
creator LAWRENCE TREAT

In the 1940's, Detective (now Inspector) Mitch Taylor and his cohorts, Lieutenant Decker and lab specialist "Jub" Freeman, were operating in New York City in the manner known as "police procedural." Anticipating the urban crisis, they moved to a small, unnamed town where life is less complicated but the crime rate is high.

Taylor is a good family man and a basically honest policeman who is human enough to avoid work when possible. He also wants the side benefits—like the legendary cop who helps himself to an apple without paying for it. Decker, still dedicated and courageous, is tired now: Freeman still performs scientific miracles with small bits of physical evidence.

TEMPLAR, SIMON
see SAINT, THE

TENNENTE, MAJOR
creator THOMAS FLANAGAN

A professional soldier, Major Tennente is also a professional policeman. He is in the service of the General who is dictator of an unidentified country in Europe. Tennente is an honorable man trying to come to terms with a dishonorable world. His philosophy is summed up in his simple statement: "There are things which have to be done." What Tennente must do, he does with compassion and justice.

THATCHER, JOHN PUTNAM
creator EMMA LATHEN, pseudonym of
Mary J. Latis and Martha Hennissart

For a widower of about sixty, John Putnam Thatcher keeps very active. Senior Vice-President of the Sloan Guaranty Trust Co., he plays tennis, goes hiking, and solves mysteries in the eastern United States. This urbane sleuth began as an expert on stocks, bonds, and trusts. He has become equally knowledgeable regarding murder, which should not be too surprising, since greed, with which he is familiar, has always been a prime cause of murder. Thatcher has surrounded himself with an interesting group of associates, ranging from aging Wall St. playboys to a serious, prissy secretary.

THINKING MACHINE, THE
creator JACQUES FUTRELLE

Professor Augustus S. F. X. Van Dusen was named "The Thinking Machine" by a newspaper when he gave a remarkable exhibition at chess, demonstrating that a man totally unfamiliar with the game could, by applying logic, defeat a champion. Professor Van Dusen is a scientist and logician who solves perplexing cases brought to him by Hutchinson Hatch, a reporter.

He is irritable, petulant, and declares, condescendingly yet quite seriously, that he would invent an airship but that he is too busy at the moment (the Van Dusen stories were written when the idea of flying was still fresh and unproven). His most remarkable physical feature is his huge head (he wears a Size 8 hat), a tall, broad brow, almost abnormal in height, crowned by a bright shock of yellow hair. He is pale and thin, his shoulders stooped in the way of the stereotyped scholar. Behind thick glasses his blue eyes are concentrated in a perpetual, forbidding squint. Despite his vast genius, he lives in modest apartments with only a housekeeper.

Although he has a small laboratory in his residence, he is generally uninterested in the external clues of a case. He merely applies logic to a problem, breaks it down into its simplest components, and arrives at a solution. He is the most intellectual of all detectives. The author, Jacques Futrelle, who wrote only four full-length books in which The Thinking Machine appears, went down with the Titanic at 37.

THORNDYKE, DR. JOHN
creator R. AUSTIN FREEMAN

Dr. Thorndyke is both doctor and lawyer, and his methods are more technical and specialized than those of the average detective. His procedure is to interrogate things rather than persons; the data he seeks are generally those which are apparent only to the eye of the medical practitioner. He searches for some fact of evidential value which can be demonstrated by physical methods and which constitutes conclusive proof of some essential point. Thorndyke's constant companion is his research kit, "the invaluable green case," with its collection of miniature instruments and array of chemicals.

He is an expert in countless scholarly fields, including anatomy, archaeology, botany, Egyptology, and ophthalmology. His approach to a problem is painstaking and humorless. He is emotionally detached, though philanthropic.

Exceptionally tall, strong, and athletic, Thorndyke has acute eyesight and hearing and unusual manual skill. He is the handsomest of all detectives, with a fine Grecian nose and classical features. He has no gifts of superhuman intelligence or intuition. His reasoning powers, however, are exceptional and he possesses a scientific imagination—the faculty to perceive the essential nature of a problem before the detailed evidence comes to light. He is quiet, reserved, self-contained (even secretive), but kindly. He is addicted to dry humor and Trichinopoly cheroots. He was about 35 when he began his first case, 50 when he solved his last.

Thorndyke's two satellites are Dr. Jervis●, who has the task of recording the exploits of the famous detective, and Polton●, his lab assistant. R. Austin Freeman was, himself, a doctor and used much of his medical background in his tales. He also personally conducted every experiment Thorndyke describes in his cases.

THURSDAY, MAX
creator WADE MILLER, pseudonym of Bob Wade and Bill Miller

Max Thursday, San Diego's leading private detective, is a tall, lean man in his thirties. He has a gaunt, rugged face, blue eyes, heavy eyebrows and a prominent, arched nose. Honest but tired and disillusioned, Max Thursday has a hair-trigger temper. He seldom carries a gun because, under pressure, he has a tendency to go berserk, shooting first and thinking later. Stabilizing this rather fallible private eye are his girl friend, Merle Osborn, a reporter on the "San Diego Sentinel," and Austin Clapp, the wise, reticent Head of Homicide for the San Diego Police.

TIBBETT, CHIEF INSPECTOR HENRY
creator PATRICIA MOYES

Inspector (later Chief Superintendent) Tibbett does not look like a great detective. He is in his mid-forties, has a slight frame, undistinguished features, mild blue eyes, sandy hair, quiet voice, and diffident manner. His subordinates, however, know he has high standards and they act accordingly.

Tibbett's wife, Emmy, is sophisticated, pleasant, with a tendency to gain weight more rapidly than she would like. The couple is inseparable and she accompanies him whenever a case takes him from their London home—the ground floor of a shabby, cheerful Victorian house in the border area between Fulham and Chelsea. In spite of their years, they are not complacent, recently took up skiing and yachting.

TIBBS, VIRGIL
creator JOHN BALL

Virgil Tibbs is considered a homicide expert by his employers, the Police Department of Pasadena, California. He is young, articulate, physically capable (a karate expert), intelligent, well read, and black. The people he meets in his investigations are disinclined to accept him as a detective and focus on Tibbs, the black man.

He has almost unbelievable patience and stoicism in the face of racial abuse. He is also practical enough to use his color if that will help him solve a case. He broke up a narcotics ring while playing the role of shoeshine boy because the drug peddler did not hesitate to transact "business" in the presence of an inconsequential Negro shining his shoes.

TOBIN, MITCH
creator TUCKER COE, pseudonym of Donald Westlake

One mistake is enough to ruin a man's life. In the case of New York policeman Mitch Tobin, the mistake was being in bed with a woman when he should have been on duty. In Tobin's absence, his partner handled an apparently routine matter alone and was killed. The ensuing investigation cost Tobin his job, despite his years of outstanding police service.

Tobin's marriage is saved only because he has an understanding wife. He is guilt-ridden and spends much of his time building a wall behind his Queens home; he finds this keeps him from brooding. He is not permitted to operate as a licensed private detective but he does use his years of police experience to investigate crimes when he is forced to by economic necessity.

TOFF, THE
creator JOHN CREASY

The Honorable Richard Rollison is a wealthy, romantic gentleman-adventurer. He is tall, "remarkably handsome," well-built, athletic, and courageous. His Mayfair flat houses a remarkable wall worthy of Scotland Yard's Black Museum—souvenirs of violence in the Toff's past escapades including a top hat with a bullet-hole in the crown, blood-stained chicken feathers, guns, knives, glass phials of multi-hued poisons, and a hangman's rope. The Toff's valet, Jolly, is intelligent, faithful and humorous.

TOLEFREE, PHILIP
creator ROBERT A. J. WALLING

The suave, well-mannered British private enquiry agent, Philip Tolefree, is perfectly comfortable at a stately house party or at a nobleman's London flat, but he never penetrates the seamy side of his metropolis. He is embodied with near-perfect purity in the long series of adventures in which Tolefree and his partner, Farrar, function.

TRACY, DICK▲
creator CHESTER GOULD

The start of the 1930's saw both the explosive spread of organized crime and the first appearance (in 1931) of newspaper strip hero Dick Tracy, who personified the new breed of police battling the gangs. In the four decades since, Tracy has been the single most popular melodrama strip in the world. He is the symbol of the clean, tough, square-jawed cop.

Tracy, his hawk nose and lean, firm lines modeled in part after Sherlock Holmes★, is the lead battler for law and order in an unnamed city (resembling Chicago) overrun by mobs. His adversaries are colorful gangsters characterized by physical or facial deformities which their names so describe: Pruneface, Flattop, The Brow. Tracy's world includes an array of interesting friends—his adopted son, Junior; B. O. Plenty and Gravel Gertie, two itinerants whom Tracy thrust together, their union producing a child, Sparkle Plenty. Diet Smith, the millionaire industrialist whose life Tracy saved, is an inventor whose gadgetry—a wrist radio and, more recently, a two-way wrist television—has always been ahead of its time, though used with the one-dimensional realism which has characterized Tracy's police work through the years.

Recently, Tracy has become frivolous and his cases less inspired. He went to the moon—in an antigravitational coupe, another of Diet Smith's inventions—and discovered a colony of beings living there in a warm valley. (Junior married the moon ruler's daughter.) His opponents have become less striking; sometimes they are the offspring of former foes—Flattop's son, the Mole's granddaughter. Dick Tracy's first name is underworld argot for police detective. Tracy has often been imitated but stands alone in terms of popularity.

TRAVERS, LUDOVIC
creator CHRISTOPHER BUSH, pseudonym of
Charlie Christmas Bush

The genial, talkative amateur detective, Ludovic Travers, is the unofficial advisor to Scotland Yard Superintendent Wharton.

Travers is tall (6'3") and very thin. The large, horn-rimmed eye-glasses he wears give him the appearance of "a benevolent secretary bird." He is intelligent, an author, and expert on social economics. Although he was born to a wealthy family, his philosophy borders on the communistic. In detection, which he has pursued for 40 years, he has little patience with routine, always seeking, usually finding, the short-cut.

TRENT, PHILIP
creator E. C. BENTLEY

Philip Trent is a successful artist who has had some success solving crime problems. He is fairly young, tall, and loosely built. His face is high-boned and appears quixotic. His hair, his short mustache, and his rough tweed clothes are reasonably untidy. Trent is friendly, pleasant, tactful, fond of good living, and extremely curious when crime problems appear. He is also a competent crime reporter (his creator spent his life as a professional journalist) whose services are requested often enough to interfere with his endeavors as a painter.

TROTTER, TUDDLETON
creator HARRY STEPHEN KEELER

A lover of homeless cats, Tuddleton Trotter is an aging, bedraggled genius who solves the most bizarre crimes with lightning-like speed and ease. Keeler's outrageous unfairness to the reader, who cannot hope to solve the mysteries, is intentional.

TROY, JEFF and HAILA
creator KELLEY ROOS, pseudonym of
Audrey Kelley and William Roos

Jeff Troy is a commercial photographer; Haila a clever and competent housewife. They make a charming amateur-detective team whose successes are a constant embarrassment to Detective Lieutenant Hankins of the Homicide Bureau, when events throw them together.

TUKE, HARVEY
creator DOUGLAS G. BROWNE

A tactless bureaucrat in London's Department of Public Prosecution, Harvey Tuke has a face like Mephistopheles and a sardonic sense of humor.

TUTT, EPHRAIM
creator ARTHUR TRAIN

Mr. Tutt is not really a detective, but a lawyer who nevertheless ferrets out crime wherever it lurks. Born on July 4, 1869, he was considered a fair combination of Lincoln, Puck, Uncle Sam, and Robin Hood. He is, quite possibly, the wisest, kindest and most eloquent lawyer in literature. The author, Arthur Train, was also a lawyer who said, "the law offers greater opportunities to be at one and the same time a Christian and a horse-trader than any other profession."

UNCLE ABNER
see ABNER, UNCLE

URSULA, SISTER MARY
creator H. H. HOLMES, pseudonym of
William Anthony Parker White

Before becoming a nun, Sister Mary Ursula, O.M.B. (Order of the Sisters of Martha of Bethany), wanted to be a policewoman. She encounters crimes in her new life, however, so she seems to have the best of both worlds. Although Sister Ursula has a weak stomach for the results of violence, she has a strong mind for solving mysteries. She is fond of reading mystery stories and is interested in church liturgy.

Lieutenant Terence Marshall of the Los Angeles Police Department is extremely fond of Sister Ursula. Marshall's wife, Leona, worked her way through college as a striptease dancer.

William Anthony Parker White also wrote under the Anthony Boucher pseudonym.

VALCOUR, LIEUTENANT
creator RUFUS KING

Later promoted to Inspector, it is as a Lieutenant of Detectives, New York Police Department, that we meet Valcour. His father was a policeman also. Valcour, a graduate of Toronto's McGill University, is Canadian born; he became a naturalized United States citizen in 1904, and soon embarked on a successful police career.

Lieutenant Valcour is a mild man with homely, but not undistinguished, features. He is friendly, has a sense of humor which can be earthy or subtle, is courteous, intelligent, and (despite his age) physically rugged. He rarely indulges himself though he does smoke cigarettes with imported Turkish tobacco and he will accept a fine cigar or a bacardi cocktail. Valcour's usual hunting grounds are Manhattan's wealthy East Side and Long Island.

VALMONT, EUGÈNE
creator ROBERT BARR

Eugène Valmont is the first French detective in English literature. He lives in England and considers the English police a dim-witted lot. He is pompous, but likeable for his fine wit and comic outlook. He is a failure in crime-solving on more than one occasion, but his conceit is never lessened. Because his name is so well known, he frequently resorts to an alias. He is a well-dressed little fellow who is vain about his clothes.

Valmont is generally considered to be the literary forefather of M. Hercule Poirot★. He is, in fact, the first in a long line of successful French detectives in English literature, virtually all of whom are comic figures.

VANCE, PHILO▲
creator S. S. VAN DINE, pseudonym of
Willard Huntington Wright

A young aristocrat who dabbled in amateur detective work at the request of his best friend, District Attorney Markham●, the debonair Philo Vance made his debut in "The Benson Murder Case." He solved this murder so easily that Markham called him to help solve many of New York's most famous and perplexing crimes. Because of Vance's nonchalant manner and pomposity, Sergeant Heath● instantly disliked him. It took readers of his exploits somewhat longer.

Vance's insufferable affectations and long-winded, pedantic discourses on esoteric subjects are received with well-restrained enthusiasm by the New York City Police force. He smiles ironically at the grimmest realities, fulfilling the role of the whimsically disinterested spectator of a world he finds merely amusing. Despite his detached and supercilious manner, he exerts an unusual fascination over those who know him.

Vance is just under six feet tall, slender and graceful. He has aloof gray eyes, a straight slender nose and a thin-lipped mouth that almost suggests cruelty. These chiselled features suggest strength but his sardonic coldness of expression precludes claims to handsomeness. He is a graduate of Harvard but the majority of his education had been acquired in Europe and he retains a slight British accent and intonation. A superb student, his thirst for knowledge is never slaked. He devotes considerable study to ethnology and psychology but his greatest intellectual enthusiasm is art. He has sufficient income to indulge a passion for collecting fine paintings and "objets d'art." It was his interest in psychology that turned his attention to crime and he is eager to test his theories.

S. S. Van Dine, the narrator of the tales, as well as the

"author," is a pseudonym for Willard Huntington Wright, who was much like Vance. Wright, too, was a poseur and a dilettante, dabbling in art, music and criticism. He lived in an expensive penthouse, was fond of costly clothes and food, and collected art. Despite his pretensions, Wright wrote the most popular mystery novels of his era but he wrote them under a pseudonym because he feared ostracism if his friends discovered he was the author.

VAN der VALK, INSPECTOR
creator NICOLAS FREELING

Inspector Van der Valk of the Amsterdam Police is a policeman, an intellectual, and an iconoclast. In addition to his appreciation of affairs of the mind, he enjoys good food, especially when it is prepared by his wife, Arlette, an excellent cook. In 1969, Van der Valk was made Chief Inspector of the Juvenile Brigade of Amsterdam after being an Inspector of Criminal Police for more than ten years. In his new assignment, he finds he has much still to learn. His long experience has not inured him to the heartbreak of crime and the drug habit when the young people are affected.

VAN DUSEN, PROF. AUGUSTUS S. F. X.
see THINKING MACHINE, THE

VAN LOAN, RICHARD CURTIS
see PHANTOM DETECTIVE, THE

VARALLO, VIC
creator LESLEY EGAN, pseudonym of Elizabeth Linington

At the age of 33, Vic Varallo resigned his captaincy on the police force of Contera because the salary was small and the chance for advancement smaller. He and his pretty wife, Laura, rented a home in Glendale, northeast of Los Angeles, and Vic joined the Glendale police force as a rather mature rookie. With his 12 years of experience, however, promotion to detective came rapidly for the big, handsome, tawny-haired Varallo and he now has a distinguished, rapidly-rising career and a growing prestige.

VERITY, MR.
creator PETER ANTONY, pseudonym of
Peter and Anthony Shaffer

Mr. Verity is described as "an immense man just tall enough to carry his breadth majestically. His face was sharp, smooth and teak-brown; his blue eyes small and of a startling brilliance.

He wore a fine chestnut Vandyke, an habitual cloak in winter, the expression of an elderly 'Laughing Cavalier.' " Mr. Verity's home is a small villa in a seaside town, Amnestie, in Sussex. He is fond of big, black Cuban cigars and swimming, still using an ancient purple bathing costume purchased 30 years ago. His villa contains a collection of sculptures and art objects—not all of which were obtained strictly legally.

Mr. Verity takes detective cases for very reasonable fees and, to the consternation of Inspector Rambler—his friendly competitor on the official police force—is invariably successful. Mr. Verity frequently operates under the alias of Mr. Fathom. Anthony Shaffer is the author of the extremely popular, perplexing "tour-de-forcè" drama, "Sleuth," of international fame.

VINE, GIL
creator STEWART STERLING, pseudonym of Prentice Winchell

The chief security officer at a swank New York City hotel, the Plaza Royale, Gil Vine doesn't resemble the conventional picture of the "house dick." He is upset by finding corpses occasionally in the expensively-priced rooms at his hotel. Gil is unusually smooth in dealing with the hotel's wealthy clientele, which ranges from elderly dowagers to business tycoons.

Gil Vine is conscientious, maintaining rooms on the second floor of the Plaza Royale to be on 24 hour call. He involves himself in everything that takes place at the hotel, with a standing rule that every item left behind by a guest be brought to him personally; it may be the first clue to a murder and as such, important.

WAGHORN, INSPECTOR JAMES
creator JOHN RHODE, pseudonym of
Cecil John Charles Street

Waghorn is a Cambridge University graduate and a product of Metropolitan Police College, where he spent 15 months learning his trade. He was immediately granted the probationary rank of Junior Station Inspector at the tender age of 27. He is an honest and fair-minded person with a pleasant, open face, shrewd gray eyes, and an easy-going manner.

At the end of his probationary period, Waghorn is promoted to Scotland Yard's Criminal Investigation Department. His early successes (closely supervised by his superior, Superintendent Hanslet●) are gained through his reliance upon Dr. Priestley★, but time and experience sharpen his powers of investigation and deduction until he relies solely on his own skills.

WARD, PETER
creator DAVID ST. JOHN, pseudonym of E. Howard Hunt

Socialite Peter Ward is a graduate of Brown University, where he starred on the hockey team, and of Yale Law School. His Washington, D.C., law practice is a "cover" for his activities as a Central Intelligence Agency agent. He is a widower; his wife was killed in an attempt on his own life while she accompanied him on assignment in Cairo. Ward now lives alone in a house in Georgetown. He is part of the most elite Washington social circles. He likes beautiful women, classical music, good food, Canadian Club whiskey, and horseback riding. He speaks many languages, including Spanish, Russian, and Italian. He is a firm believer in and staunch supporter of the C.I.A.

WATTS, WALLY
creator PAUL W. FAIRMAN

One of the youngest detectives in adult fiction, Wally Watts is eighteen years old. Wally is a correspondence school detective, following in the footsteps of Philo Gubb★ and P. Moran★. His stories take the form of letters he exchanges with the Watchful Eye Detective School of New York City. Young Mr. Watts lives in upstate New York in the town of Lettyville, population 3,000. He earns money for his correspondence course by working as a grocery clerk-delivery boy.

WELT, NICKY
creator HARRY KEMELMAN

Nicky Welt, born around the turn of the century, is a white-haired professor with a gnome-like face. He teaches English Language and Literature at a New England college and his interests and manner reflect his academic surroundings. He solves mysteries as would a professor lecturing not-too-bright college freshmen. His "pupil" (and chronicler of his cases) is the District Attorney of Suffolk County, Massachusetts. They play chess every Friday night, and the District Attorney frequently concludes the evening in possession of the solution to a mystery he had described before the game began.

WENNICK, PETER
creator ERLE STANLEY GARDNER

Ostensibly a law clerk and process-server for a prestigious West Coast law firm, Pete Wennick actually has the function of going outside the law to get cases resolved in the firm's favor. Often at odds with the police, his adventures were found in pulp publications of the 30's.

WENTWORTH, RICHARD
see SPIDER, THE

WEST, HONEY
creator G. G. FICKLING, pseudonym of
Gloria and Forrest E. Fickling

One of the few female private detectives in mystery fiction, Honey West is tough but will occasionally admit to what she calls "feminine feelings of weakness." A beautiful blonde in her late 20's, Honey has an eye-catching figure. She is 5'5" tall and weighs 120 pounds with 38-22-36 measurements. Though by the very nature of her profession she is personally "liberated," her body is exploited throughout the series of books in which she appears. She is often forced to strip off her dress at gunpoint, and she has lost the top half of her bathing suit several times during seaside struggles.

Honey lives and works in Long Beach, California; she was graduated from Long Beach City College but became a detective to try to find her father's killers. He had been a private detective until he was killed, while on a case, behind the Los Angeles Paramount Theater. Honey's great and good friend, Lieutenant Mark Storm of the Long Beach Sheriff's Office, has tried to get her to give up her dangerous profession and has proposed marriage to her "thousands of times." To date, Honey has steadfastly remained single and independent.

WEST, ROGER
creator JOHN CREASEY

"Handsome" West is big, broad and, of course, really handsome. He looks younger than his years; his keen blue eyes are always alert, his fair hair hides the gray. Roger ages through the series of books about his career. He begins as an Inspector in 1942, and, now Chief Superintendent at Scotland Yard, is still active. At one time, he nearly left his wife, Janet, but now relies on her for advice on some cases and trusts her discretion on others. His teenage sons, Martin and Richard, intrude on his crime-fighting career less than do other family problems.

WESTBOROUGH, PROFESSOR
creator CLYDE B. CLASON

An expert on Roman history and professor of classics, Theocritus Lucius Westborough is a frail, white-haired gentleman who, on bizarre crime puzzles, serves as unofficial advisor to the police. The cases of the gentle old academician frequently involve Oriental elements.

WESTLAKE, DR. HUGH
creator JONATHAN STAGGE, pseudonym of several authors and collaborations, primarily Richard Wilson Webb and Hugh Wheeler

In an age when most medical detectives are specialists in pathology or psychiatry, Dr. Hugh Cavendish Westlake is an anachronism: a poor, hardworking general practitioner. Westlake's practice is in the small eastern town of Kenmore, where he resides with his young daughter, Dawn. Westlake has been a widower for a number of years. Dr. Westlake is still a young man; he was only 31 at the time of his wife's death. In his later cases (dating from about 1939 or 1940) he shows a reawakening interest in women.

Dawn and he share the propensity for getting involved in murder cases, keeping him too busy to be caught by someone looking for an eligible widower. The doctor frequently visits the larger town of Grovestown, where he shares an occasional highball, and a murder investigation, with Inspector Cobb, his friend.

WIGGINS, GRAMP
creator ERLE STANLEY GARDNER

The granddaughter of 70-year-old Gramp Wiggins is married to Frank Duryea, District Attorney of Santa Delbarro County, California. Foxy Grandpa has no fixed address, lives in a trailer and travels throughout the United States and Mexico. He has more pride in his housekeeping abilities than in his crime-solving talent; his trailer is always spic and span, he mixes a powerful martini and is a superb cook. Although generally on the side of law and order, Gramp is not averse to bringing illegal liquor and sugar into the United States on his return from Mexico.

WILLING, DR. BASIL
creator HELEN MC CLOY

Born in Baltimore to a Russian mother and American father, Basil Willing left home to serve in the United States Army Medical Corps in World War I, and developed an interest in psychology. After leaving the service, he returned to Baltimore, was graduated from Johns Hopkins Medical School, continued his studies in Paris and Vienna. Dr. Willing and his servant, Juniper, then moved to New York City, where he led a bachelor's life until his marriage to Gisela von Hohenems, an Austrian refugee.

The 5'11", slender, distinguished doctor became chief of a psychiatric clinic, and Medical Assistant to the District Attorney of Manhattan—a position he has held for many years. During World War II, he worked with the Federal Bureau of Investigation and served in the United States Naval Intelligence. Dr. Willing brings his training to the questioning of suspects, following the theory that "lies are psychological facts."

WILSON, SUPERINTENDENT HENRY
creators G. D. H. and M. I. COLE

At one time, the chief official of Scotland Yard was the conscientious Superintendent Henry Wilson. Totally dedicated, Wilson was called to duty at any moment of the day or night; when the bachelor relaxed without leaving his phone number at the Yard, he invariably felt guilty.

Then, his outstanding detective work proves an ex-Home Secretary guilty of a crime, and politics force him to resign. He quickly becomes the foremost private detective in England, getting assistance from his friends at Scotland Yard. When the political climate changes, Wilson, is reinstated at Scotland Yard.

WIMSEY, LORD PETER
creator DOROTHY L. SAYERS

In 1890, Peter was born to Mortimer Gerald Bredon Wimsey, 15th Duke of Denver, and his wife, Honoria. The boy was educated at Eton and Balliol College, taking 1st class honors in modern history, in 1912. He also acquired affectations, an exaggerated Oxford manner, and a monocle.

At this time, love and World War I came into Lord Peter Wimsey's life. He had planned to marry but he was about to enter the army, and felt it would be unfair to a wife if he came back from the war mutilated. When he returned to England on leave in 1916, he found the girl he loved had married another.

He returned to the war and recklessly earned the Distinguished Service Order. He also nearly lost his life behind German lines. His experiences left him with what was then called "a nervous breakdown." He recovered and moved into a London flat. There he pursued his interests in history, bibliophily, cricket, music (the piano and campanology), and criminology.

In 1935, he married mystery writer Harriet Vane. A son, Bredon Delagardie Peter, was born to the couple the following year, and later they had twins. Lord Peter is attended by the ultimate valet, Bunter●.

WINTRINGHAM, DR. DAVID
creator JOSEPHINE BELL, pseudonym of Dr. Doris B. C. Ball

The active, perceptive young physician, David Wintringham, is Junior Assistant Physician at Research Hospital in London. He is athletic, fond of swimming and the outdoors—he enjoys camping in Sussex in a caravan (trailer) with his wife, Jill, and infant son Nicholas. The Wintringhams are wealthy enough to have a nanny for their son and a maid. Often David will discuss a case with his wife, who frequently makes useful suggestions. The young amateur detective's eye is equally keen spotting questionable medical diagnoses, discovering physical clues to a crime, and recognizing imitation jewelry at a glance.

WITHERALL, LEONIDAS
creator ALICE TILTON, pseudonym of Phoebe Atwood Taylor

Gentleman scholar and headmaster of an exclusive New England boys' academy, Leonidas Witherall is also the pseudonymous author of the popular exploits of Lieutenant Haseltine. Witherall's chief recreation seems to be trying to extricate himself and his friends from farcical problems of a homicidal nature while he struggles to maintain his dignity. He is referred to as "Bill" because of his resemblance to Shakespeare.

WITHERS, HILDEGARDE▲
creator STUART PALMER

Miss Hildegarde Withers was born in Dubuque, Iowa but has spent most of her life as a New York school teacher. A "lean, angular spinster lady," her unusual hats and the black cotton umbrella she carries are her trademark. She becomes involved in many cases because of her friendship with Inspector Oscar Piper, New York Police Department. He proposed to her once, but retracted the offer at the last minute. "She's just a meddlesome old battle-axe who happens to be the smartest sleuth I ever knew."

Hildegarde collects tropical fish, abhors alcohol and tobacco, and appears to have an irritable disposition. However, she is a romantic at heart and will extend herself to help young lovers. She has crossed the path of hard-drinking Chicago lawyer John J. Malone and they have worked well together. Even after her retirement Hildegarde cannot resist murder investigations.

WOLFE, NERO
creator REX STOUT

Possibly the world's foremost practicing detective, certainly the largest, Nero Wolfe has his office and home in a brownstone house on West 35th Street in New York City. He is elephantine, carrying one-seventh of a ton on his 5'11" frame. "I carry this fat to insulate my feelings," he says. Many years ago, he decided he was too heavy and determined to take daily exercise, which consisted of throwing darts (he called them "javelins") for 15 minutes a day.

He is a self-admitted genius but detests work. Wolfe keeps Archie Goodwin● on the payroll primarily to prod him to undertake cases—which generally guarantee a rich fee—enabling him to indulge his hobby, orchid growing; his necessity, gourmet food, as prepared by Fritz Brenner●; and his luxurious residence. Wolfe never leaves his house, except under extreme provocation or "to meet personal contingencies," and cannot abide moving mechanical devices, such as automobiles—he will not ride in a taxi under threat of death; and Archie is the only driver he will consider for a trip, however short. A bomb in his study might occasion a change in his daily routine, but only briefly.

His command of the English language is exemplary, almost legendary; he also speaks seven foreign tongues: French, Spanish, Italian, Hungarian, Bari, Albanian, and Serbo-Croatian, and he has a good knowledge of Latin. He curses occasionally, but his favorite expletive is "Pfui!"

If Archie is unavailable for certain chores, Wolfe hires other operatives to work for him, usually Saul Panzer●, Orrie Cather● and Fred Durkin●. The official police, with whom he maintains a love-hate, hot-cold relationship, are most usually represented by Inspector Cramer●, by Lieutenant Rowcliff● and Sergeant Stebbins●.

Wolfe's brown hair is neatly trimmed and carefully brushed; his teeth are so white they gleam. He dresses conservatively, except when in bed, where he wears bright yellow pyjamas. His shirts are almost always yellow (his favorite color) and he changes them twice a day; he wears a tie and a vest year-round. He is generally master of his emotions, and only Archie can guess, with any accuracy, what Wolfe is thinking. He laughs about once a year; it sounds like a snort. When his eyes are wide open, he is either very sleepy or totally indifferent. When they are nearly closed, forming little slits, he is most alert—and most dangerous. When he is really thinking, his eyes close and his lips compress, pushing out and pulling in.

More than one female client has called Wolfe handsome. He is ostensibly antagonistic towards women but will admit, in a moment of candor, that this is merely a defense mechanism. Wolfe is reticent about his early years; this has led many to believe he is the illegitimate son of Sherlock Holmes.

YAMAMURA, TRYGVE
creator POUL ANDERSON

Karate expert Trygve Yamamura is truly an exotic private detective: born in Hawaii, he is half Norwegian and half Japanese. He is happily married, eschewing the drunkenness and woman-chasing popular among others in his profession. He works in a modest little office in Berkeley.

ZALESKI, PRINCE
creator M. P. SHIEL

Prince Zaleski, the noble Russian exile, is perhaps the most erudite and remote detective in literature. He leaves his couch in only one adventure, and his devoted Ethiopian servant, Ham, is grief-stricken until the master returns.

The splendid apartment of Zaleski is unmatched in terms of barbaric, bizarre beauty. He sits, in solitude, surrounded by Flemish sepulchral brasses, Egyptian mummies, gem-encrusted medieval reliquaries, Brahmin gods, runic tablets, miniature paintings, winged bulls, Tamil scriptures on lacquered leaves of the talipot. He is lulled by the "low, liquid, tinkling of an invisible musical-box," while in "the semi-darkness a very faint greenish lustre radiated from an open censer-like 'lampas' of fretted gold in the centre of the domed encased roof." In this setting, Zaleski indulges in a drug—the "base of the 'bhang' of the Mohammedans."

Since he does not conduct his investigations outside his dwelling-place, Zaleski must exercise extraordinary powers of concentration whenever Shiel (both narrator and author), brings him another grotesque case. Shiel says: "(Zaleski) seemed . . . to possess the unparalleled power not merely of disentangling in retrospect but of unravelling in prospect, and . . . to relate coming events with unimaginable minuteness of precision." Zaleski also had a "fineness of intuition" with his subtle reasoning.

ZOOM, SIDNEY
creator ERLE STANLEY GARDNER

"I live life as I see it" is the philosophy of Sidney Zoom, a detective who cares little for the opinion of others. He is a tall, lean, hawk-eyed investigator, given to prowling the streets at night. He is particularly fond of rainy nights as, with his police dog, Rip, he seeks adventure and oddities of human behavior. The detective business is not an economic necessity for Zoom, who lives on a palatial yacht. He carries a special badge and commission given him by the Chief of Police, allowing him access where private citizens were forbidden entry.

ROGUES & HELPERS

Criminals, both sympathetic
and sinister; villains, arch
and ordinary; supporters,
recorders and aides of
the great detectives.

ADLER, IRENE
creator SIR ARTHUR CONAN DOYLE

To Sherlock Holmes★, Irene Adler will always be *the* woman. Born in New Jersey in 1858, she became prima donna at the Imperial Opera of Warsaw, where she was involved with the King of Bohemia; later, she married Godfrey Norton, a lawyer. Holmes fell in love with the exquisitely beautiful Irene and, rumor has it, they had a brief affair, culminating in the birth of a child. Holmes called her "the daintiest thing under a bonnet on this planet." She died in 1903.

BANTZ, HAROLD
creator ELIZABETH DALY

The assistant of Henry Gamadge★ claims to have been taken off the streets as a destitute youth by his mentor. Harold Bantz became a valuable aide to Gamadge, saved his life in one case and helped him kidnap a client in another.

BATHGATE, NIGEL
creator NGAIO MARSH

Nigel Bathgate, a young journalist on the "London Clarion," is invited to a house party where he renews his acquaintance with the vivacious Angela North. Angela, a bit wild, scares Nigel by driving a car recklessly but, nonetheless, intrigues him. They ultimately get married. Murder occurs during the weekend, and Bathgate meets the Scotland Yard Inspector sent to investigate, Roderick Alleyn★. Bathgate is an ingenuous, robust young man with a reddish face, brushed-up mustache, and a neatly barbered look. He becomes Alleyn's good friend and chronicles his adventures.

BARON, THE
see under "DETECTIVES"

BOURKE
creator LOUIS JOSEPH VANCE

A quick, compact, dangerous little safecracker, Bourke met Michael Lanyard▲ (The Lone Wolf) in Paris, and taught him the fine art of the master cracksman. Having received most of his education at Dublin University, Bourke could speak the purest English, and his French was good enough to pass unchallenged in Paris. He had an ever-alert eye for pretty girls, a heart bigger than himself, no scruples worth mentioning, a secret sorrow and a pet superstition. His secret despair was the bright red color of his hair, which identified him so readily. His superstition was that, as long as he refrained from practicing his skills in Paris, that city would provide a refuge.

After teaching Lanyard his skills, he left with his disciple for Switzerland, to die of consumption in 1910—Lanyard at his side to the end.

BRENNER, FRITZ
creator REX STOUT

More than the cook in Nero Wolfe's★ household, Fitz Brenner is the major domo. He keeps the famous brownstone in perfect order. He has been with Wolfe even longer than Archie Goodwin●, the master's confidential assistant. Brenner is a superb chef who could work in New York's best restaurant for double his current salary (which exceeds $1,000 a month).

While actually cooking, in chef's hat and apron, he will neither talk nor listen to anyone. When alone, he likes to sit in the kitchen with his shoes off, listening to the rado and playing solitaire. He is Swiss, speaks French and reads French newspapers. He is very fond of his pet turtle. All people who wear skirts are ladies to him and he blushes easily in their presence.

BUNN, SMILER
creator BERTRAM ATKEY

Smiler Bunn, known also as Mr. Wilton Flood, is a genial, middle-aged, fat, wealthy gentleman who "makes his living off society in a manner always devious and sometimes dark, but never mean." He is an ingenious crook, blessed with great courage, resourcefulness and a keen sense of humor. He is described as a "condor-eyed, electric-witted and amazingly successful prowler among the perilous labyrinths of the shady side of life." Smiler loves to eat and drink, regarding each meal as an enjoyable experience.

Bunn and his friend, Lord Fortworth, have lived in bachelor partnership for years, specializing in securing portable property (such as cash and jewels) from those who have no right to it, thereby avoiding encounters with the police. Bunn's morose partner, also known as Henry Black or the Squire, is described by Bunn: "A rum 'un, the Squire always was, always will be. Got nothing, nothing in the world but the stark-naked, bullheaded courage of a rhinoceros."

BUNTER
creator DOROTHY L. SAYERS

If there is a more perfect man Friday than Lord Peter Wimsey's★ Bunter, he is unknown. Lord Peter appreciates this and, in 1923, paid him the then-princely sum of 200 pounds a year. Bunter, a brave man, had served as sergeant under Wimsey's captaincy in France. He stayed loyally with His Lordship when the Armistice brought lessened dangers. Bunter, that "invaluable fellow," has talents not usually possessed by the average butler. He is an expert in photography and is well-founded as a bibliophile. In fact, when we first meet him, Lord Peter is delegating him to attend a sale of rare books. But it is Bunter's abilty to brew perfect coffee which probably earns the greatest praise from his master, gourmet Lord Peter.

BURGER, HAMILTON▲
creator ERLE STANLEY GARDNER

On more than 50 occasions, Los Angeles County District Attorney Hamilton Burger has matched wits with Perry Mason★, but with no success. At first, Perry found the broad-shouldered, thick-necked bachelor D.A. to be a "pretty decent chap." Later, as Mason's victories mounted, he realized Burger hated him, even trying to have him disbarred. Generally, Perry remains patient when Burger throws an easily-ducked punch at him, countering only with a warning. Mason is even solicitous of his opponent's health, warning the red-faced Burger to lose about 30 pounds. By the mid-1960's, there is some evidence of mellowing. The District Attorney shakes hands with Perry and calls him by his first name.

CATHER, ORRIE
creator REX STOUT

Private detective Orrie Cather has virtually no talents except that people like to tell him things. He can't ask good, clever quesions and isn't smart enough to be cunning. It's just that people think he looks like someone in whom one can confide. Nero Wolfe★, who hires him as a freelancer, has no affection for him.

CLAY, COLONEL
creator GRANT ALLEN

Colonel Clay is the first short-story thief in detective literature, preceding the first book about Raffles• by two years. He is a master of disguise, changing unrecognizably from a Mexican seer to a Scottish parson while pursuing the fortune of his own special victim—Sir Charles Vandrift, the African millionaire. Clay is not a large man and his fresh, clean face exudes innocence. He has fun laughing at police as well as victim.

CLEEK, HAMILTON
creator THOMAS W. HANSHEW

Cleek, The Man of the Forty Faces, is a gentleman with a remarkable ability to contort his face, changing its appearance a dozen times in as many moments, so that in one instant it has the full roundness of a John Bull and in the next the haggard expression of a poor East Indian. This weird gift enables him to set a living mask over his features without the aid of make-up.

He is tall and slim, with a thin nose and a clear-cut aristocratic face. He had been a thief since childhood but, when he was between 25 and 35 years old, he decided to eschew his life of crime and become a detective. He is perfectly dressed, faultlessly mannered, with the fine articulation of a man of "birth." His eyes are honest and straight; his face, smooth and clean-shaven, undeniably handsome.

In his prime, he was the boldest, most impudent criminal with whom Scotland Yard ever had to cope. He resented the newspapers of London calling him a "cracksman," likening that sobriquet to calling Paganini a "fiddler." He asked that, instead of referring to him as "The Vanishing Cracksman," they refer to him as "The Man Who Calls Himself Hamilton Cleek." In return for that courtesy, he promised to send them information as to the place and time of his next robbery and, on the morning following the crime, to present a small portion of the loot to Scotland Yard as a souvenir of his performance. This he does, with unchecked success, until he falls in love and turns over a new leaf.

Although Cleek has many aliases, including George Headland, Lieutenant Deland and Captain Burbage, he is really the Prince of Mauravania. He ultimately spurns the throne of that Graustarkian kingdom to marry Ailsa. His adventures are aided by Dollops, a London street-boy.

CRAMER, INSPECTOR L. T.
creator REX STOUT

Inspector Cramer is the head of New York City's Homicide Squad and is frequently forced to ask Nero Wolfe★ for help or is called in by Wolfe to make an arrest when a case is wrapped up. He is red-faced, sour and usually angry. He chews a cigar (almost never smokes one) and, as he gets more and more exasperated with Wolfe or Archie Goodwin• he chews the cigar more and more vigorously, sometimes throwing the mangled remains at a wastebasket—not bothering to pick it up when he misses. He is not the typical dunder-headed police official of literature, although Wolfe once told him, "Your acceptance of your salary constitutes a fraud on the people of New York and you are a disgrace to an honorable profession." This is unfair of Wolfe, since Cramer functioned well in the single case in which he appears alone, "Red Threads" (1939).

DOVE, FIDELITY
creator DAVID DURHAM, pseudonym of
Roy Vickers

Fidelity Dove is a female larcenist who heads a highly successful gang of male thieves. They're all faithful to Fidelity and would gladly give up their lives for her. Even her greatest foe, Detective-Inspector Rason, has a generous opinion of the female counterpart of Raffles●. He has been too late each time he has tried to catch her and concedes she is "the coolest crook in London and then some." Rason, whose record improved when he joined "The Department of Dead Ends"★, admitted he had been on Fidelity's track dozens of times and had never been able to prove anything, saying, "In a way, she's a great woman."

DRACULA, COUNT▲
creator BRAM STOKER

Count Dracula is, in the words of Jonathan Harker, a "very peculiar man." To his neighbors in Transylvania, Dracula is a nobleman; to everyone else, he is a vampire. One particular quirk in the Count's life-style is sufficient to excite curiosity even among the most blasé: he is never seen to eat or drink. Also of some interest is the fact that he has no reflection in a mirror.

Dracula is a tall old man, clean shaven except for a long white mustache (unlike Bela Lugosi, whose portrayal of the sinister Count made motion picture history). Dracula dresses in black from head to foot. His hands are coarse, with fat, stubby fingers; there are hairs in the center of the palm. His handshake is strong enough to make men wince. The fingernails are long and fine, with a splendid manicure that ends each nail in a sharp point. The touch of that hand is cold as ice— "more like the hand of a dead man."

His face is long and thin, with a narrow nose and strangely curved nostrils. His eyebrows are thick and nearly meet over his nose. His mouth is thin-lipped and cruel-looking, with unusually sharp, white teeth that partly protrude over his bright red lips. His ears are pale and end in sharp tips, giving him a satanic appearance.

DRAKE, PAUL▲
creator ERLE STANLEY GARDNER

An able detective in his own right, Paul Drake has always been eclipsed by his good friend, Perry Mason★▲. This may be intentional since Mason provides 75% of the Drake Detective Agency's business, which is located on the same floor as Mason's law offices. Little is known of Drake's early history, beyond the fact that he is a small-town boy who was jilted by a girl when he was younger. He has never married. He is tall and has poor posture, often sitting sideways and slouched in a chair. He is a nervous man, and the long hours he works for Mason have caused him considerable stomach distress.

DURKIN, FRED
creator REX STOUT

A free lance detective who is sometimes called in on a case by Nero Wolfe★, Fred Durkin is the second-best "tailer" around (next to Saul Panzer●). According to Archie Goodwin●, Wolfe's assistant, Fred was "as honest as sunshine, but he wasn't so bright as sunshine." Wolfe cannot tolerate having Fred dine with him because Durkin adds vinegar to his food. As he breezes into Wolfe's office, Fred likes to toss his hat so it hooks on the back of Archie's swivel chair.

EGYPT, HARRY
creator DANIEL BROUN

Mild-mannered, gentle Harry Egypt, with his pleasant New Orleans drawl, is short and barrel-like, though without excess fat. His brown eyes peer benignly from steel-rimmed bifocals. Before World War II, he had been a soldier of fortune in Burma, Spain, and Hong Kong. During the war, he displayed his bravery at Dieppe. His experiences qualified him for a life as a detective or as a thief; he chose to operate outside the law. Advance planning is the hallmark of Egypt's success. Whether kidnapping or stealing millions in old Civil War gold, Egypt will begin no operation until he has studied it carefully.

FLAMBEAU
creator G. K. CHESTERTON

Flambeau is a colossus of crime; "a figure as statuesque and international as the Kaiser." He is a Frenchman of gigantic stature, fantastic physical strength, a robust sense of humor, the agility of an acrobat, and extraordinary courage and daring. His great strength is generally demonstrated in comical acts, rather than bloody ones, as when he turned a magistrate on his head "to clear his mind," and when he ran down a street with a policeman under each arm. His great crimes were robberies —ingenious and numerous. Though he is a master of disguise, the one thing Flambeau cannot hide is his great height; he is 6'4''. His enemy was Valentin●, the Chief of the Paris Police.

Eventually, Flambeau repents and reforms, opening an office as a private detective under the guidance of Father Brown★, whose help is always available (and usually required).

FOUR SQUARE JANE
creator EDGAR WALLACE

Four Square Jane is a girl who steals only from those with bloated bank accounts—the grossly rich who had, moreover, acquired their wealth through shady means. The money she steals is immediately donated to charitable institutions. Though many people have seen Jane, no one really knows what she looks like. She is a master of disguise, passing equally well for a little girl in a short skirt or an elderly lady in a veil.

Superintendent Dawes, the bright young pride of Scotland Yard, calls her the cleverest criminal he has ever encountered. Though she is considered a female Robin Hood by many, to one Chief Inspector at the Yard she is a common thief, and to Dawes she is the one thing he has dreaded—a criminal with a brain.

FU MANCHU, DR.▲
creator SAX ROHMER, pseudonym of
Arthur Sarsfield Ward

The evil Dr. Fu Manchu is a tall, slender Oriental with a brow like Shakespeare's and a face like Satan's. He usually wears a long yellow robe but sometimes dons a black robe with a silver peacock embroidered on the front. On his close-shaven skull he generally wears a black cap surmounted by a red ball. His eyes are long and magnetic—the true cat-green—and so piercing they can be felt even when unseen. He wears no mustache (contrary to some reports) because it would interfere with his disguises— at which skill he is a master.

He has a cruel cunning and a giant intellect, with all the resources of science, both past and present, at his disposal. His mastery of the secret sects of the East—Dacoits, Thugs, Phansigars, Hashishin—and his command of every Tong in Asia are the tools he employs in his quest to become Emperor of the World, which brings him into many battles with Sir Dennis Nayland Smith★.

While the ubiquitous doctor is the most sinister and powerful villain in literature, he adheres strictly to the rules of the game and his word may be accepted as a gentleman's. Although he rose from the ghettos of Limehouse, Fu Manchu is believed to be of noble birth, related to members of the famed Manchu Dynasty.

GODAHL, THE INFALLIBLE
creator FREDERICK IRVING ANDERSON

The Infallible Godahl is the American counterpart to Great Britain's Raffles• as the consummate criminal, the perfect thief. Godahl never fails; consequently, no one knows how great he is, his name never having appeared on the police blotter. Only he knows. He is a scientific thief of incredible genius, a Thinking Machine★ on the wrong side of the law.

The Infallible Godahl is a flamboyant young New Yorker who has amassed a great fortune (enough to be called one of "the fifty little millionaires" of the Pegasus Club) with a succession of brilliant robberies. He breaks each problem into its essentials in a clear-cut, precise manner, then uses his giant intellect to consummate his robbery. He believes that superstition is foolish, intuition useless. He prefers the certainty of the marked card, the sureness of pure reason. Though he believes himself the intellectual superior of any opponent, he fears the afflicted, believing that anyone who has lost the use of any of his senses acquires greater sensitivity in those that remain.

The creator of The Infallible Godahl, Frederick Irving Anderson, is regarded, with Melville Davisson Post, as one of the great writers of American mystery short stories.

GOLDFINGER, AURIC▲
creator IAN FLEMING

Only a super-criminal is worthy of a battle with James Bond★ ▲, and Auric Goldfinger, villain incarnate, is such a man. This noxious manipulator of men is less than five feet tall, his stumpy body jammed almost directly into his shoulders. His huge, almost perfectly round head is crowned by a bright, carrot-red crewcut. The moonshaped face has a fine, high forehead, and a fleshily acquiline nose between high cheekbones. "The mouth was thin and dead straight, but beautifully drawn. The chin and jaws were firm and glinted with health." He wears a flesh-colored hearing aid in his left ear. The most startling feature of his face is a pair of pale, china-blue eyes "that stared right through a face to the back of the skull." Thin, sandy brows were level above the large, piercing eyes fringed with pale lashes. It is "the face of a thinker, perhaps a scientist, who was ruthless, sensual, stoical and tough."

GOODWIN, ARCHIE
creator REX STOUT

With the exception of Nero Wolfe★, his confidential assistant
Archie Goodwin, is probably the best detective in the business.
Wolfe is an acknowledged genius but he is extraordinarily lazy
and reluctant to take a case. Archie is paid a considerable sum
ostensibly to work as Wolfe's secretary, chauffeur, errand boy,
accountant, office manager, and bodyguard, but his major value
lies in his ability to nudge Wolfe to action. Virtually all contact with the interesting sex is handled by Archie. Wolfe is
usually uncomfortable and/or exasperated in the presence of
females and he believes Archie has merely to lift a finger to
have women flock to him.

While not entirely accurate, this belief is not too far afield;
Archie is tall, broad-shouldered, narrow-hipped, and very handsome. He has brown hair and eyes, his nose is a bit flat and he
possesses a pleasant baritone voice. The lion's share of his
salary goes for good clothes and tickets to sporting events. He
is very strong and is an accomplished fighter who sometimes
fights cleanly; he has saved Wolfe's life on more than one occasion. His memory is practically photographic—he can recall
an hour-long conversation with five people nearly verbatim. His
wit is unexcelled by any other detective's chronicler.

GUTMAN, CASPER▲
(The Fat Man)
creator DASHIELL HAMMETT

The ruthless adventurer who for 17 years has coveted the Maltese Falcon■ only to be thwarted by Sam Spade★, Casper Gutman is flabbily fat with bulbous pink cheeks, lips, chins and
neck, and a great soft egg of a belly that was his entire torso.
When he walked, all his bulbs bounced and shook separately,
like "clustered soap bubbles not yet released from the pipe
through which they had been blown." His eyes, made small by
the fat around them, are dark and sleek. Dark ringlets thinly
cover his scalp. His voice is a throaty purr. His foppish dress
includes a black cutaway coat, black vest, black satin ascot tie
held by a pinkish pearl, striped gray trousers and black patent-
leather shoes.

HANSLET, SUPERINTENDENT
creator JOHN RHODE, pseudonym of
Cecil John Charles Street

Early in his career, Superintendent Hanslet met Dr. Priestley★,
who was delighted to help solve the crime problems brought to

him by the then-young inspector. Brisk, methodical and meticulous, Hanslet often minimized Priestley's efforts, only to find himself proven wrong.

HASTINGS, CAPTAIN
creator AGATHA CHRISTIE

Captain Hastings embodies the essential ingredient of the true Watson● (i.e. the loyal, not very bright companion to the eccentric detective). Early in World War I, Hastings is at Styles on sick leave, invalided home from the Belgian front to a convalescent home. The exact war injury is not clear, since he is able to do considerable walking and play tennis as well.

It is at Styles that he renews his acquaintance with Hercule Poirot★, whom he met in Belgium. Hastings finishes his military service, is discharged as a Captain, and agrees to share a flat with Poirot in London. He works as secretary to a Member of Parliament, choosing not to return to his pre-war job at Lloyds of London.

Hastings, an incurable romantic, readily fell in love with most of the attractive women in his cases. He married in 1925 and moved to Argentina, returning to Europe and resuming his partnership with Poirot on several occasions.

After the death of his wife, Hastings returns to Styles for what, poignantly, will be the last case on which he and Poirot will work. He is anxious to return there because his favorite child, his eldest daughter, is working nearby, and he fears she has become romantically involved with a married man. His main purpose, however, is to recapture the past and be reunited on a case with Poirot, the man with whom he has shared so many detective adventures.

HEATH, SERGEANT ERNEST▲
creator S. S. VAN DINE, pseudonym of
Willard Huntington Wright

The hard-working but extraordinarily inept Sergeant Heath of the New York City Homicide Bureau was openly antagonistic to Philo Vance★ when they first met, but Vance's successes eventually aroused a curious feeling of good fellowship in the breast of the doughty policeman. His broad, pugnacious features and his imperturbable blue eyes, with their habitual penetrating intentness, were reflections of his innate tenacity and honesty.

HOLMES, MYCROFT
creator SIR ARTHUR CONAN DOYLE

Mycroft Holmes is the older brother, by seven years, of Sherlock Holmes★ ▲. Unlike his more-famous brother, Mycroft is huge; Sherlock says encountering Mycroft is like meeting "a tram car coming down a country lane." He walks around the corner to his office each morning, returns each night; he takes no other exercise from one year to the next. Totally without ambition, Mycroft is content to earn 450 pounds a year as a government accountant and advisor.

He is the only man in the world whose powers of observation and deduction exceed those of Sherlock Holmes. "If the art of the detective began and ended in reasoning from an arm chair," says Sherlock, "my brother would be the greatest criminal agent that ever lived." Because of his lack of energy and ambition, however, Mycroft would not "go out of his way to verify his own solutions, and would rather be considered wrong than take the trouble to prove himself right."

He is founder-member of the Diogenes Club, which contains the most unsociable and unclubbable men in London. His marked resemblance to Nero Wolfe★ has been noted.

HOONG LIANG
creator ROBERT VAN GULIK

Trusted advisor to Judge Dee★ and Sergeant of the Tribunal, Hoong Liang dies in service while trying to aid the Judge in solving a criminal case.

HUDSON, MRS. MARTHA
creator SIR ARTHUR CONAN DOYLE

The long-suffering, able landlady of Sherlock Holmes★ at 221 B Baker Street is Mrs. Hudson, a kindly, aging woman who has endured the eccentric habits of the famed detective, "the worst tenant in London," for many years.

JERVIS, DR. CHRISTOPHER
creator R. AUSTIN FREEMAN

Dr. Jervis is an aide of the famed criminal investigator, Dr. Thorndyke★. He chronicles Thorndyke's cases, observing and recording all the facts, then failing magnificently to perceive their significance. He falls in and out of love with regularity, to the exasperation of Thorndyke.

KANG, DR. LIN
creator VICTOR CANNING

Dr. Lin Kang is, basically, a petty crook. Born in China in 1885, he has earned his Ph.D. at Peking University, with the help of hard working parents. There is no indication that he ever helped them. He was, from youth, stout (even pudgy) with a placid, Buddha-like face. Behind his warm smile and enigmatic dark eyes is an always-scheming brain. However, his plots are usually small-time.

Dr. Kang never makes a great deal of money, often being reduced to cheating at cards. His schemes frequently backfire and, while he avoids imminent, apparently inevitable death, it is usually more by luck than by skill.

KARMESIN
creator GERALD KERSH

Karmesin is "either the greatest criminal or the greatest liar of our time." Should the former be the case, he certainly is "The Compleat Criminal," since he has been at various times a murderer, jewel thief, swindler, bank robber, confidence man, racketeer, and blackmailer. Apparently, crime really does not pay since Karmesin is usually broke. Basically Karmesin is on the side of the law.

LANYARD, MICHAEL▲
see LONE WOLF, THE

LESTRADE, INSPECTOR
creator SIR ARTHUR CONAN DOYLE

A quick, energetic worker, Inspector Lestrade is incredibly slow to grasp the importance of clues brought to his attention by Sherlock Holmes★. To his credit, however, he comes to Holmes for help when Scotland Yard is baffled, and he rarely interferes with Holmes' work. He and his fellow policeman, Inspector Gregson, are anxious to take credit for Holmes' solutions. Lestrade and Gregson are called "the pick of a bad lot" by Holmes and Dr. Watson● describes Lestrade as "sallow, rat-faced, dark-eyed."

LITTLE CAESAR
creator W. R. BURNETT

"Wanted for murder: Cesare Bandello, known as Rico. Age: 20. Height: 5 ft. 5 in. Weight: 125. Complexion: pale. Hair: black and wavy. Eyes: light gray or blue. His face is thin and he walks with one foot slightly turned in. Does not take up with strangers. Solitary type, morose and dangerous. Reward: $7,000 . . . for capture dead or alive."

This is the description of Rico, also known as Little Caesar, after his plunge from the top of Chicago's underworld hierarchy. On his way up, when he was just a member of Sam Vettori's gang, he was known as the best gunman in Little Italy. He possesses a menacing gun, reckless courage and an insatiable urge to be first, to win at everything—even in a friendly card game.

His desire to succeed is so intense that he is incapable of relaxing. He sleeps, eats, and makes love in a tense, rigid manner that allows for no pleasure. He does not live in the present, but regards life as a weary, drab journey to a vague place in the future where he will be Number One. Rico is, basically, a simple man, with only three loves: himself, his hair and his gun; he takes excellent care of all three. He has a nervous habit of combing his luxurious black hair with his ivory pocket comb. He does not drink nor care much about women, except as occasional objects of gratification. He trusts no one; women even less than men.

LONE WOLF, THE▲
creator LOUIS JOSEPH VANCE

Raised as Marcel Troyon, a drudge and scullion in Troyon's, a disreputable Parisian hotel, Michael Lanyard learned to steal and cheat at an early age. He used the money to buy food, since the selfish proprietress of the hotel gave him little besides beatings. By the time he reached the age of 15, he had developed a long, lanky, boorish look. His face was pallid, his mouth sullen, and hot black eyes were set deeply in his face.

After working all day, he was locked into his room, but scrambled through a window and roamed the streets of Paris, which he came to know intimately. He stole books from one end of the city, surreptitiously read them in a corner of his room, then sold them to a dealer in another district. Thus he learned to read English—the language he believed to be his true one—before he could speak it.

While cleaning rooms, he would steal one or two coins from a guest's pockets, but he once made the mistake of attempting to pilfer a gold louis from a man known as Bourke●. He was caught but, instead of being punished, Lanyard was taught to be the master criminal Bourke always aspired to be. The young lad soon became an expert mathematician, a connoisseur of armour-plate and an adept with explosives. He could grade precious stones at a glance, developed a passion for good paintings and learned to be at ease in every grade of society. He also learned the "three cardinal principles of successful cracksmanship: know your ground thoroughly before venturing upon it; strike and retreat with the swift precision of a hawk; be friendless. And the last of these is the greatest." He heeds this advice and becomes The Lone Wolf—a sophisticated, debonair gentleman by day and a daring, debonair burglar by night.

LUPIN, ARSÈNE
creator MAURICE LEBLANC

Arsène Lupin is the Prince of Thieves, the French counterpart of the British Raffles● as the consummate criminal. He is not a suave character, however, but a street urchin-type who thumbs his nose, literally, at the police.

He is a master of disguise (so skilled that he took the identity of Lenormand, chief of the Sûreté, and directed police investigations into his own activities for four years). His disguises are numerous—so varied that one never really knows which character in a story is Lupin, or even if the one called Lupin, is, in fact, the famed gentleman-cambrioleur. His aliases are legion —during his adventurous career he has been called, at various times, Prince Renine, Luis Perenna, Jim Barnett, Paul Sernine, Captain Jeanniot, Horace Velmont, Paul Daubreuil, Bernard d'Andrezy, Désiré Baudru, Cavaliere Florianai, Jean Daspry, Ralph de Limezy, Jean d'Enneris, Victor Hautin, and le Duc de Charmerace, as well as Lenormand.

Lupin is uniquely French, with unexcelled "joie de vivre," a superb sense of humor and unparalleled conceit. To him, the police are a group of dunderheads who are incapable of understanding him, much less of arresting him. He is a friend of the Prefect but has little respect and no admiration for him. Lupin and his gang lead the police a merry chase for the pleasure of the crimes rather than for personal gain or for more noble motives. He is amoral, turning to crime for the fun of it. He is young, quick-witted, handsome, brave, and full of spirit.

After unmatched success for many years as a criminal, Lupin turns to the side of the law (for personal reasons) and aids the police in their investigations—usually without their knowledge. Later still, he turns his full time and talent to detective work, bringing a sharp, penetrating mind, as well as years of first-hand experience, to his work. He is not, however, a first-rate detective. He cannot overcome the handicaps of his many years as a daring criminal: inability to resist love affairs, and over-fondness for jokes.

Maurice Leblanc, the creator of Arsène Lupin, was a police reporter for a French newspaper when a new journal asked him for a fictional crime story and, without previous experience, Leblanc created the famous character.

MADVIG, PAUL
creator DASHIELL HAMMETT

A tall, heavy-set, handsome blond, Paul Madvig is a friend of Ned Beaumont★ in Hammett's classic, "The Glass Key"■. A machine-made politician, he was once a runner of errands; now he is the city's political boss. His clothes are saved from flashiness by their quality and by the way he wears them. He is 45 years old, his light hair parted in the middle and brushed close to his head.

MALVINO THE MAGICIAN
creator FREDERICK IRVING ANDERSON

People said Malvino had no eyes. He is a sleight-of-hand artist, born to eternal darkness, who always wears a black silk mask over his face. Malvino the Magician is also a thief skillful enough to warrant unstinted praise from The Infallible Godahl●, the only man who recognized Malvino's greatness.

Malvino is tall and slender, always dressed in black. Head erect and shoulders squared, his bearing is military. He carries a slender ebony cane, with which he taps the street in front of him. Malvino frequently displays his manual dexterity, which is so great that when Godahl tried to imitate him, he almost failed.

MANDERS, BUNNY
creator E. W. HORNUNG

Bunny Manders is the fellow-adventurer and chronicler of the nefarious exploits of Raffles●. He is typically British in appearance and could not be called especially quick-witted, even by the most generous standards. He is penniless and joins Raffles in his robberies, though he detests the idea. He had been Raffles' schoolmate and had done menial chores for him. When they met again as adults, loyalty and affection were rekindled in Manders to the point where he practically idolized the great cracksman. Despite his hatred of their illegal profession, Bunny serves Raffles devotedly and his bravery sees them through many close calls. He had literary talent in his younger years, had edited the school magazine—experience which served him well when he turned to narrating Raffles' adventures.

MANDRELL, AUGUSTUS
creator FRANK MC AULIFFE

Mandrell is a smooth, cold, professional assassin and a connoisseur of beautiful possessions and women (both of which he can well afford considering his fees). He is also a devotee of sardonic gallows humor, which sparkles throughout his self-narrated "commissions."

MARKHAM, JOHN F. X.▲
creator S. S. VAN DINE, pseudonym of
Williard Huntington Wright

Markham is Philo Vance's★ ▲ best friend, though totally unlike his aristocratic companion in tastes and ethical outlook. As
District Attorney, Markham is called to the scene of many of
New York's most spectacular crimes and enjoys having his
clever friend along to offer advice. Markham's manner is forth-
right and brusque—even, on occasion, domineering. He is grim
and serious about life. He is honest, incorruptible and untiring
in the performance of his duty, following the dictates of his
legal conscience in the face of every temptation and obstacle.
Despite his virtues, he is at times, unable to cope with the intricacies of a case. He served only one term in office, being
defeated in his bid for reelection on a hopelessly split ticket.

MASON, RANDOLPH
creator MELVILLE DAVISSON POST

Randolph Mason is an unscrupulous lawyer who uses the in-
adequacies of the law to defeat justice. In his mid-forties, Mason
is tall and broad-shouldered. His now-sparse brown hair is
streaked with gray; his high forehead is a bit reddish. His face
is quite ugly; his nose is too big and his eyes too small, their
inky blackness always alive and nervous-looking. The eyebrows
are thick and bushy. He has a large, square jaw and a straight,
thin-lipped mouth. If one looks him square in the face, his expression seems to be sneering, fearless, animated; if looked at
from above, it appears cynical and sly; from below, it looks
cruel, vindictive, almost savage. He likes to clasp his long white
hands behind his back.

In a courtroom, he appears bored while listening to the prosecution. Hated and feared by other members of his profession,
Mason is a man of giant intellect and one of the country's great
lawyers. Though he was a criminal lawyer originally, giant
corporations recognized his talents and hired him to find methods of by-passing statutes, so that they could comply with the
letter of the law, yet violate its spirit with impunity—bending
the law without breaking it. In the cases in which Mason becomes involved, the criminal makes no effort to avoid being
caught for his crime, concentrating instead on the evasion of
punishment. Mason once explained his immoral philosophy:
"No man who has followed my advice has ever committed a
crime. Crime is a technical word. It is the law's term for certain
acts which it is pleased to define and punish with a penalty.
What the law permits is right, else it would prohibit it. What
the law prohibits is wrong, because it punishes it. The word

moral is a purely metaphysical symbol." Later in his career, Mason went over to the side of justice.

The author, Melville Davisson Post, spent several years practicing criminal and corporate law, providing him with rich background for the tales of Mason. Though moralists complained that the stories gave too much advice to potential criminals, Post argued that nothing but good could come from exposing the defects of the law.

MEREFIELD, HAROLD
creator JOHN RHODE, pseudonym of
Cecil John Charles Street

Young, ambitious secretary to Dr. Priestley★, Harold Merefield narrated many of his mentor's early exploits. He executes commissions that are of immeasurable aid in the solution of crime problems. Frequently referred to as "my boy" by Dr. Priestley, Merefield handled all his employer's telephone communications.

MORESBY, INSPECTOR
creator ANTHONY BERKELEY, pseudonym of
Anthony Berkeley Cox

A Scotland Yard official of ordinary appearance and behavior, Inspector Moresby is totally unlike one's conception of a professional detective. He often matches wits with Roger Sheringham★ but is astute enough to ask for help and tolerant enough to endure the insufferable amateur.

MORIARTY, PROFESSOR JAMES▲
creator SIR ARTHUR CONAN DOYLE

The great adversary of Sherlock Holmes★, and the most dangerous man in London, Professor James Moriarty, works like a spider at the center of a web of crime which embraces the entire city. The true nature of his activities is recognized only by Holmes. Indeed, Holmes has little success convincing Scotland Yard officialdom of the professor's criminality. The world sees him only as a mild-mannered mathematics professor who had made a brief academic splash with a paper on the dynamics of an asteroid.

Moriarty is "clean-shaven, pale, and ascetic-looking . . . and is forever slowly oscillating from side to side in a curiously reptilian fashion." He is, says Holmes, "The Napoleon of crime . . . He is a genius, a philosopher, an abstract thinker . . ." Yet, Holmes welcomes the challenge of Moriarty as an adversary worthy of his own intellect, suggesting to Watson that life would be dull without such challenges.

In his eagerness to win the battle, Holmes moves in too

close and the Professor decides to eliminate him. In "The Final Problem," he makes several attempts on Holmes' life, forcing the detective and Watson to flee England. Holmes and Moriarty finally meet, alone, at the edge of the Reichenbach Falls in Switzerland. After a brief struggle, they fall over the brink—the arch villain apparently to his death, the detective miraculously escaping with his life.

Moriarty set the standard for all the criminal geniuses and master villains who followed. The phrase "Napoleon of Crime" has been applied to several fiends since Moriarty.

O'SHAUGHNESSY, BRIGID▲
creator DASHIELL HAMMETT

The gorgeous red-head who masquerades as Miss Wonderly to become Sam Spade's★ client in "The Maltese Falcon,"■ Brigid O'Shaughnessy, is described by Spade's secretary, Effie Perine, as "a knockout." Her blue eyes are both shy and probing; her body erect and high-breasted; her legs long; her hands and feet narrow; her hair, curling from beneath a blue hat, dark red; and her lips full, colored a bright red, with white teeth glistening through her smile.

"PACK, THE"
creator LOUIS JOSEPH VANCE

"The Pack" is an assembly of the leaders of the world's underground, who try to force Michael Lanyard (The Lone Wolf●) to join them. The group includes Wertheimer, representing the "swell-mobsmen of England"; Count De Morbihan, "standing for the gratin of Paris"; Popinot, speaking for the Apaches; and the mysterious Mr. Smith from America.

PANZER, SAUL
creator REX STOUT

Saul Panzer is a free-lance detective who is frequently called in by Nero Wolfe★ to help on a tough case. Both Wolfe and Archie Goodwin● think he's the best but Saul says only, "I've developed my faculties." He has a nose that obscures the rest of his wrinkled little face; he always needs a shave, his suit is never pressed, and he looks like a rummy down on his luck. However, he commands double the rate of other private detectives, is worth it, drinks only champagne and owns at least two houses in Brooklyn.

He has a great deal of pride in his ability. He once told Wolfe, "This is the third time I've flopped on you in ten years and that's too often. I don't want you to pay me, not even expenses."

PARKER
creator RICHARD STARK, pseudonym of
Donald E. Westlake

One of the toughest men in mystery fiction is Parker, the professional thief with no first name. Nothing is left to chance when Parker plans a big caper. The country's best gunmen, safecrackers and the like, are enrolled, a split-second schedule is planned and countless rehearsals are held. Parker becomes so emotionally involved during the planning of a crime that he becomes impotent—a situation which changes drastically after the job is completed.

Despite precision planning, something usually goes wrong and Parker is lucky to escape with his life. There have been misunderstandings with the huge crime syndicate that occasionally finances his operations. In one instance, he had to flee, leaving all his money behind, because his wife had "fingered" him to the syndicate. Later she killed herself; Parker has never remarried. He has had plastic surgery, so he is no longer recognized by his enemies.

PARKER, DR. LYNDON
creator AUGUST DERLETH

Dr. Lyndon Parker is a solid, middle-class, unimaginative Englishman who lives at No. 7 Praed Street, London, with Solar Pons★ and recounts the famous detective's adventures. He is loyally and deeply attached to Pons and England, though he undoubtedly spent many years of his early life in the United States—a time about which he has never spoken. He is generally two steps behind Pons and one behind the reader when a case is in progress, though he tries his best to appear quick-witted.

PARKINSON
creator ERNEST BRAMAH, pseudonym of
Ernest Bramah Smith

The punctilious attendant of Max Carrados★, Parkinson serves as the eyes of the blind detective. He is a quiet, deliberate servant whose voice reflects the respect he has for Carrados. Regarding Parkinson's intellect, Bramah wrote: "It is doubtful if anyone had yet plumbed the exact limits to the worthy fellow's real capacity. There were moments when he looked more sagacious than any mortal man has hope of ever being, and there were times when his comment on affairs seemed to reveal a greater depth of mental vacuity than was humanly credible."

Parkinson's occasionally brilliant understatements provide a genteel humor.

PETRIE, DR.▲
creator SAX ROHMER, pseudonym of
Arthur Sarsfield Ward

Born in Egypt in 1884, Dr. Petrie, in addition to helping Sir Nayland Smith★ in his battles with Dr. Fu Manchu●, became a chemist of such profound knowledge he earned the respect of Fu Manchu himself. While Petrie describes himself as "only an ordinary practitioner," he is an internationally-recognized authority on tropical diseases. He married the beautiful Karamaneh in Egypt in 1917, and they had a daughter the following year. Before their marriage and after, the sensuous Oriental beauty saved Petrie's life (and Smith's) countless times.

PHOTOGRAPHER, THE
(Manuel Andradas)
creator JAMES HOLDING

There are many series detectives, even some series burglars, but Manuel Andradas (The Photographer) is a series murderer. Photography is only a sideline for this professional assassin, whose services are available to organized crime in Brazil, where he lives. He can be reached at a small café, where the name of the intended victim is written on the menu. The contact must pay in advance half of the Photographer's considerable fee.

POLTON, NATHANIEL
creator R. AUSTIN FREEMAN

Polton is Dr. Thorndyke's★ laboratory assistant, butler, photographer, and jack-of-all-trades. He possesses boundless ingenuity and technical resources. His crinkly countenance belies his sporadic fervors of the heart, which frequently intrude on Dr. Thorndyke's investigations. Polton resides at 5A King's Bench Walk with the noted medico-legal expert.

PRINGLE, ROMNEY
creator CLIFFORD ASHDOWN, pseudonym of
R. Austin Freeman and Dr. John James Pitcairn

Romney Pringle, in the Raffles● tradition of "gentleman crook," hides behind the respectable front of literary agent. He is a charming scoundrel who made enough money by nefarious means to retire to Sandwich for a life of ease and comfort. During his "working days," Pringle was a tall, slim, wholesome-looking man with a fair complexion and youthful appearance.

He is able to stay healthy with minimum effort by rising early, getting to bed before two in the morning, and smoking Havana cigars instead of cigarettes. His leisure time is spent reading, cataloguing his antique gems, and cycling.

PRY, PAUL
see under "DETECTIVES"

RAFFLES, A. J.
creator E. W. HORNUNG

Raffles is the greatest criminal in the literature of roguery. The famed "Amateur Cracksman" is a gentleman, as comfortable in the society of England's wealthiest families as he is on the cricket field or at a burglar-proof safe. He is tall and handsome, with curly black hair and a lean, athletic frame. His jaw is firm and his mouth strong, if somewhat unscrupulous. His eyes are a cold, hard, beautiful blue that has attracted more than one female. His clean-shaven features are pale and sharp—a face that reveals little mercy or sympathy. He was captain of his team at school and went on to become one of the greatest cricket players in England, a skill that earned him entrance to some gatherings which he otherwise might not have penetrated.

Raffles is polished, debonair, sophisticated; he looks as if he were born in evening clothes. His charming personality and great wit make him a desirable guest among the upper strata of society but his personal code of honor forbids stealing from his host (though his fellow-guests do not enjoy that same self-imposed protection). He also eschews violence.

The safe has not been made that can stop Raffles and no thief has ever matched his courage and daring. While he prefers to map out carefully a plan of action, he has been known to commit a spur-of-the-moment theft on a whim. He has the instinctive secretiveness of the inveterate criminal, rarely telling his plans to his friend, helper and chronicler, Bunny Manders●.

Raffles steals sometimes for the fun of it, sometimes to give the proceeds to a friend in need, sometimes as an intellectual exercise, sometimes to right a wrong, sometimes to keep the creditors away from his door. His fancy address and life-style (for instance, he smokes only Sullivan cigarettes, the most expensive brand sold) require a considerable income, and Raffles will not work at menial employment. Though he has many talents (he could have been a successful poet, however unremunerative that field may be), he prefers to live by his wits and his skill as a cracksman.

Raffles turned to crime while playing cricket in the Colonies. Penniless, his only way out of an embarrassing situation was to steal. He had intended it to be an isolated act, caused by unusual circumstances, but "tasted blood" and decided this was the life for him. "Why settle down to some humdrum, uncongenial billet," he asks Bunny, "when excitement, romance, danger and a decent living were all going begging together? Of course it's very wrong, but we can't all be moralists, and the distribution of wealth is very wrong to begin with." Late in his career, however, Raffles aligns himself with the side of law and order, turning to the detection of crime. A bullet in the Boer War ends his life.

The creator of Raffles, Ernest William Hornung, was the brother-in-law of Sir Arthur Conan Doyle. In turn-of-the-century England, Sherlock Holmes★▲ was the most popular and familiar figure in literature, Raffles was second. After Hornung died, Barry Perowne continued to provide readers with exploits of Raffles, first in a long series of stories that put the gentleman thief in a contemporary setting, later in stories that once again saw Raffles working by gaslight.

ROWCLIFF, LIEUTENANT GEORGE
creator REX STOUT

Lieutenant Rowcliff is more detested by Nero Wolfe★ and Archie Goodwin● than are most criminals. To Wolfe, he'll always be "the officer who came here once with a warrant and searched my house"—an unthinkable affront. When Archie dies and has a choice of Heaven or Hell, he'll simply ask, "Where's Rowcliff?" He is big and handsome, has been decorated for personal bravery and is one of the most ambitious cops on the force. When confronted by Archie, he gets so irritated that he stutters; Archie knows him so well that he starts to stutter just before Rowcliff does. This infuriates the policeman so much that he stutters worse than before.

SAINT, THE
see under "DETECTIVES"

SAVAGE, RENA
creator BAYNARD KENDRICK

Attractive and efficient secretary to Captain Duncan Maclain★, Rena was hired by his partner, Spud Savage●, who quickly married her. She feels personally responsible for her employer's morale and well-being.

SAVAGE, SAMUEL "SPUD"
creator BAYNARD KENDRICK

The partner and long-time best friend of Captain Duncan Maclain★, "Spud" Savage is noted for his intelligence, his loyalty to Maclain, his natural athletic ability, and his yellow eyes.

SEEGRAVE, SUPT.
creator WILKIE COLLINS

Seegrave is the dull-witted Superintendent of the Frizinghall police. Tall and portly, his brusque manner comfortingly military, his commanding voice and resolute eye demanding respect, he is a thoroughly imposing figure. In Franklin Blake's words, "That man is no earthly use to us. Mr. Seegrave is an ass." His negative approach to the principals in the case and the conclusions he draws support Blake's theory.

STEBBINS, SERGEANT PURLEY
creator REX STOUT

Inspector Cramer's● assistant, Stebbins doesn't like private detectives much, but sometimes he forgets and makes an exception of Nero Wolfe★ and Archie Goodwin●. He is bigger and stronger than Archie, but not handsome, being saddled with inordinately large ears and a bony, square-jawed face. He has no humor but he is not stupid. Archie and Wolfe can tolerate Stebbins.

STREET, DELLA▲
creator ERLE STANLEY GARDNER

Perry Mason's★ famous Girl Friday was born in 1906, apparently to a wealthy Beverly Hills family. Her parents separated early and her mother died "of a broken heart." When her father lost his money during the depression, Della was forced to earn a living.

There is evidence that she was once in show business, performing a strip-tease act. This is certainly plausible, considering the charms of the attractive, slim, 5'2½", 112-lb. Miss Street. She eventually went into more sedentary (albeit more dangerous) secretarial work. She has been arrested at least five times in connection with Perry's cases. She has also been in danger of losing her life in the line of duty.

That Della is in love with her boss is evident. After early attempts to change him failed, she accepted the fact that they could never be happily married, refusing many proposals from him so she could retain her job. Many men have admired her (including Archie Goodwin● and Ellery Queen★) but her loyalty to Mason and her work for him have always been her foremost concern.

TRENT, ANTHONY
creator WYNDHAM MARTYN

The son of a dedicated country physician, Anthony Trent has expensive tastes. A Dartmouth graduate, he starred in Ivy

League football and acted in school plays while there. He is interested in golf, tennis, art, and music. At the age of 30, a poorly paid writer of crime stories, he decides upon a life of crime to get "the good things in life." He takes a new identity, an apartment on Central Park West, and a discreet elderly housekeeper, Mrs. Kinney. Safes are no problem to the mechanically-adept Trent; he robs only unattractive rich people who can afford the loss. He is above middle height, slim and wiry. His face has strong features, a humorous expression and a large, hawk-like nose. A patriot, he turns down a commission to enlist as a private in World War I.

VALENTIN, ARISTIDE
creator G. K. CHESTERTON

Valentin was the Chief of the Paris Police and the most famous investigator in the world at the time of his attempts to achieve his greatest ambition—the arrest of the notorious Flambeau●, colossus of crime ultimately thwarted by Father Brown★. Valentin was unfathomably French, and his successes were arrived at by plodding logic, though he was not a thinking machine. He was a thinking man but a plain man at the same time, so all his wonderful successes, that seemed like magic tricks, had been gained by ordinary, clear French thought. He was not above committing murder in his pursuit of justice.

VALENTINE, JIMMY
creator O. HENRY, pseudonym of
William Sydney Porter

Jimmy Valentine is at the top of his profession, which happens to be burglary. He is good looking, a stylish dresser, well-mannered, and a most agreeable, charming young man who can make the day brighter for a warden, a fellow criminal, or a pretty girl. His proudest possession is his unique set of burglar tools, worth $1,000, which he had custom-made to include two or three items he invented himself.

The author, William Sydney Porter, is believed to have written under the pseudonym O. Henry because Orrin Henry, a guard at the prison in which he was serving time for embezzlement, had been kind to him.

VELVET, NICK
creator EDWARD D. HOCH

Nick Velvet is a unique thief, uninterested in such pedestrian plunder as jewels or money. He steals the bizarre and his fee is a flat $20,000 (with an extra $10,000 if the task is especially hazardous). He has stolen a tiger from a zoo, a stained-glass window from a museum, all the water from a swimming pool, and an entire major league baseball team. Between assignments he relaxes by sailing on Long Island Sound, drinking beer, and enjoying the company of Gloria, his girl friend.

VON GROOT, KARL
creator ERNEST BRAMAH, pseudonym of
Ernest Bramah Smith

An adversary of Max Carrados★, von Groot is a German spy masquerading as a Dutch curator. Born in Prussia about 1880, educated at Heidelberg, he entered the German Navy as torpedo-lieutenant in 1907. In 1910, he resigned under curious circumstances, to enter the espionage system. He speaks German, French, Dutch, Russian, and English. He is blond, tall, with gray eyes and a diagonal swordcut along his left cheek.

WALLINGFORD, GET-RICH-QUICK
creator GEORGE RANDOLPH CHESTER

James Rufus Wallingford is one of the outstanding confidence men in literature. Using purely (or nearly) legal business practices, he manages to earn vast fortunes, which he promptly spends on costly food, drink, and clothes. His pretty young wife, Fannie, wants to believe her husband is honest, suspects otherwise, and feels guilty about mistrusting him.

Wallingford has every appearance of an eminently successful man, one of those suave and sophisticated beings for whom the world's finer things are obviously intended. He never walks; he strides. He never eats; he dines. He never asks; he commands. He is a gentleman whose word is as good as his cash (which he distributes generously and flamboyantly—when he has it).

A large man, whose high silk hat makes him appear even taller, his enormous shirt-front enhances his confidence-inspiring appearance as a prosperous businessman. He is the center of attention in any gathering. The wealthiest and most influential people of every town are as anxious to make his acquaintance as he is anxious to involve them in his latest business scheme.

WATSON, DR. JOHN H.▲
creator SIR ARTHUR CONAN DOYLE

The diligence and deep devotion of Sherlock Holmes'★ faithful friend and amanuensis, Dr. Watson, were so profound that his name has become synonymous with the classic detective's helper. Born in 1852, Watson chose the career of an army surgeon, enrolling at the University of London Medical School, where he earned his degree. Attached to the Fifth Northumberland Fusiliers as assistant surgeon, he sailed for India when the second Afghan War broke out. At the battle of Maiwand, he was wounded by a Jezail bullet and would have fallen into the hands of the murderous Ghazis but for the courage of Murray, his orderly. His life was despaired of but, after months of fever and delirium, he was sent home to England.

Poor, friendless, his health impaired, he was set adrift in London, where he met Holmes and took rooms with him at 221B Baker Street. He established a small medical practice but spent a great deal of time helping Holmes fight crime. He recorded these adventures and, with the aid of a literary agent, Sir Arthur Conan Doyle, published them, supplementing his income.

Watson was slow-witted, especially compared to his friend, but did not resent Holmes' laughter or annoyance when he was slow to perceive a clue or understand a line of reasoning. Watson, himself, says: "I was a whetstone for his mind. I stimulated him. He liked to think aloud in my presence . . . if I irritated him by a certain methodical slowness in my mentality, that irritation served only to make his own flame-like intuitions and impressions flash up the more vividly and swiftly." Holmes appreciates Watson, saying: "I am lost without my Boswell."

The good doctor also serves a useful function when dealing with females; Watson admitted to having gained a knowledge of women on three continents. He was married to the lovely Mary Morstan but they had only a few years together before she succumbed to an illness. He is believed to have remarried but no positive proof exists. The handsome doctor has an athletic, if somewhat heavy, physique. His brown hair and mustache, dark brown eyes and regular, gentle features inspire affection and confidence in women. He is kindly, warm, friendly —traits one would hope to find in a pet dog, to which, unjustly, the good doctor has been compared.

ZAROFF, GENERAL
creator RICHARD CONNELL

Tall, handsome, past middle age, General Zaroff has white hair, thick black eyebrows, and a pointed military mustache. His eyes are black and very bright. His cheek bones are high, his nose is sharply cut, and he appears to be an aristocrat. Zaroff's passion is hunting. He has had so many victims that ennui causes him to seek the most dangerous game of all—man. He finds a perfect match for his skills in Sanger Rainsford, a celebrated professional hunter.

CASES

A selection of some of the most memorable crimes, puzzles, solutions and adventures from the extensive literature of detective and mystery fiction.

"Absent-Minded Coterie, The" (1906)
ROBERT BARR

Spenser Hale of Scotland Yard visits Eugène Valmont★ to enlist his help in stopping a counterfeiting ring. The curious Mr. Summertrees, who lives at a fancy Park Lane address, is suspected. Summertrees has all the newspapers delivered, though they seem to go unread, and locks himself in his room every morning—to write, he says. The industrious Summertrees turns out to have more than one pseudonym, more than one job and source of income.

"Adventure of the Late Mr. Faversham, The" (1929)
AUGUST DERLETH

Professor F. V. Faversham of Merk College stepped into his house one foggy night, never to be seen or heard of again. The police are baffled, so two of the professor's colleagues ask Solar Pons★ to take up the case. Not only has Faversham disappeared, but 10,000 pounds of the school's funds went with him. Leaving his house with Professor Hans von Ruda, Faversham had stepped onto his front steps, seen the damp night, and re-entered to get his rain coat. After waiting on the front steps an inordinate amount of time, Professor von Ruda re-entered to see what was delaying his friend. Every door and window of the house was locked and bolted; the only egress was through the front door, which had never escaped von Ruda's sight. A detailed inspection of the house revealed no secret passages, no other openings large enough for a man to pass through, and no Faversham.

ADVENTURES OF ROMNEY PRINGLE, THE (1902)
CLIFFORD ASHDOWN

Romney Pringle●, at his death, left several manuscripts recounting his "adventures in chicanery"; this volume contains the first six to be released. Most noteworthy of the tales is "The Assyrian Rejuvenator," in which Pringle's target is a crook selling an incredible product: M-U-D. The mud is supposed to remove wrinkles and restore youth to its user. Pringle buys a jar, but let the seller beware.

ALIAS JIMMY VALENTINE●
(see "A Retrieved Reformation")

AMATEUR CRIME, THE (1927)
A. B. COX

Several crime enthusiasts stage a "murder" as their idea of a practical joke. The victim of the hoax, staid Mr. Priestley, thinks he has killed a blackmailer. To evade the consequences, he determines to escape with a beautiful young lady—to whom he is handcuffed. English title: Mr. Priestley's Problem

AND THEN THERE WERE NONE (1939)
AGATHA CHRISTIE

Ten citizens, far from exemplary, are invited to a lonely island mansion by a mysterious host who fails to appear to greet them. Terror and suspense mount as the guests are murdered, one by one, by a remorseless and maniacal killer, fulfilling the words of an old nursery rhyme. English title: Ten Little Niggers

ANTAGONISTS, THE (1964)
WILLIAM HAGGARD

World-famous scientist Dr. Alexander Gorjan, residing in Great Britain, is a danger to one of England's rival powers. The best way to eliminate such threats is through violence. A second major power, formerly allied to England, intervenes and attempts to subvert Dr. Gorjan to its own ends. A power struggle ensues on British territory. The government does not stand by idly while events take their course, assigning Colonel Charles Russell★ to the case.

ANTHONY TRENT, MASTER CRIMINAL (1918)
WYNDHAM MARTYN

This episodic novel introduces one of the best rogues on the American scene. Anthony Trent● is a modern Robin Hood who robs only from the rich and, occasionally, gives to the poor. Against the background of New York City during the first World War, Trent frequently foils German spies. He is a patriot, even in the trenches in France.

APPLEBY AT ALLINGTON (1968)
MICHAEL INNES

Retired Sir John Appleby★ visits a neighboring estate being restored to past glories by its owner. While Appleby is exploring a gazebo, his curiosity leads him to a bundle in the corner—a dead body still warm. Pipe-smoking, contemplative Sir John is soon on a retired busman's holiday as he solves a mystery involving an old castle, buried treasure, a village charity ball and many odd people. American title: Death by Water

AROUND DARK CORNERS (1970)
HUGH PENTECOST

A collection of short stories and novelettes in which a 12-year-old boy helps his uncle, George Crowder★, solve mysteries in rural Connecticut. "In the Middle of Nowhere" is outstanding.

ASHENDEN or THE BRITISH AGENT (1928)
W. SOMERSET MAUGHAM

A writer with knowledge of several languages, Ashenden★ has excellent qualifications for entrance into the secret service. R, Chief of Intelligence, offers Ashenden this advice before he is added to the staff: "If you do well you'll get no thanks, and if you get into trouble you'll get no help." These words often return to Ashenden's mind as he attempts to rid England of the menace of Chandra Lal, the leader of a group of Indian conspirators against England, operating in Berlin. A dedicated spy, Chandra had been faithful to his wife in India until he fell in love with Giulia Lazzari, a dancer and prostitute. British agents assign Ashenden the task of using the beguiling Giulia to set a trap for the dangerous Chandra.

ASPHALT JUNGLE, THE (1949)
W. R. BURNETT

A gang of small-time crooks, under the direction of a criminal mastermind, plans an almost fool-proof robbery. All goes well until one mistake interrupts their plans and they scatter in all directions while the police hunt down the ring.

AT BERTRAM'S HOTEL (1965)
AGATHA CHRISTIE

Attempting to recapture an earlier time in her life, Miss Jane Marple★ revisits Bertram's, a dignified, quiet, expensive hotel in London. Although she realizes times are changing, she is nostalgic for the earlier, simpler days. Her reminiscences and the quiet of the hotel are interrupted by murder involving some of the "beautiful people" of the "Jet Set."

AT THE VILLA ROSE (1910)
A. E. W. MASON

At the Villa Rose, a beautiful young girl is involved in a heinous murder through a cunningly conceived web of suspicion. Her lover, convinced of her innocence, persuades the great French detective, Inspector Hanaud★, to take the case and find the villain. Jealousy, greed, ambition and love play important parts in the novel.

AVENGING SAINT, THE (1931)
LESLIE CHARTERIS

A tale of international intrigue in which Simon Templar, The Saint★, employs his wits and his fists in an attempt to avert another World War.

BANKING ON DEATH (1961)
EMMA LATHEN

The Schneider family was wealthy; therefore, the distribution among them of a relative's trust fund seemed a simple matter. True, one beneficiary had been missing for forty years but it seemed simple merely to split his share among the family. However, when John Putnam Thatcher★ investigates, he locates the missing heir—murdered, his head smashed. He also finds that no one in the suspicious family has a valid alibi.

BAT, THE (1926)
MARY ROBERTS RINEHART

The courageous Miss Cornelia receives anonymous notes, presumably written by the sinister Bat, threatening her with death. She refuses to leave her house. A nasty detective, summoned from New York specifically to guard the house against the pseudonymous criminal, does not prevent a double murder the night he arrives. Suspicion is directed at her niece and the girl's fiancé, but Miss Cornelia holds her own in an intellectual tussle with the Bat.

BEAST MUST DIE, THE (1938)
NICHOLAS BLAKE

Felix Lane has a believable and justifiable motive for murder: a reckless driver killed his small son, then sped from the scene of the accident. The grief-stricken father recovers from a mental breakdown with one all-pervading idea: the man who killed his son must be identified, hunted down, and killed. Detective Nigel Strangeways★ enters the intricate case.

BEFORE THE FACT (1932)
FRANCIS ILES, pseudonym of
Anthony Berkeley Cox

Young and innocent, Lina McLaidlaw had married Johnnie Aysgarth, whose sole asset was his charm. It took eight years for Lina to realize that her husband was a scoundrel, and probably a murderer. Ominous signs suggest that Johnnie is going to commit another crime—and his wife is slated to be the victim. Filmed by Alfred Hitchcock as "Suspicion," with a revised ending.

BEGGAR'S CHOICE (1953)
H. C. BRANSON

Wealthy, aged Augustus Lefever was suffering from a serious heart ailment. Therefore, when he was found dead, his demise was attributed to his heart condition. Lefever's family physician refuses to sign the death certificate, insisting Lefever did not die of natural causes but was suffocated. The doctor points the finger of guilt at the dead man's "wild" niece, his heir. Detective John Bent★ works to find the truth.

BEHIND THAT CURTAIN (1928)
EARL DERR BIGGERS

One January night, when the streets of London are shrouded with fog, Harry Galt is shot through the head in his private office. Oddly, his shoes are discovered on the desk, his feet are shod in a pair of Chinese slippers embroidered with Chinese letters. The mystery remains unsolved for 16 years. Then, a famous Scotland Yard detective is shot in the heart in the midst of a dinner party in San Francisco while wearing the same Chinese slippers—which soon vanish from sight. Charlie Chan★ of the Honolulu Police is assigned to the case.

BELLAMY TRIAL, THE (1926)
FRANCES NOYES HART

Stephen Bellamy and Susan (Mrs. Patrick) Ives, two prominent members of Long Island society, are accused of murdering Stephen's wife, Madeleine. The State contends the defendants were having a clandestine love affair and, when caught by Mrs. Bellamy, killed her. Although circumstantial evidence seems to be against them, public sympathy is with the young couple after they tell their stories from the witness box.

BENSON MURDER CASE, THE▲ (1926)
S. S. VAN DINE

Amateur psychologist-detective Philo Vance★ is able to test his theories when District Attorney Markham● invites him to observe the methods of the New York Police in the murder case of Alvin Benson, who was found shot to death in his West 48th Street apartment. Vance spots the murderer almost immediately but doesn't reveal him, allowing Markham and Sergeant Heath● to fix the guilt on five successive persons by circumstantial evidence.

BIG SLEEP, THE▲ (1939)
RAYMOND CHANDLER

Private detective Philip Marlowe★ is hired by wealthy, proud General Sternwood, a dying old man who lives in a hothouse. The General has two immoral daughters: the younger, on drugs, poses in the nude. The daughters are connected with a number of people who are after the General's money. The group includes a blackmailer, a pornographer, a gambler, an ex-bootlegger, and at least one killer. This is the first Philip Marlowe case.

"Bird in the Hand" (1932)
ERLE STANLEY GARDNER

This is considered one of the best of the 75 novelettes in which Lester Leith★ appears. A smuggler is murdered and the trunk in which he was hiding a shipment of gems is missing. In his search for the jewels, Leith plans to use a bird cage and a "bloodhound canary."

"Bird in the Tree, A" (1942)
ERIC AMBLER

Maurice Wretford, out cycling, was shot to death with a .22 caliber bullet while 19-year-old Thomas Wilder was shooting at birds with a .22 caliber rifle. Scotland Yard was satisfied it had the culprit. To the discomfort of Assistant Commissioner Mercer, Dr. Jan Czissar★ busybodies his way into the case and into Mercer's office. He clicks his heels, announces himself and provides the correct solution to the case.

BISHOP MURDER CASE, THE▲ (1929)
S. S. VAN DINE

The murderer in this story has an uncommon sense of humor and of sportsmanship. In a nonstop trail of successive murders, a note is discovered at each scene. Each note contains a nursery rhyme with a false clue and is signed "The Bishop." Philo Vance★ finally puts a stop to the fun, which had included a generous sprinkling of archery, chess, and astronomy, mixed with poison and bloodshed.

BLACK CAMEL, THE (1929)
EARL DERR BIGGERS

The famous and beautiful movie actress, Shelah Fane, is stabbed to death in a quiet, peaceful area of Waikiki Beach. Charlie Chan★ investigates amid public clamor demanding that the murderer be found and punished immediately. "Death is the black camel that kneels unbidden at every gate," Chan tells the suspects.

BLACK GLASS CITY, THE (1964)
JUDSON PHILIPS

A movie company, shooting an expensive sex epic, invades a sprawling Connecticut estate. One-legged journalist-detective Peter Styles★ searches for a brutal murderer who paints clown faces on the bodies of his victims.

BLACK MOUNTAIN, THE (1954)
REX STOUT

This is a rare case in which the corpulent, sedentary detective, Nero Wolfe★, leaves not only his house but the country. With his assistant, Archie Goodwin●, he flies to Montenegro to solve a case in the shadow of Mount Lovchen, the Black Mountain. Wolfe adopts a disguise to deal with sinister international intriguers and to cope with an enemy to whom murder is trivial.

BLEAK HOUSE (1852-1853)
CHARLES DICKENS

The inheritance case of Jarndyce and Jarndyce had dragged through the courts for generations, entangling persons of varying degrees of importance. The accidental discovery of a late will settles the suit but, by then, the entire fortune has been consumed by the costs of the case.

The would-be heirs have spent their lives waiting for the great Jarndyce fortune to be distributed. Tom Jarndyce finally blows his brains out. Miss Flite had visited the court daily, expecting a judgment that would bring her great wealth. Also involved were John Jarndyce (great-nephew of Tom and the owner of Bleak House in Hertfordshire), and John's cousins, Richard and Ada Clare Carstone. Interested, too, were Sir

Leicester and Lady Dedlock of Chesney Wold, whose solicitor, Tulkinghorn, was involved in the suit.

Forgery, drugs, murder, and blackmail run rampant until Inspector Bucket★ puts a stop to it. "Bleak House" is the first novel in which a detective plays a significant role.

"Blind Man's Buff" (1914)
FREDERICK IRVING ANDERSON

Malvino the Magician●, born to eternal darkness, is awarded the ultimate accolade when he is called superior to The Infallible Godahl● by Godahl himself. Malvino is engaged to perform for the "fifty little millionaires" at the Pegasus Club, of which Godahl is a member. The black-masked magician is to be paid $1,000 for an exhibition of his famous magic tricks. In addition, he is to be locked in a room for five minutes; if he escapes, he may keep all that he has managed to steal in the course of the evening. Malvino exacts a promise from Godahl not to be present at the performance. Malvino has a trick up his sleeve for the members of the club, who have planned a ruse for Malvino, and Godahl enjoys one of his most profitable nights in this tale that chortles at the concept of "honor among thieves."

"Blue Cross, The" (1911)
G. K. CHESTERTON

Valentin●, Chief of the Paris Police, seeking to make the arrest of the century, searches in England for the notorious Flambeau●. The latter is on the trail of a priceless silver and sapphire cross in the care of kindly Father Brown★. With no clues, Valentin begins his search in the most haphazard way, turning into every unlikely *cul-de-sac* and down every dark alley, trusting his instincts to pick up the trail of the thief. He is attracted by a peculiar yellow-and-white-striped restaurant where sugar is in the salt cellar, salt is in the sugar pot. When he learns that two priests scurried away after throwing a bowl of soup at the wall, he takes off in pursuit, following a trail of absurdities: an overturned applecart and switched signs at a greengrocer's, an enormous bill and a smashed window in a restaurant, and a mysterious package mailed from a puzzled confectioner's shop. The trail inevitably leads to the two priests: Father Brown and Flambeau.

BOOK OF MURDER, THE (1930)
FREDERICK IRVING ANDERSON

This is the only book collected from a decade of Deputy Parr★ stories which appeared in "The Saturday Evening Post." In

1941, Howard Haycraft praised these stories as timeless. They are still praiseworthy for the nostalgia they evoke of a long-gone New York and New England.

BOWSTRING MURDERS, THE (1933)
CARTER DICKSON, published originally as
by Carr Dickson

Eerie Bowstring Castle is the setting for an almost-perfect locked room mystery. The corpse of a strangler's victim is found in a room where the dust is undisturbed on all windows and sills. The door has been under constant observation, with no one seen either to enter or leave. John Gaunt★ arrives to investigate and solve this and several other intricately conceived murders.

BRIDE WORE BLACK, THE (1940)
CORNELL WOOLRICH

A grief-crazed woman assumes several identities to enter the lives of five men and kill them, one by one. A homicide detective stalks the huntress through the years. Their confrontation is the ironic climax of the first suspense novel by the author who has been called the greatest suspense writer of all.

BROKEN VASE, THE (1941)
REX STOUT

Although he is second string on the Rex Stout team (behind Nero Wolfe★), Tecumseh Fox★ is a first-rate detective. He investigates the murder of a musician at a concert auditorium resembling New York's Carnegie Hall. In a frantic automobile race against a New York Central train, Fox breaks fictional speed records.

BY THE PRICKING OF MY THUMBS (1968)
AGATHA CHRISTIE

Miss Christie dedicated this book to readers who wondered what had happened to Tommy and Tuppence Beresford★. They are alive and well, albeit older, and still involved in mysteries. Curiosity makes them wonder about an old lady who has disappeared from a rest home. The death of another, Tommy's aunt, triggers their concern, and there is no stopping until a solution is found.

CALAMITY TOWN (1942)
ELLERY QUEEN

In this, the first of the author's novels of naturalistic Americana, Ellery Queen★ comes to the peaceful New England town of Wrightsville to work on a novel. He finds himself entangled in a web of family relationships that leads to murder. The characters and the small-town setting are particularly vivid.

"Can You Solve This Crime?" (1950)
JEROME and HAROLD PRINCE

This was one of the earliest mysteries to make use of the new television medium. A live panel show, which bears the name of this short story, has as its panelists three amateurs and one professional, Inspector John B. Magruder★ of Homicide. The idea of the show is to re-enact a crime to see if the solution can be deduced before millions of viewers. The crime depicted on this program happened ten years ago and is one on which Magruder had worked without success. He believes now he knows the solution.

CANARY MURDER CASE, THE▲ (1927)
S. S. VAN DINE

Sophisticated Philo Vance★ is invited to aid District Attorney Markham● and Sergeant Heath● of the Homicide Bureau in the effort to trace a murderer. The Canary, a noted blonde Broadway entertainer, is strangled to death in her apartment, the only entrance to which is through the main hall in view of the telephone operator's booth. The number of suspects is narrowed to four known to have been enamored of the Canary.

CAPE COD MYSTERY, THE (1931)
PHOEBE ATWOOD TAYLOR

A best-selling novelist is murdered during an unusually warm Cape Cod weekend. The victim was deservedly unpopular but Asey Mayo★ will not let murder go unpunished. He sets out to clear up the mystery in this, his first appearance.

CASE OF THE BARKING CLOCK, THE (1947)
HARRY STEPHEN KEELER

In this burlesque of the classic innocent-man-condemned situation, it takes detective Tuddleton Trotter★ the first two-thirds of the book to get into the death house to visit his client. The final third of the book contains countless intricacies of plot, dialect humor, outrageous coincidences, and bizarre elements.

CASE OF THE COUNTERFEIT EYE, THE (1935)
ERLE STANLEY GARDNER

Peter Brunold has a bloodshot glass eye to use the "morning after." It is distinctive, closely identified with him, and thus quite a handicap when a corpse is found clutching a bloodshot glass eye. Later, another corpse is found, with another bloodshot glass eye in hand. Perry Mason★ is in almost as much jeopardy as his client: the lawyer's fingerprints have been found on one of the alleged murder weapons.

CASE OF THE HOWLING DOG, THE▲ (1934)
ERLE STANLEY GARDNER

When a potential client wants to see Perry Mason★ about a howling dog and a will, the attorney is not interested. He does not enjoy drawing wills, and wonders if the man shouldn't see a veterinarian. However, when the man asks whether a will is legal if the person who made it had been executed for murder, immediately Mason becomes interested. He finds, in addition to the will and the dog, a man who had run away with the wife of another, and a sexy housekeeper.

"Case of the Middle-Aged Wife, The" (1934)
AGATHA CHRISTIE

In answer to Parker Pyne's★ advertisement, the unhappy Mrs. Parkington visits him to see if he can help her. Her once-attentive husband has become entangled with his typist, "a nasty, made-up little minx." Without a second's hesitation, Mr. Pyne states that he can cure the situation but he must be paid a substantial fee in advance. Mrs. Parkington agrees and is sent to hair dressers, beauty specialists, and dress-makers; she is introduced to a handsome young gentleman, Claude Luttrell, and the two spend a great deal of time together. She encounters her husband and his typist on a dance floor and, instead of experiencing burning jealousy, she feels sorry for "poor old George." A "cure" is achieved.

CASE OF THE PERJURED PARROT, THE (1939)
ERLE STANLEY GARDNER

One of Perry Mason's★ trademarks is his ability, in court, to switch the physical evidence in a case. This is generally done with guns or bullets and confuses the jury, to his client's advantage. In this case, Perry offers a coroner's inquest two parrots, one of which swore like a muleskinner and was found near the body of a millionaire hermit who had been murdered.

CASE OF THE SEVEN SNEEZES, THE (1942)
ANTHONY BOUCHER

The time is May, 1940, the early days of World War II in Europe. A group is gathered to celebrate the 25th anniversary of a wedding which had taken place against the background of another war in Europe. This is macabre, since one of the members of the party was murdered shortly after the wedding. The setting for the 1940 party is an island off the California coast. Fergus O'Breen★ is present because he knows several members of the party and his services have been sought by one of them. Several murders occur and the guests are cut off from the mainland.

"Case of the Tragedies in the Greek Room" (1920)
SAX ROHMER

One morning, the distorted body of the night watchman at the Menzies Museum is discovered in the Greek Room. Though the room is impenetrable at night, there is evidence of a struggle: one glass case is smashed and another, containing the museum's prize Athenean Harp, is unlocked. Moris Klaw★ offers to help perplexed Scotland Yard by sleeping in the room. That night, his psychic dream tells him a woman in white had lifted the harp from its case shortly before the watchman was killed. A new watchman also meets a strange death. Dry plaster of Paris spread around the priceless instrument reveals the footprints of little bare feet.

"Case of the Two Questions, The" (1959)
E. X. FERRARS

Old Jones P. Jonas★ recalls two questions his client wanted answered, both related to impossibilities: could an anemic, chain-smoking, middle-aged woman run several hundred yards, commit a murder, then appear not even slightly short of breath? Second, could a car be driven through a watersplash and back again without getting its tires wet? With the answers comes the solution to a murder.

CASE PENDING (1960)
DELL SHANNON

Lieutenant Luis Mendoza★ of the Los Angeles Police Department searches for the link between two female corpses, each with one eye mutilated. Interwoven with the murder case are counter-plots involving illegal adoption, the attempt to dispose of a blackmailer, a narcotics drop, and Mendoza's love-life.

CASK, THE (1920)
FREEMAN WILLS CROFTS

Most of the action in this case takes place in Paris around 1910–12. M. Chauvet and the Sûreté cooperate with Scotland Yard in tracking one of "the most callous and cold-blooded criminals of the century." Inspector Burnley slowly, methodically destroys an unbreakable alibi. One alibi, dependent on a performance of Berlioz' "Les Troyens," reflects Croft's musical interests, as well as his relentless factuality.

CAT OF MANY TAILS (1949)
ELLERY QUEEN

An insane murderer known as The Cat stalks New York City. With cords of Indian silk, he strangles victims selected seemingly at random. The city's resources are mobilized as the city's millions panic. Ellery Queen★ is pitted against one of his wiliest adversaries.

"Chain of Witnesses" (1954)
PHYLLIS BENTLEY

Cumulative effect has always intrigued Miss Bentley. In this story, she portrays the snowballing results of a single event on the lives of many people in a small English town. The leading character, Miss Marian Phipps★, first appeared in 1937; she did not appear again until this short story which won a prize in the Ellery Queen Mystery Magazine annual contest.

CHILL, THE (1963)
ROSS MAC DONALD

Dolly, the beautiful young bride of Alex Kincaid, runs away from him after their marriage. Alex asks private detective Lew Archer★ to find her. The problems of the newlyweds are mixed with a trail of murder that spans a continent.

Complicated family and unfamiliar relationships keep Archer guessing until the final dramatic act reveals an unlikely murderer.

CHINESE BELL MURDERS, THE (1958)
ROBERT VAN GULIK

A vicious rape-murder, a Buddhist temple with a closely guarded secret, and a mysterious skeleton are the ingredients of crime problems that Magistrate Jen-djieh Dee★ of the Poo-yang district of China must ponder in the year 668 A.D.

CHINESE GOLD MURDERS, THE (1959)
ROBERT VAN GULIK

The newly appointed magistrate of the Peng-lai district of China assumes his first official post. He is greeted with crime problems involving a previously-murdered magistrate, a disappearing bride, and a butchered bully. Solving these interrelated cases, difficult for an experienced official, is a triumph for Judge Dee★ early in his career.

CHINESE PARROT, THE▲ (1926)
EARL DERR BIGGERS

The Jordan ranch in the California desert is the scene of strange and unexpected crimes. A parrot screams, "Help! Murder! Put down that gun!" for no logical reason. It is poisoned. A bullet hole is found in a wall, a gun is missing, a Chinese cook is stabbed, and a gun and some pearls are missing. The keen Charlie Chan★ unravels a tangled web of character, situation, and motive.

CIRCULAR STAIRCASE, THE (1908)
MARY ROBERTS RINEHART

A middle-aged spinster is persuaded by her niece and nephew to rent a country house for the summer. The house they choose belonged to a bank defaulter who had hidden stolen securities in the walls. The gentle, peace-abiding trio is plunged into a series of crimes solved with the help of the aunt. This novel is credited with being the first in the "Had-I-But-Known" school.

CLEEK, THE MASTER DETECTIVE (1918)
THOMAS W. HANSHEW

Hamilton Cleek●, the master criminal, decides to reform in order to be worthy of the girl he loves. He goes to his former adversary, Inspector Narkom of Scotland Yard, to ask for a chance to work on the side of the law. Narkom gives Cleek a herculean set of riddles to solve.

"Common Stock" (1923)
OCTAVUS ROY COHEN

Gerald Corwin is sent to California to secure a vital proxy for the New York stockholder's meeting of the K.R. & P. Railroad. The Quincy-Scott gang has initiated a drive to gain control of the railroad and must prevent the proxy from reaching its destination. Jim Hanvey★ is sent to protect Corwin from the emissary of the Quincy-Scott group, Billy Scanlan. To Corwin's frustration and puzzlement, Hanvey introduces Scanlan to him, tells Scanlan their train and compartment number, and seems to make the would-be thief's assignment easy. Hanvey explains: "The less trouble Billy has to take the more time he'll have for thinkin', an' the more he thinks the worse off he is. Thinkin', son, has ruined a heap of happy homes, an' don't you forget it."

CONVERTIBLE HEARSE, THE (1957)
WILLIAM CAMPBELL GAULT

Los Angeles is "Cartown, U.S.A." and the used-car business is a way of life in the city. Gang warfare begins when some used car dealers increase their profit margins by selling stolen cars. Brock Callahan★ finds a corpse in a "hot" car and realizes his life and integrity are in danger.

CORK ON THE WATER (1951)
MAC DONALD HASTINGS

A dubious insurance claim sends the suspicious Mr. Montague Cork★ from the London music halls to the hills and rivers of Scotland. Mr. Cork goes fishing, is shot at, and scrambles up and down the Scottish Highlands to protect his company's interests.

CORPSE AT THE CARNIVAL (1958)
GEORGE BELLAIRS

While vacationing on the Isle of Man, Inspector Littlejohn★ finds his services required to help solve the murder of an old man on the boardwalk. He renews his acquaintance with an old friend, Archdeacon Kinrade, and gains the friendship of local Inspector Knell. Littlejohn, successful in his detective work, is reassured that he is not past his peak, as he'd feared.

"Corpus Delicti, The" (1896)
MELVILLE DAVISSON POST

Life is good for the man known as Samuel Walcott; he has wealth, the respect and affection of his fellow-men, and is in love with Virginia St. Clair, the most beautiful girl in New York. Receiving a letter that threatens his idyllic existence, he tells his story to Randolph Mason●: many years ago, he had killed the real Samuel Walcott in a brawl. At the urging of Nina San Croix, Walcott's wife, he had assumed her husband's identity, returned to New York, and claimed Walcott's inheritance. Nina wanted them to be married but "Walcott" put her off until she threatened to expose him as an impostor and a killer. Mason tells the unhappy man there is only one solution: Nina must be killed. The publication of this story helped bring about much-needed reforms in criminal jurisprudence.

CRIME OF VIOLENCE (1937)
RUFUS KING

Miss Josephine Galt, a sixtyish social secretary, prides herself upon her ability to remain calm during an emergency. However, her nerves are tested when she comes upon the body of Horace Worthington, his piglike eyes still open and staring. The investigation of this death brings the Pine family under police investigation: Mrs. Pine had offered her daughter in marriage to Worthington so that her dipsomaniac son would be assured of a life of wealth. Lieutenant Valcour★, solves the case, only after amiably offering to share his glass of milk with the murderer.

CRIMINAL CONVERSATION (1965)
NICOLAS FREELING

Inspector Van der Valk★, poses as a patient to conduct an unofficial investigation of a Doctor Van der Post, who is suspected of murdering a painter. Van der Valk explores the art world of Amsterdam as he pursues his quarry.

CRYSTAL STOPPER, THE (1912)
MAURICE LEBLANC

The machinations of a master villain entangle a beautiful girl and endanger the life of Arsène Lupin●, who is almost out of his depth. A mysterious object which appears to be a crystal stopper is the object of an intellectual tug-of-war. It is won and lost in virtually alternating chapters of the story, though the true significance of the object is not known until the end.

CUE FOR MURDER (1942)
HELEN MC CLOY

The scene is New York in the early days of World War II. Dr. Basil Willing★, on duty with the Federal Bureau of Investigation, investigates murder on stage at a Broadway theater.

CUNNING AS A FOX (1965)
KYLE HUNT

Problems both domestic and mental in a London family lead to murder, and call on the talents of Emmanuel Cellini★, a psychiatrist who functions also as a detective. He can retain his objectivity and still sympathize with a family in trouble.

"Customs of the Country, The" (1956)
THOMAS FLANAGAN

The Republic which Major Tennente★ serves as Chief of Military Police is in fact a dictatorship. Tennente, although opposing the dictator, is incorruptible. Contraband is being smuggled into the Republic and the Major is sent to find out why the culprits cannot be caught. The situation calls for an honest man.

DANCE OF DEATH (1938)
HELEN MC CLOY

The over-heated body of a yellow-faced girl is discovered in a snowdrift. Psychiatrist-detective Dr. Basil Willing★ encounters such clues as fatal reducing pills, fading roses, and an unwound watch, before he learns the truth.

DARK LIGHT, THE (1949)
BART SPICER

An elderly black deacon asks Carney Wilde to locate his pastor, a self-appointed clergyman who vanished while on his way to deliver a radio talk. The trail leads Wilde to several murders and a few guilty secrets.

DARK POWER, A (1968)
WILLIAM ARDEN

Industrial spy Kane Jackson★ is hired by a New Jersey pharmaceutical combine to recover a missing sample of a drug potentially worth millions. Several bodies soon come into view.

DAUGHTER OF ANDERSON CROW, THE (1907)
GEORGE BARR MC CUTCHEON

Rosalie is the adopted daughter of Anderson Crow★ in Tinkletown, New York, where a series of exciting events occurs, including a daring train robbery and a strange kidnapping. Crow, humiliatingly defeated by the train-robbing gang, finally brings them to justice. He uses his experience and knowledge, and luck plays a role. Rosalie's true parentage ultimately is discovered.

DAUGHTER OF TIME, THE (1951)
JOSEPHINE TEY

Bed-ridden Inspector Alan Grant★ is physically immobile, and bored. A chance gift rescues him from apathy and sets him to investigating the 400-year-old alleged murder by Richard III of the Princes in the Tower. Without leaving his bed, Grant in-vestigates the evidence and arrives at a convincing solution by means of acute historical detection, in a tale which Anthony Boucher called "one of the permanent classics in the detective field," and which Dorothy B. Hughes has termed "not only one of the most important mysteries of the year, but of all years of mystery."

DEAD ERNEST (1944)
ALICE TILTON

The cadaver of Ernest Bostwick Finger, found lying in the deep freeze, disrupts the writing of the latest book by Leonidas With-erall★. Witherall is headmaster of an exclusive boys' prep school, who writes popular detective stories under a carefully protected pseudonym. He attempts to maintain his dignity while solving some of the most ludicrous crimes.

DEADLINE AT DAWN (1944)
WILLIAM IRISH, pseudonym of
Cornell Woolrich

A frightened young couple, trapped in a web of greed and murder, haunt the night streets of the city in a desperate race against the sunrise.

"Death at the Porthole" (1938)
BAYNARD KENDRICK

The trans-Atlantic voyage of the S.S. Moriander is interrupted by the cry, "Man overboard!" Violence is rampant as Cliff Chandler★ discovers many of the passengers are carrying weapons.

DEATH FROM A TOP HAT (1938)
CLAYTON RAWSON

When death attacks a series of magicians, conjurers and fortune tellers, magicians become leading suspects. The Great Merlini★ is brought into the case, perhaps on the theory that it takes a magician to catch one. How he solves this mystery is narrated by free-lance writer Ross Harte. As the story opens, Harte is writing a magazine article on the modern detective story, and most of this article-to-be is included in the first chapter.

"Death Had a Voice" (1948)
CHARLES B. CHILD

In this story, perhaps the best of the tales about the dapper little Iraqi Police Inspector Chafik J. Chafik★, mob violence threatens Baghdad. An unknown man has inflamed the crowds, shouting, "Kill in the Prophet's name!" His voice is compelling and there are enough poor, hungry people to follow him. Before Chafik can stop these riots, he must determine if the motives are religious, political, or personal.

"Death in Australia" (1957)
VICTOR CANNING

It is 1920, and Dr. Lin Kang★ is temporarily down at the heels, stranded in Australia. An epidemic of malaria threatens a ship in the harbor and Dr. Kang goes aboard, pretending medical knowledge he does not possess. The ship has a safe in which is locked a collection of pearls, opium, and $2,000 in American money. Dr. Kang has his eye on this loot and on the keys to the only car in town.

DEATH IN THE FIFTH POSITION (1952)
EDGAR BOX

Press agent Peter Sargeant★ is hired to provide good publicity for a ballet troupe which is being harassed by witch-hunters for having a "communist" choreographer. When the star of the new ballet is murdered onstage, Sargeant proves he can detect as well as he can publicize.

DEATH IS THE LAST LOVER (1959)
HENRY KANE

A gorgeous blonde calls on susceptible private detective Peter Chambers★ and asks him to prove her wealthy protector innocent of the charge of murdering a dance hall hostess. Resourceful Chambers has only 24 hours to find the criminal. The police are breathing down his client's neck while Chambers constantly is distracted by a pair of beautiful girls.

DEATH KNELL (1945)
BAYNARD KENDRICK

At the Jordans' cocktail party people are talking, laughing, enjoying their drinks; gorgeous Troy Singleton appears and an ominous silence descends. Troy soon is found with a bullet hole over her heart, and Captain Duncan Maclain★ must find her murderer.

DEATH OF A BUSYBODY (1943)
GEORGE BELLAIRS

Genial Inspector Littlejohn★ of Scotland Yard goes to the village of Hilary Magna to discover how the local voyeur drowned in the vicar's cesspool. A vivid picture of an English country hamlet in wartime enhances the proceedings.

DEATH OF A CITIZEN (1960)
DONALD HAMILTON

When Washington asks Matt Helm★ (code name: Eric) to undertake a mission, it means giving up a career as photographer, his home, wife and family. His wife, learning that he killed during the war and is ready to kill again, feels she can no longer live with him. Committed to the new assignment and to the resumption of his prior career, Helm wanders throughout the southwestern United States. To stay alive, he must learn whom he can trust and which innocent-appearing people really are Russian spies.

DEATH OF A GHOST (1934)
MARGERY ALLINGHAM

When the famous British painter John Lafcadio died, his will stipulated that there be a gathering every year, at which one of his paintings, previously unseen, would receive its first exhibition. These gatherings proved to be macabre rituals of homage, attended by the strangely assorted members of the Lafcadio household, as well as by some of the leading artists in Europe. At the eighth of these showings, murder took place. Fortunately Albert Campion★ was on the scene.

DEATH OF A LAKE (1954)
ARTHUR W. UPFIELD

The blazing sun beats down on Lake Otway in Australia; no relief of the drought is in sight. Rumors point to the lake as the final resting place of a man, missing for three months, who had absconded with $75,000. Suspense mounts and the tempers of the seven suspects fray while the sun dries up the lake. Inspector Napoleon Bonaparte★ solves this heat-baked mystery.

DEATH UNDER SAIL (1932)
C. P. SNOW

Seven people go on a sailboat cruise along the Norfolk Broads in England. The captain is found with a bullet in his heart, and the holiday-makers must remain in a nearby cottage where living conditions are primitive. Hardships, coupled with murder investigation, produce the inevitable tensions that can be resolved only by unmasking the criminal. On hand to investigate is Detective-Sergeant Aloysius Birrell, who has read everything ever written about crime—fictional and factual. He is perhaps the most cocksure detective in recorded history. More helpful is a civil servant named Finbow, on leave from duties in Hong Kong, whose aid is requested by one of the suspects. Finbow is a shrewd psychologist, able to see through the conflicting loves, hates, and jealousies to a surprising solution.

DEPTHS, THE (1963)
JOHN CREASEY

Dr. Palfrey★ and his Z5 organization are at war with the mad-scientist ruler of an undersea kingdom. The madman has discovered the secret of prolonging life indefinitely. He can also create tidal waves powerful enough to wreck any ship or seacoast.

"Diamond Links, The" (1897)
GRANT ALLEN

Sir Charles Vandrift, in Switzerland with his wife and his secretary, makes the acquaintance of a charming little Scottish parson and his pretty bride. They seem poor, but the simple minister wears a beautiful pair of diamond cuff links at dinner. Amelia Vandrift desperately wants them, to complete her necklace. The curate assures his new acquaintances they are merely paste but, as heirlooms, have sentimental value to him. With diligent effort, Wentworth, the secretary, secures the stones for a lordly price of 2,000 pounds and discovers they were, indeed, made for Amelia's necklace. Colonel Clay● is the rogue of this tale.

DIAGNOSIS: HOMICIDE (1950)
LAWRENCE G. BLOCHMAN

Each of the stories in this collection has a medical background. Set in the midwestern United States and contemporary in idiom, nevertheless they follow the tradition of the English medico-detective stories of about half a century ago. In these American stories the acute mind of Dr. Daniel Webster Coffee★, in and out of the laboratory, enables him to solve crimes for his policeman friend, Lieutenant Max Ritter.

DR. PRIESTLEY INVESTIGATES (1930)
JOHN RHODE

When young Tom Awdrey is arrested for reckless driving under the influence of liquor, the police find a dead body in his car. Until Dr. Lancelot Priestley★ enters the case, the evidence seems conclusive that the body had been hit by Awdrey's car. English title: Pinehurst

"Doomdorf Mystery, The" (1914)
MELVILLE DAVISSON POST

Doomdorf had come from some remote, barbaric corner of Europe to settle in Virginia on a small wedge of property between two land grants. He established a log still and brewed a liquid that attracted the idle and vicious from miles around. Soon the peaceful community was racked with violence and riots. Uncle Abner★ and Squire Randolph, setting out to destroy the still and evict Doomdorf, find him murdered, in a room with a heavily bolted door and window frames cemented shut. Thick layers of undisturbed dust lie on the sills. Two people confess to the killing, and Abner must lay a strange ambush for the real assassin.

DOORBELL RANG, THE (1965)
REX STOUT

A wealthy woman offers Nero Wolfe★ the largest retainer of his career. She claims she is being harassed by the Federal Bureau of Investigation, that agents are following her and members of her family, that her telephone has been tapped and that her privacy is being invaded. With some hesitation, Wolfe accepts the case and discovers the FBI may know more about a murder than they want to have divulged.

DOUBLE OR QUITS (1941)
A. A. FAIR

The mysterious death of a client forces Donald Lam★ and Bertha Cool★ into a legal battle with an insurance company over double indemnity, a game of wits with a trio of fortune hunters, and a search for missing jewelry, while constantly avoiding the clutches of the police.

DRACULA▲ (1897)
BRAM STOKER

Jonathan Harker, an English solicitor, is sent to transact business with Count Dracula●, master of Castle Dracula in Transylvania. Harker suspects evil when he discovers the Count lying in a coffin-like box, apparently dead. Phantom-women walk about the castle; Harker learns he is a prisoner and finds that he has lost most of his strength. The Count moves to London. When victims are reported with two tiny punctures on their throats, Dr. Van Helsing warns that the attacks are the work of a vampire able to live for centuries on the blood of its victims.

DRINK·TO YESTERDAY (1940)
MANNING COLES

At the outbreak of World War I, Michael Kingston changes his name to William Saunders and lies about his age to enter the British Army. A brilliant language student, with excellent knowledge of German, he is offered a job with British Intelligence and goes behind the German lines as the nephew of Major Tommy Hambledon★. The young man's sense of humor, charming good looks and quick wit endear him to Max Von Bodenheim, an officer in German Intelligence. Von Bodenheim is impressed with the boy's perceptive mind and sends him to spy on the English. As Hambledon and "Saunders" continue their work, the difficulty of their jobs and the danger of their positions increase until escape from Germany is imperative. They learn there is no safety for a man in Intelligence.

"Dublin Mystery, The" (1909)
BARONESS ORCZY

"Millionaire Brooks," one of the few millionaires in Ireland, has two sons: Murray, his father's favorite, and Percival, a wastrel enamoured of a dance hall girl. Brooks dies suddenly of a stroke; shortly thereafter, Patrick Wethered, his lawyer, is found murdered. The will left by Brooks provides an income of 100,000 pounds a year to Percival; Murray receives a beggarly 300 pounds per annum. Percival adheres to the letter of the will, giving his brother the crumbs from his extravagant table. Everyone—police, press, public—makes the same assumption: that Percival forged the will; everyone, that is, except the Old Man in the Corner★.

DUKE OF YORK'S STEPS, THE (1929)
HENRY WADE

A successful financier, known to have a heart condition, collapses and dies at the foot of the London monument, "The Duke of York's Steps." A shadowy figure had jostled him before he fell, and Scotland Yard's Inspector John Poole★ is summoned to investigate.

EGYPTIAN CROSS MYSTERY, THE (1932)
ELLERY QUEEN

A series of bloody, bizarre murders, each victim beheaded and fastened to a cross, engages the attention of Ellery Queen★ and his father, Inspector Richard Queen. A nudist camp, a Balkan blood-feud and a demented Egyptologist are some of the elements in this complex problem.

EIGHT FACES AT THREE (1939)
CRAIG RICE

John J. Malone★, rumpled Chicago lawyer, teams up with press agent Jake Justus and eccentric heiress Helene Brand, to discover who killed a vicious dowager and why the murderer then made up the beds in the victim's house and stopped the clocks at 3:00.

EIGHT MURDERS IN THE SUBURBS (1954)
ROY VICKERS

This volume is a collection of stories about the little-known branch of Scotland Yard, the Department of Dead Ends★, which gets the cases on which everyone else has given up. Among the best of these tales are "The Case of the Perpetual Sneer" and "Miss Paisley's Cat."

813 (1910)
MAURICE LEBLANC

Arsène Lupin● is accused of murder. All the evidence points to him, so he undertakes to head the police investigation, to find the true murderer. A clock on which the number "813" has particular significance is a vital element in the case, as is a packet of letters written to Bismarck of Germany, who must make several journeys (incognito) to help clear up the mystery. The death-rate, via murder and suicide, is high.

ELECTION BOOTH MURDERS, THE (1935)
MILTON M. PROPPER

Sidney Reade, the reform party's choice for District Attorney, is shot as he enters an election booth to cast his ballot. Two suspects jump into a car, try to escape from the scene of the crime, but are captured by an alert policeman. Two more murders follow; Tommy Rankin★ and the Philadelphia Police follow a trail through a maze of political chicanery to solve this case.

EMPEROR FU MANCHU (1959)
SAX ROHMER

The Chinese province of Szechuan, near the border of Tibet, is cut off from the Western world by the "bamboo curtain." London and Washington can only guess at what lies behind that curtain, but Nayland Smith★ of the British Secret Service has no doubts. Reports of a legendary figure called The Master had been filtering through to the West, recalling the memory of the evil Oriental genius, Dr. Fu Manchu●. Smith knows the implications of Fu Manchu's presence in this remote area. A man with a thorough knowledge of the Chinese is needed to steal into the region. Tony McKay is the choice; he has the qualifications, as well as a private score to settle. Disguised as a Chinese fisherman, McKay begins his first solo mission as an undercover agent, and Fu Manchu spreads the net for his capture.

ENGLISH MURDER, AN (1951)
CYRIL HARE

It was going to be a pleasant weekend but this typical English Christmas party found itself snowbound in a castle, with Death as an uninvited guest. It takes the combined efforts of Dr. Bottwink, a Czech refugee, and Sergeant Rogers of Scotland Yard to solve three baffling murders.

EXIT THIS WAY (1945)
M. V. HEBERDEN

The client of private eye Desmond Shannon★ is a Syndicate overlord awaiting execution for the murder of a Vice Squad policeman—the one crime he swears he didn't commit. The investigation is marked by a machine-gun tempo and a harsh, naturalistic picture of power politics.

FABULOUS CLIPJOINT, THE (1947)
FREDRIC BROWN

Eighteen-year-old Ed Hunter★ joins forces with his uncle, carnival-pitchman Ambrose Hunter★, to track the person who bludgeoned Ed's father (Am's brother) to death in a dark Chicago alley. Later Ed and Am open their own detective agency and are involved regularly in murder.

FARMHOUSE, THE (1947)
HELEN REILLY

On the day a young woman leaves Manhattan to move into a house in Dutchess County, a man plunges to his death from a skyscraper. The trail of murder leads upstate and Inspector McKee★ follows in its wake to rescue a heroine in distress.

FEARFUL PASSAGE, THE (1945)
H. C. BRANSON

Private investigator John Bent★ receives a mysterious, anonymous phone call requesting him to go to a small town in upper New York State. He investigates the murder of a distinguished art critic and historian whose young, beautiful wife is in love with Tom Shepherd, a boy her own age. Everyone tries to protect Tom, despite his place atop the list of logical suspects.

FEMALE OF THE SPECIES, THE (1928)
"SAPPER"

Carl Peterson, a long-time villain, has been killed by Bulldog Drummond★ but Peterson's mistress escapes and turns the tables on the detective. She kidnaps Drummond's bride and plays a nerve-jangling game of hide-and-seek.

FINAL COUNT, THE (1926)
"SAPPER"

A scientist has invented a poison which will end war. He is seized, along with large quantities of the poison (which causes instantaneous death wherever it is sprayed). The kidnapper, an old enemy of Bulldog Drummond★, intends to use the deadly invention for his own foul ends.

FINAL DEDUCTION, THE (1961)
REX STOUT

A woman receives a note informing her she will never see her husband alive unless she pays a ransom of $500,000. She seeks the advice of Nero Wolfe★. As the case unfolds, a woman is demolished by a car, a man is crushed by a huge statue, and Archie Goodwin● loses his temper.

FINGERPRINT, THE (1956)
PATRICIA WENTWORTH

An anonymous letter causes an old man to change his will. The man is murdered, near the ashes of his new will, and Scotland Yard has a prime suspect. Miss Maud Silver★ disagrees and puts aside her knitting needles only long enough to find the murderer.

"First Stone, The" (1931)
ERLE STANLEY GARDNER

The lure of adventure sends Sidney Zoom★ and his dog, Rip, outdoors on a rainy night. Sidney becomes involved with a corpse and some scattered rubies, and soon finds he is in conflict with the local police. Reprinted as "The Case of the Scattered Rubies"

FISTFUL OF DEATH (1958)
HENRY KANE

When a well-dressed, prosperous-looking citizen walks into Peter Chambers'★ office one morning, it looks like a good business day. In this case, there is to be a $200,000 payoff, as well as a lot of pretty girls. There are three corpses, and someone tries to make Chambers number four.

FRIDAY THE RABBI SLEPT LATE (1964)
HARRY KEMELMAN

The body of a young woman is found on the grounds of the Temple of Rabbi David Small★. His car, seen at the Temple at the time of the murder, makes him a suspect. His Talmudic training qualifies the shy, scholarly rabbi to practice his deductive reasoning. He not only exonerates himself, but ensures renewal of his contract in the small suburban town that had, previously, remained cool to his unconventional attitudes despite his devotion to his flock.

GAME WITHOUT RULES (1967)
MICHAEL GILBERT

This collection of spy stories, set in the Cold War era, includes such tales as "Trembling's Tours" and "Heilige Nacht," which take place in divided Germany. Detectives: Samuel Behrens★ and Daniel Calder★.

GARSTON MURDER CASE, THE (1930)
H. C. BAILEY

The psalm-spouting, hypocritical British criminal lawyer, Joshua Clunk★, gets caught in the affairs of the munitions-manufacturing Garston family. An obscure chemist has vanished, some cheap jewelry has been stolen, an aged matriarch has been strangled; Clunk's assignment is to connect the events and solve the murder. English title: Garstons

"Gateway of the Monster, The" (1913)
WILLIAM HOPE HODGSON

The Grey Room of an old house has every appearance of being haunted. Each night, the door is securely locked but later is heard to slam loudly, sometimes for many hours, and next morning the bedclothes are found hurled into a corner. The room's history dates back 150 years—a man, his wife and child were strangled in it, and no one had slept in the room since. Carnacki★ is called: he seals the windows, closets, door and lock, then runs ribbons across the floor and walls. In the morning, the seal to the door, which again had slammed all night, is broken, but the keyhole has remained sealed; the ribbons are intact, but the bedclothes are in a bundle in their customary corner. A search of the room reveals no opening through which any animate being could pass. Carnacki resolves to spend a night in the room, protected by an Electric Pentacle, an excellent defense against certain manifestations.

"Gay Falcon" ▲ (1940)
MICHAEL ARLEN

Gay Falcon★ breaks into the bedroom of the beautiful and startled Diana Temple—one of the world's 10 best-dressed women. Falcon burglarizes her safe, confident she won't call the police. The next day, he takes his haul to the board of a large insurance company, which is delighted to retrieve stolen jewelry on which it had paid claims of 100,000 pounds during the past few years. Falcon has dinner with the lovely Diana, who confesses to her life of crime and who is frightened of something —or someone.

GET-RICH-QUICK WALLINGFORD (1908)
GEORGE RANDOLPH CHESTER

J. Rufus Wallingford●, with less than $100 in his wallet, strides into the best hotel in town with poise and flair worthy of

the richest financier in the country. He rents the finest suite
and orders rich food, tipping everyone generously. Wallingford
has no fear about the bills, however, since his next scheme has
been formulated. He finds investors for his new carpet tack company, which is sure to make everyone connected with it quite
rich. The Universal Carpet Tack Company is dedicated, "To
the live business men of America—those who have been stung
and those who have yet to undergo that experience."

GILBERT'S LAST TOOTHACHE (1949)
MARGARET SCHERF

A rector and his wife die "accidentally" at a diocesan convention. Reverend Martin Buell★ is left holding the baby, who
may be the missing heir to a large estate. Typical clues are a
watch in the catsup and a sweater in the flour bin.

"Girl Who Married a Monster, The" (1954)
ANTHONY BOUCHER

Doreen was marrying Luther Peabody, knowing well the list of
girls who had died under suspicious circumstances shortly after
they had married him. Lieutenant MacDonald asks Nick
Noble★, as the latter sits in his usual cafe drinking cheap
sherry, "Why should a girl deliberately marry a Bluebeard?"

GLASS KEY, THE▲ (1931)
DASHIELL HAMMETT

Political boss Paul Madvig● fights to maintain control over his
empire with the help of Ned Beaumont★, a hard-drinking,
hard-gambling political hanger-on. Senator Ralph Henry is Madvig's distinguished candidate for re-election. When Beaumont
finds Taylor Henry, the Senator's son, dead in the street, Shad
O'Rory tries to frame Madvig. O'Rory is a gangster and ward
boss with his own candidate for the Senate. Both Madvig and
the Senator confess to the murder.

GOLDEN TRIANGLE, THE (1917)
MAURICE LEBLANC

It is Spring of 1915. Paris is filled with spies, traitors, and
wounded soldiers. The villainous financier Essares Bey is married to "Little Mother Coralie" of the hospital wards—the object of Captain Patrice Belval's love. An intricate plot that
threatens the girl is too complicated for the wounded Captain
to solve, so Arsène Lupin●, using one of his many false names,
arrives to delve into the devious machinations, which threaten
the financial heart of France, itself.

GOLDFINGER▲ (1959)
IAN FLEMING

Obsessed with the desire for gold, Auric Goldfinger● conceives of a foolproof plan to rob Fort Knox. He enlists the aid of the top criminals in the United States. Secret agent James Bond★ must draw on all his ingenuity and talent to foil the plan; a bevy of beauties from the Bronx helps.

"Great Horseshoe Mystery, The" (1962)
LLOYD BIGGLE, JR.

It is an old-fashioned rural Fourth of July in Borgville, Michigan (population: 800) and a new park is to be dedicated. It had been hoped that the Governor would speak but the County Drain Commissioner substitutes. Grandfather★ Rastin is amazed to hear that his teenage grandson has never heard of pitching horseshoes, and undertakes to fill this breach in the boy's education. Shortly thereafter, a local store is robbed and Grandfather's horseshoes are stolen. Is there any hidden connection?

"Green-and-Gold String, The" (1948)
PHILIP MAC DONALD

At a California circus sideshow, Dr. Alcazar★, a clever charlatan, tells the fortune (and past) of a British-born maid. When she is murdered and a large reward is offered by her employer, Alcazar enters the case. He poses as a professor of the occult, possessing special powers, but must use his deductive skills to solve the crime and collect the reward. His cohort in detection here is Avvie du Pois, who works as a weight-guesser.

GREEN FOR DANGER (1944)
CHRISTIANNA BRAND

At Heron's Park Hospital, victim number one dies of unnatural causes on the operating table. Victim number two, a young lady, is found with two deep wounds on her chest. A clever and diabolical murderer will commit crime number three unless the police can stop him. Detective: Inspector Cockrill★.

GREENE MURDER CASE, THE▲ (1928)
S. S. VAN DINE

The gloomy Greene mansion, a walled-in estate on New York's East River, is the scene of a double tragedy. The eldest sister is shot and killed; the youngest, an adopted sister, is wounded by an intruder. While Philo Vance★ and District Attorney Markham● are at work on the case, the two Greene brothers also are shot and killed. The only survivors in the sinister household are the mother, a helpless invalid; Sibella, her daughter; and Ada, the adopted sister. Psychologist-detective Vance discovers the villain in time to save the last member of the family.

GREENMASK (1964)
ELIZABETH LININGTON

The author, a mystery fan herself, used the world of detective fiction as an integral part of the plot in this novel. Basic to the story is a series of murders in Hollywood which have parallels to Agatha Christie's "The A.B.C. Murders"▲. As American equivalents of the British Railway Guide, Los Angeles County Guides are found placed on top of each corpse. Sergeant Ivor Maddox★ and his colleagues on the Los Angeles Police Department are in a quandary until luck comes their way. Anthony Boucher called this book "a mystery reader's mystery novel."

"Gutting of Couffignal, The" (1925)
DASHIELL HAMMETT

This novelette is set on "Couffignal," a small, wedge-shaped island off the California mainland with more than its share of wealthy residents. The Continental Op★ is on the kind of assignment he doesn't relish: guarding expensive presents at a wedding. A storm arises, followed by the landing of a gang of thieves armed with machine guns. Their object: robbery on a large scale. The detective is forced to wage virtually a one-man war against an invading criminal well-equipped army.

"H as in Homicide" (1964)
LAURENCE TREAT

A shy young lady reports to Mitch Taylor★ that her girl friend has vanished. Mitch is not very interested until the murdered body of a girl appears, when he is able to come up with one of the bushel-full of ideas he always claims to carry in his head held in reserve until needed.

HAND OF FU MANCHU, THE (1917)
SAX ROHMER

Nayland Smith★ and Dr. Petrie●, aided by Scotland Yard, battle the evil genius, Fu Manchu●, and his mysterious, world-wide organization, the Si-Fan. The scene in London ranges from foreign embassies to the underworld; the stakes are no less than world domination. Using weapons that range from crude missiles to occult animal magnetism, the Orientals threaten to extinguish the white race and to make Dr. Fu Manchu Emperor of the World.

"Hands of Mr. Ottermole, The" (1931)
THOMAS BURKE

In 1949, a panel of distinguished critics, including Carr, Queen, and Boucher, selected this as the greatest mystery short story of all time. Undoubtedly, they were impressed by the atmosphere of terror emanating from this tale of murder in the London streets. There is an air of black magic about these murders (London's Strangling Horrors, as they are called by the press). Each murder is committed at a time when the scene of crime is devoid of any murderer, yet the number of corpses mounts.

HANGOVER SQUARE (1941)
PATRICK HAMILTON

Solid George Harvey Bone's life in Earl's Court, London, is tormented by his passion for a worthless trollop, Netta Longdon. She has led him a merry chase while betraying him with one of his best friends. Bone's agony is complicated by his schizophrenia, which forces him to revenge.

HARDLY A MAN IS NOW ALIVE (1950)
HERBERT BREAN

A body is found in a disused old New England well by reporter Reynold Frame★ and his beautiful fiancée, Constance Wilder. They want only to be married, but, problems involving theft, abduction, ghosts, and a 175-year-old unsolved murder case prevent the wedding until a seance helps unravel the mystery.

HEADS YOU LOSE (1941)
CHRISTIANNA BRAND

The aristocratic Miss Morland said, "Do you call that a hat? I don't call it a hat at all. Good heavens, I wouldn't be seen dead in a ditch in a thing like that." The next morning, Miss Morland was found lying by a ditch, the absurd hat perched grotesquely on her severed head. Detective: Inspector Cockrill★.

HECKLER, THE (1960)
ED MC BAIN

The Heckler unleashes a reign of terror on the people of "Isola." It starts with threatening phone calls and continues with unusual ads in the local newspapers. These are just a foretaste of what this criminal genius has planned. There will be murders, bombings and a "big caper." The Heckler scatters his diversions well and the 87th Precinct★ is spread too thin to cope with his well-conceived plans.

HEIR PRESUMPTIVE (1935)
HENRY WADE

His expensive tastes and rapidly-dwindling funds put Eustace Hendel in a desperate situation. Only his cousin and the cousin's invalid son stand between Eustace and the vast Hendel estate and title. The only solution to his urgent problem is the execution of two perfect murders.

HENDON'S FIRST CASE (1935)
JOHN RHODE

Fledgling Inspector Jimmy Waghorn★ investigates the affair of Bernard Threlfall, a noted research chemist who has died of ptomaine poisoning. A burgled laboratory, a threatening letter from the dead man's wife, and a disappearing nephew complicate a complex and baffling crime. Waghorn must call upon the keen mind of the famous sleuth, Dr. Lancelot Priestley★, to provide a solution.

"His Heart Could Break" (1943)
CRAIG RICE

John J. Malone's★ client, in the Death House of the Illinois State Prison, has reason for optimism: the lawyer has uncovered sufficient evidence for a new trial. Yet, when Malone arrives at the prison to talk to him, the client has hanged himself. Malone demands an investigation and finds himself acting as a detective instead of a lawyer.

HOLLOW NEEDLE, THE (1909)
MAURICE LEBLANC

A robbery and murder have been committed, and Arsène Lupin●, fleeing, is shot from the balcony of a French chateau by a beautiful girl. A young detective, assigned to arrest the villain, is foiled at every turn. He manages finally to trap Lupin in "the hollow needle," a secret cavern known only to French kings since the time of Charlemagne. A fantastic escape in a submarine follows. Lupin, in love with the girl, intends to give up his life of crime.

HOUND OF THE BASKERVILLES, THE▲ (1902)
SIR ARTHUR CONAN DOYLE

Young Sir Henry Baskerville, who has spent most of his life in Canada, is heir to a fortune when Sir Charles Baskerville is killed by a phantom hound—a legendary beast which had already dispatched an 18th century ancestor. Henry tells Sherlock Holmes★ that someone has stolen his boot, and the detective immediately suspects the ghostly animal may strike again. Suspects, convicts, inexplicable apparitions abound on fog-shrouded Grimpen Mire, which borders the ancestral Baskerville Hall, the setting for perhaps the most famous mystery novel of all time by one of the most famous writers of the genre.

HOUSE OF CLYSTEVILL, THE (1940)
BERTRAM ATKEY

Smiler Bunn● and Lord Fortworth, having carefully surveyed their financial resources, decided to buy a country estate. Horcheddor Hall was large and gloomy when they purchased it; within months it was transformed into a splendid, congenial house. Instead of enjoying it, Smiler and Fortworth became involved in fighting a bitter private war against their neighbors—two brothers known as the werewolves of Clystevill—and their unusual "house guests."

HOUSE OF THE ARROW, THE (1924)
A. E. W. MASON

Inspector Hanaud★, the famous French detective, and Jim Frobisher, junior member of a prominent London law firm, attempt to solve a complicated problem. A wealthy client of Frobisher's firm, Mrs. Harlow, had died, apparently of natural causes. Suddenly, her niece, Betty, is charged with murdering the aunt. Although the body is exhumed and no traces of poison are discovered, Hanaud claims Mrs. Harlow met death at the hands of someone in the household.

HOUSE ON TOLLARD RIDGE, THE (1929)
JOHN RHODE

The elderly Mr. Barton, who had lived alone and kept to himself, is murdered. The only relative, his wayward son, Arthur, is arrested and tried for the murder. Mrs. Hapgood, the daughter of Barton's former partner, believes in Arthur's innocence. She goes to her death trying to prove it. Dr. Lancelot Priestley★ must find the culprit.

HOUSE WITHOUT A KEY, THE▲ (1925)
EARL DERR BIGGERS

Old Dan Winterslip was rich, handsome, and respected, but there were ugly rumors about his unsavory past that no one dared repeat to him. One quiet, moonless night, Winterslip is murdered. The clues consist of a brooch, a page from a guest book, a cigarette stub, and an illuminated wristwatch. This is the first recorded case of Charlie Chan★, all of whose intelligence is necessary to defeat a wily murderer.

HUNT THE TOFF (1952)
JOHN CREASEY

When Richard, The Toff★, Rollison produces an alibi for a girl accused of murder, he finds she has been framed so skillfully that he must go into hiding to avoid being charged as her willing accomplice.

ILL MET BY MOONLIGHT (1937)
LESLIE FORD

This book records the first meeting of Colonel Primrose★ and the attractive widow, Mrs. Grace Latham★. The setting is the summer colony of April Harbor on Chesapeake Bay, during the dog days of August. Nerves are strained as a thunderstorm approaches but other motives, mostly from the past, must be sought to account for the murder of an attractive and charming, though predatory, woman.

I'LL EAT YOU LAST (1941)
H. C. BRANSON

A suspicious death by drowning brings the bearded intellectual sleuth, John Bent★, to a small lakeside community, where a complex web of crimes and counterplots has been designed to put a fifty-million-dollar estate into wrong and unscrupulous hands.

I'LL SING AT YOUR FUNERAL (1942)
HUGH PENTECOST

Lydia Egan either had jumped or had been pushed from a high hotel window. The possible suspects included her generous mentor, the wealthy Emily Stoddard, and her troupe of friends, business associates and discoveries. These include an ex-riveter turned singer, a voice teacher, a theatrical coach, a numerologist and an Indian chief. Inspector Luke Bradley★ is summoned from police headquarters to discover the guilty party and to close the case.

I MARRIED A DEAD MAN (1948)
WILLIAM IRISH, pseudonym of
Cornell Woolrich

After a train wreck, a girl with nothing to live for is mistaken for another, who was killed in the wreck. She grasps this providential new identity and falls in love. The past returns to destroy her.

"Imponderables, The" (1944)
PAT HAND

Professional gambler Careful Jones★ has been concerned only with his own welfare. However, it is World War II, and he shows patriotic concern when dishonest card-sharps try to bilk an Air Force hero home on leave. The brave but unwise hero is in danger of losing all the money he had saved for his wedding. Then, Jones takes a hand in the game.

"Impossible Crime, The" (1954)
GERALD KERSH

Karmesin★ has told of many crimes in which he was involved; none were as ambitious as this. Karmesin plans to steal the Crown Jewels from the historic Tower of London.

"Infallible Godahl, The" (1914)
FREDERICK IRVING ANDERSON

Among the great thieves in literature, The Infallible Godahl● must hold a record for masterminding a crime in a story in which he does not appear! A gentleman giving the name of J. Borden Benson introduces himself to Oliver Armiston, the creator of Godahl. The two men exchange cards, neither knowing who the other is. Benson provides Armiston with a problem for the next story about Godahl. He tells of a sacred white ruby allegedly in the possession of Billy Wentworth, a fabulously rich adventuress whose home is an impregnable fortress. A room, guarded by solid steel walls and door, contains a treasuretrove unequalled in the world; the mythical gem is concealed therein. Benson explores the room with the lady acting as guide. He determines to have Godahl crack the impenetrable room in his next story. The day after it is published, a man is found dead, the gem gone.

INFORMATION RECEIVED (1933)
E. R. PUNSHON

The receipt of two free tickets to a revival of "Hamlet" brings terror to Sir Christopher Clarke, one of the wealthiest, most powerful men in London. Sir Christopher calls his solicitor, to change his will. That request is the catalyst for a series of events in which at least three people lose their lives. Bobby Owen★ is the first policeman at the scene of the first crime; before the case is resolved, he will have come to the attention of important people at Scotland Yard.

IN THE HEAT OF THE NIGHT (1965)
JOHN BALL

Black detective Virgil Tibbs★ is traveling in the Deep South to visit his mother when a murder is discovered. Because of his color, he is a suspect. Professional courtesy is extended to him as a member of another city's police department, mainly so he can help solve the crime. (This Edgar-winning novel was a distinguished film.)

INSPECTOR FRENCH'S GREATEST CASE (1924)
FREEMAN WILLS CROFTS

Early one morning, a police constable is summoned into the offices of a Hatton Street diamond merchant. The policeman finds the firm's safe door open and the murdered head clerk beside it. The constable informs his superiors and a manhunt is begun for a thief and murderer. Detective: Inspector Joseph French★.

INSPECTOR MAIGRET
AND THE STRANGLED STRIPPER (1954)
GEORGES SIMENON

A striptease girl who works at "Picratt's," a small night club in Montmartre, overhears two men planning to murder a character called the Countess. She tells the police what she overheard, but she is the victim of foul play soon afterward. Inspector Maigret★ investigates, and a second murder, followed by a breathtaking chase, occurs before Maigret can solve two violent crimes. English title: Maigret in Montmartre

IRON GATES, THE (1945)
MARGARET MILLAR

Lucille Morris, an attractive, wealthy, married woman, is serene, self-possessed. One December day, the delivery of a package transforms her into a whimpering, frightened creature who must be hospitalized. The description of life in a sanatorium is set against a chilling tale. The detective on the case is Inspector Sands★.

IRON SPIDERS, THE (1936)
BAYNARD KENDRICK

Many elements are woven into the fabric of this mystery set in the Florida Keys: economic depression, voodoo, a locked room, and a tropical storm. Solved by Stan Rice★.

I, THE JURY▲ (1947)
MICKEY SPILLANE

Mike Hammer★▲ vows to track down and kill the murderer of his wartime buddy, a man who had lost an arm saving Hammer's life. Mike succeeds in his quest. The last two lines of the book have become famous: The dying murderer says, "How could you?" Hammer replies, "It was easy."

"Ides of March, The" (1899)
E. W. HORNUNG

Bunny Manders●, having dissipated a considerable inheritance, sinks to writing bad checks to pay gambling debts. In despair, he goes to his schoolmate, Raffles●, and asks for help. Raffles confesses that despite his appearance of affluence he, too, is badly off, but claims he can get the desperately-needed cash "from an old friend." At night, Raffles' unknown "friend," a jeweller, becomes an unconscious benefactor.

KINDS OF LOVE, KINDS OF DEATH (1966)
TUCKER COE

A disgraced New York policeman, Mitch Tobin★, close to isolating himself from reality, receives an offer to investigate the murder of a girl in a Pennsylvania motel. The roots of the crime are in New York City's organized underworld. Tobin, with a code of honesty peculiar to himself, accepts the challenge and returns to the world.

LAST HERO, THE (1930)
LESLIE CHARTERIS

Simon Templar, The Saint★, takes the law into his hands when Scotland Yard fails to rid London's underworld of some of its most despicable characters. Dr. Marius, the greatest villain of all, taxes The Saint's ingenuity and resources.

LAUGHING FOX, THE (1940)
FRANK GRUBER

Johnny Fletcher and Sam Cragg find a dead man and a dead fox in their hotel room. The case takes them to an agricultural fair and to a crap game. They must deal with a missing heir problem, sell muscle-building books and indulge in some fancy footwork to dodge bill collectors before they solve the problem in their own way.

LAURA (1942)
VERA CASPARY

Famous New York columnist Waldo Lydecker begins to write the epitaph of the recently-murdered Laura Hunt when he is interrupted by detective Mark McPherson★. Lydecker answers questions, gives detailed accounts of the days immediately preceding the murder, paints a vivid picture of the beautiful girl and a less than complimentary portrayal of her intended bridegroom, Shelby Carpenter. During the investigation, McPherson picks up clues that define Laura's relationships with Lydecker and Carpenter and, before long, the detective becomes emotionally invoved with the dead girl. During a savage rainstorm, a visitor turns up in Laura's apartment and the path is cleared for another murder.

LEAGUE OF FRIGHTENED MEN, THE (1935)
REX STOUT

Novelist Paul Chapin is crippled as the result of "a boyish prank" played on him by his Harvard classmates. They form a "League of Atonement" for Paul and, with their help, all seems to go well for him. Then, one member of the League is found at the foot of a cliff, his body smashed to bits by the surf-pounded rocks. The survivors each receive a set of verses boasting of the murder. Only one person could have written the verses: Paul Chapin. Following the death of Judge Harrison, terror grips the surviving members when Eugene Dryer, the art dealer, is poisoned; then psychologist Andrew Hibbard disappears. The official police seem out of their depth, so Nero Wolfe★ must be relied on by 26 frightened men to end the crimes. He identifies the murderous poet but he knows the crimes can never be proven.

LEAVENWORTH CASE, THE (1878)
ANNA KATHERINE GREEN

Rich old Mr. Leavenworth, at the point of signing his new will, is murdered. Ebenezer Gryce★ is called in to solve the case.

Evidence and the testimony of expert witnesses show the cause and time of death, the murder weapon is positively identified and accusing fingers point to Mary Leavenworth as the culprit. ("The Leavenworth Case" is credited with being the first American detective novel and the first detective novel written anywhere, in any language, by a woman.)

"Lenton Croft Robberies, The" (1894)
ARTHUR MORRISON

A series of thefts at his home in Lenton Croft sends Sir James Norris to Martin Hewitt★ for help. Three times in less than a year, guests at his house have had pieces of jewelry stolen from their rooms by a silent thief—who, in each theft, leaves a single, burned match inches from the original resting place of the missing jewelry. Norris and his secretary, Vernon Lloyd, are unable to comprehend how a burglar could enter a room with a locked door, steal just one piece of jewelry, and escape.

LITTLE CAESAR (1929)
W. R. BURNETT

During a night-club holdup Rico, known as Little Caesar●, shoots and kills a policeman. The act gives him the power to challenge Sam Vettori for the leadership of Vettori's gang. His ruthlessness and cunning move Rico up the ladder in the Chicago underworld, until one of the gang involved in the holdup squeals and Rico has to flee.

This story of a Chicago hoodlum and his gang, told from the gangster's point of view and in his language, is the first important novel of its kind and marked an epoch in the crime story. It was made into a popular motion picture and served as the prototype for scores of similar stories.

LONE WOLF, THE▲ (1914)
LOUIS JOSEPH VANCE

Michael Lanyard spends his childhood as a drudge in a Paris hotel, learning to steal for self-preservation. In his 16th year, he is caught as he attempts to steal a gold coin from Bourke●, a master thief. Instead of being punished, Michael is taught the finer arts of what is to become his profession. He becomes The Lone Wolf●▲, traveling alone and prospering. His successful career is threatened, however, on two different fronts. The underworld, aware of his success, threatens to reveal his identity unless he joins the "Pack"●. On the other hand, he meets Lucy Shannon, the beautiful girl for whom he is willing to forget his earlier vow of solitude.

LONE WOLF'S SON, THE (1931)
LOUIS JOSEPH VANCE

Michael Lanyard, The Lone Wolf●, with his 20-year-old son are aboard a trans-Atlantic liner when the famed Habsburg emeralds are stolen. The Lanyards match wits with the more sophisticated circles of gangdom.

LONG GOODBYE, THE▲ (1953)
RAYMOND CHANDLER

Philip Marlowe★ becomes involved in the murder of a millionairess who has had six husbands. Though he has seen her only once, Marlowe is a murder suspect and is thrown into jail because of his unwillingness to betray a client. Marlowe trusts no one, and is surprised by nothing; before he solves the murders in this case, he will be surrounded by more wealth, corruption, and cruelty than even he is used to.

LOSS OF THE JANE VOSPER, THE (1936)
FREEMAN WILLS CROFTS

Four violent explosions send the freighter Jane Vosper and her half-million-dollar cargo to the bottom of the sea. The insurance company's suspicions are aroused, but an investigation by the British Board of Trade fails to reveal evidence of foul play. However, the strange disappearance of one of the investigators causes Scotland Yard to make a further investigation, leading to disclosures of sabotage and murder. Detective: Inspector Joseph French★.

LOST GALLOWS, THE (1931)
JOHN DICKSON CARR

On a visit to London, the inscrutable Henri Bencolin★ is pitted against a mad, avenging hangman who has the power to penetrate locked rooms and to drive automobiles with no one to be seen behind the wheel.

LURE OF THE BUSH, THE (1928)
ARTHUR W. UPFIELD

John Thornton, owner of one of the largest homesteads in New South Wales, Australia, was a man to be envied, the only cloud on his happiness a continuing argument with his son. Disaster strikes when King Henry, the chief of a nearby group of aborigines, is found dead in a rainstorm. There is evidence of

foul play. Detective: Inspector Napoleon Bonaparte★. English
and Australian title: The Barrakee Mystery

MAIGRET AT THE CROSSROADS (1932)
GEORGES SIMENON

The body of an unidentified diamond merchant from Antwerp
is found in a car which doesn't belong to him, parked in a small
garage 20 miles south of Paris. Commissaire Jules Maigret★
investigates but is unable to find anyone who knows anything
about the crime. He is stalemated. When the murdered man's
widow is shot down at his feet, Maigret leaps into action.

MAIGRET GOES HOME (1932)
GEORGES SIMENON

Commissaire Jules Maigret★ is warned that a woman will soon
be killed in his own home town, Saint-Fiacre. He heeds this
warning, returning for the first time in many years. When he
attends the local church services, the murder is committed right
before Maigret's eyes.

MAIGRET'S MISTAKE (1964)
GEORGES SIMENON

The body of a demi-mondaine is found in a luxury apartment
house in a well-to-do section of Paris. Why was she living
there? A distinguished doctor and his wife, who reside in the
same building, and a disappearing musician, reputed to be the
dead girl's lover, are three of the suspects who must be questioned by Commissaire Maigret★.

MAIGRET MYSTIFIED (1932)
GEORGES SIMENON

Monsieur Couchet, dead of a gunshot wound, is still seated in
an armchair in the office of his pharmaceutical firm; 300,000
francs are missing from the safe. The evidence shows the theft
had taken place just before the murder, but why had M. Couchet done nothing but sit in his armchair? Detective: Commissaire Jules Maigret★.

MALTESE FALCON, THE▲ (1930)
DASHIELL HAMMETT

After private detective Sam Spade★ takes a case for a beautiful
redhead, his partner, Miles Archer, is killed. Setting out to find
the killer, Spade runs afoul of the police and finds himself involved with an odd assortment of characters, all searching for

a black statue of a bird, about a foot high and said to be worth some two million dollars. Among those searching for the valuable statuette are Brigid O'Shaughnessy● who, in masquerading as Miss Wonderly, had become Spade's client: her employer, Fat Man Casper Gutman●; Joel Cairo, the flashily-dressed, effeminate agent of Gutman; and Wilmer Cook, Gutman's nervous, trigger-happy bodyguard.

MAN LAY DEAD, A (1934)
NGAIO MARSH

At a weekend house party, the guests of Sir Hubert Handesley play at a parlor sport they call "The Murder Game." The lights are turned out, and when they are relit, a corpse is found at the foot of the stairs, a jewelled dagger between his shoulder blades. Local police ask Scotland Yard for help and Chief Inspector Roderick Alleyn★ is detailed. He finds unusual motivation, considerable evidence, a devious killer with an almost foolproof method—and personal danger.

MAN ON THE BALCONY, THE (1967)
MAJ SJÖWALL and PER WAHLÖÖ

Detective Superintendent Martin Beck★ is one among hundreds of Swedish police involved in a hunt throughout Stockholm for a psychopath who has been strangling and raping little girls, leaving the bodies in parks. A masterful police procedural novel, this novel has the detailed realism of a documentary.

"Man Who Spoke Latin, The" (1911)
SAMUEL HOPKINS ADAMS

Average Jones'★ curiosity leads him to do research as a mute in the household of Colonel Graeme, a Latin professor. The Colonel's house guest, Lucius Livius, has a bump on his head, speaks only Latin, and claims to be an ancient Roman. Graeme's large and disorganized collection of rare books becomes the focal point of a search for one particular volume—a recent, inexpensive acquisition. Jones considered this case his only failure.

MASK OF FU MANCHU, THE▲ (1932)
SAX ROHMER

The diabolical Dr. Fu Manchu●, whose magic elixirs have made him younger, more clever and more sinister than ever, searches for the lost tomb of the "Hidden Prophet." The treasures of the great Mohammedan master, particularly a gold mask, will make Fu Manchu ruler of a fanatical sect. A handful of Englishmen stand in his way: Sir Nayland Smith★, Dr. Petrie●, Sir Lionel Barton, Dr. Van Berg and Shan Greville. The drug of forgetfulness, the cord of a spider, the bone that whistled in the night like a doomed soul, and a beautiful, evil daughter, are only part of Fu Manchu's arsenal of force.

"Meanest Man in Europe, The" (1924)
DAVID DURHAM, pseudonym of
Roy Vickers

Fidelity Dove★ displays social conscience as she tackles Mr. Jabez Crewde. When Crewde tries to cheat a hospital, Fidelity teaches him a lesson.

MEET THE TIGER (1928)
LESLIE CHARTERIS

Simon Templar, The Saint★, and a lovely young girl, Patricia Holm, survive a series of horrors; they gain the loot in the Tiger's lair.

MEMOIRS OF ARSÈNE LUPIN, THE (1925)
MAURICE LEBLANC

Arsène Lupin●, under the name of Ralph d'Andrezy, had never been in love until he met the exquisitely beautiful Josephine Balsamo, Countess of Cagliostro. The lovers try to solve a mystery that had its origins in the Middle Ages.

METHOD IN MADNESS (1957)
DORIS MILES DISNEY

A lonely old lady dies in a nursing home, and the policy she carries with Commonwealth Insurance seems to be at the root of her death. Jeff DiMarco★ investigates. He is as concerned with human elements as he is with protecting his company's interests. Normally phlegmatic, DiMarco is angered when he confronts cruelty. He is also touched by the poignancy of loneliness.

MIDNIGHT MAN, THE (1966)
HENRY KANE

A raid on an after-hours nightclub spins Inspector McGregor, New York Police Department (retired), into a battle of wits against an untouchable ganglord. A private murder scheme involves a particularly ingenious weapon.

MISSING PARTNERS, THE (1928)
HENRY WADE

Two partners suddenly fade into thin air. Subsequently, one is found murdered; the other is presumed guilty. The survivor reappears, is sent to jail, but manages to prove his innocence. It is up to Superintendent Dodd to find the guilty.

"Mom Sings an Aria" (1966)
JAMES YAFFE

Murder occurs at the Metropolitan Opera House. An interesting, seldom-used theme is explored in a story of the hatreds raging among the fans of different opera singers. Detective: Mom★.

MONSIEUR LECOQ (1869)
ÉMILE GABRORIAU

This lengthy melodrama, set in Paris and its environs, features Lecoq★, frequently in disguise. This is a strangely balanced book; the first half contains all the detection. The second half is family chronicle, featuring much scandal, as demanded by the readers of Gaboriau's day.

MOONSTONE, THE (1868)
WILKIE COLLINS

Franklin Blake delivers a sacred, priceless moonstone to Rachel Verinder at her birthday party. Later, Rachel announces the gem has been stolen from her room. Superintendent Seegrave● is called to find the culprit. While he bungles along, Blake wires Scotland Yard for help and Sergeant Cuff★, the finest detective in England, arrives. He uncovers a valuable clue—a smudge on Rachel's freshly-painted door. To everyone's surprise, the girl refuses to allow a search for the stained garment that could identify the thief. Sergeant Cuff suspects her of having staged the robbery. He quits the case. Blake, with whom Rachel has fallen in love, leaves England because she treats him abominably. Rachel's maid commits suicide, leaving a note for Blake, in which he learns that Rachel suspected him of the crime. He returns, with Sergeant Cuff, to solve the case.

The Moonstone has been called by T. S. Eliot the first and the best detective novel ever written.

"Most Dangerous Game, The" (1925)
RICHARD CONNELL

Sanger Rainsford, a big-game hunter on a trip up the Amazon, falls off his yacht and swims for Ship-Trap Island. There, in the midst of dense jungle, he finds a palatial chateau, built by a General Zaroff●. The sinister Zaroff is owner of the island, a pack of savage dogs, a grotesque museum and a unique training school. He has a passion for hunting, but traditional big-game hunting has become a bore, so he invented a new sport. Rainsford, supplied with hunting clothes, food, a knife and moccasins, becomes the prey.

MOVING TOYSHOP, THE (1946)
EDMUND CRISPIN

Poet Richard Cadogan, arriving in Oxford for a holiday, finds a dead woman in a room above a toyshop. A blow from a blunt instrument renders him unconscious. When he recovers, Cadogan finds not only that the dead woman has vanished, but the toyshop has turned into a grocery store. Detective: Gervase Fen★.

MR. JUSTICE RAFFLES (1909)
E. W. HORNUNG

A young cricket player is caught in the tentacles of a cruel, greedy moneylender. To see justice done, Raffles▲ kidnaps the notorious Shylock, uses cool nerve and his own sensitive fingers to open a safe, and eludes the police.

MRS. MEEKER'S MONEY (1961)
DORIS MILES DISNEY

Postal Inspector David Madden★ investigates an attempt to defraud by using the United States mails. He finds murder. Madden is aided by student Inspector Tod Chandler who tends to lose objectivity when he meets a pretty suspect.

MURDER AT THE VICARAGE (1930)
AGATHA CHRISTIE

One of the district's least popular men is murdered. He is so hated that almost everyone in the town of St. Mary Mead is suspect. Miss Jane Marple★ investigates; she is occasionally "upstaged" by her nephew, a young novelist, and by the vicar. A map of St. Mary Mead proves useful.

MURDER FOR TWO (1943)
GEORGE HARMON COXE

The homefront during World War II is the scene as Jack "Flashgun" Casey★, rejected by the army, vents his anger on a murderer who is also a spy. This plot weaves through wartime Boston and the operations of a newspaper in a large city.

MURDER IN CANTON (1966)
ROBERT VAN GULIK

The year is 680 A.D., and the setting is the Chinese port city of Canton. Judge Dee★ arrives from Peking to find the missing Imperial Censor, an important personage in the higher strata of the Palace. The Censor appears—as a corpse.

MURDER IN THE BASEMENT (1932)
ANTHONY BERKELEY

Mr. Reginald Dane's first house is ideal, except for a slight depression in the basement floor. Investigation discloses the body of a woman wearing only a pair of gloves; a bullet is in her skull. Further investigation must uncover a wily murderer, as well as the identity of the victim. Detective: Roger Sheringham★.

MURDER IN THE BOOKSHOP (1936)
CAROLYN WELLS

Sewell's Bookstore on Manhattan's Lexington Ave., specializing in rare and valuable books, caters to collectors. One evening, bibliophile Philip Balfour and his librarian, Keith Ramsay, visit the shop. Death strikes Balfour in the back room. At the same time, a book valued at $100,000 is missing. Fleming Stone★ is called in to solve the baffling mysteries.

MURDER IN THE CALAIS COACH (1934)
AGATHA CHRISTIE

Hercule Poirot★ is riding the fabled Orient Express on his return from the Middle East. A snowstorm halts the train in Yugoslavia and a murder takes place among the stranded passengers who represent truly an international mélange. English title: Murder on the Orient Express

MURDER IN THE MAZE (1927)
J. J. CONNINGTON

A garden maze is the setting for a crime of violence, as both twin Shandon brothers are victims of a clever murderer whose trail is as tortuous and difficult to follow as the maze. Detective: Sir Clinton Driffield★.

MURDER MUST ADVERTISE (1933)
DOROTHY L. SAYERS

At Pym's Advertising Agency, a man is killed in a headlong fall down a flight of stairs. At about the same time, Bredon, a young man about whom little was known, joins the firm. Events connect the respectable advertising firm with a group given to engaging in midnight orgies, a Chief Inspector of Scotland Yard is assaulted, another corpse is found and Lord Peter Wimsey★ becomes a prime murder suspect.

MURDER OF QUALITY, A (1962)
JOHN LE CARRÉ

The death of a schoolteacher's wife brings ex-spy George Smiley★ into the wealthy, snobbish precincts of Carne School in Dorsetshire. He is involved in the feud between the local Anglicans and Baptists before the murderer is revealed.

MURDER OF ROGER ACKROYD, THE (1926)
AGATHA CHRISTIE

Hercule Poirot★, recalled from retirement, undertakes the investigation of a brutal murder. He is assisted by Dr. Sheppard, the local physician. A dictaphone is cleverly employed; all clues pointing to the culprit are there for the reader to use in attempting a solution.

This is the most widely discussed of Miss Christie's stories involving M. Poirot. Since its publication, readers have argued passionately about whether the solution is a fair one.

MURDERS IN PRAED STREET, THE (1928)
JOHN RHODE

Six residents of Praed Street are murdered in serial fashion by a cunning killer. Relationships could be established between some, but not all, victims: Police efforts establish no motive. Dr. Lancelot Priestley★ investigates; the name of one victim reminds him of a courtroom drama buried in the mists of time. He perceives the motive and establishes the name of the next potential victim—himself.

"Murders in the Rue Morgue, The" (1841)
EDGAR ALLAN POE

An old woman and her daughter are found brutally murdered in their room on the Rue Morgue. It appears to be hermetically sealed. In their confusion, the police of Paris arrest an innocent person, to whom all superficial evidence points. C. Auguste Dupin★ draws deductions from evidence overlooked by the police and discovers a mode of entrance into the room.

This, the first detective short story, constitutes a virtual manual of theory and practice for the form and is highly regarded even today.

MURDERS IN VOLUME 2 (1941)
ELIZABETH DALY

The serenity of the rich, stuffy Vauregard clan is threatened by a young woman claiming to be the reincarnation of a family governess who had disappeared over one hundred years ago. One member of the family, who believes the lady's story, dies of poison. The "ghost" disappears again, leaving a void in a set of Lord Byron's poems. Detective: Henry Gamadge★.

MYSTERY OF EDWIN DROOD, THE (1870)
CHARLES DICKENS

A young engineer, Edwin Drood, is engaged to Rosa Bud. Their fathers, close friends, had wanted the two young people to marry, but Edwin and Rosa soon realize they are not in love, and agree to remain friends. Jack Jasper, Drood's uncle and guardian, is in love with the pretty Rosa but she fears him because he is an opium addict. Neville Landless falls in love with Rosa; she reciprocates. He resents Drood's casual attitude to the girl and almost kills him.

One Christmas morning, Drood is reported missing. Jasper says he had seen Drood and Landless together the previous night, heading toward the river, where Drood's watch and tie pin are discovered. Though Drood's body is not found, Landless is suspected of murder. Jasper tells Rosa that he has sufficient evidence to hang Landless, implying that he will use this knowledge unless Rosa returns his passion.

A white-haired stranger named Datchery arrives, and sits for hours behind his open door in a house opposite Jasper's residence. Every time he hears Jasper's name mentioned, he makes a chalk mark inside his closet door.

The story ends here, for Dickens died before he could complete the novel. Who the mysterious Datchery is, who killed Drood, if he was, in fact, killed at all, and other problems must remain unanswered forever. Dickens left no notes to show how he intended to end the story, believed to have been potentially Dickens' finest work and perhaps the greatest detective novel written.

"Mystery of Marie Roget, The" (1842)
EDGAR ALLAN POE

This story consists entirely of a series of newspaper clippings concerning the disappearance and murder of a shopgirl, interspersed with the comments of C. Auguste Dupin★. Unlike most detective stories, it contains no solution; in fact, it contains no formal ending. There is a valid reason for this. The crime was genuine, as was the girl—Mary Cecilia Rogers—and the newspaper clippings were authentic. Since the crime was unsolved (and has remained so), the publication printing Poe's story was reluctant to add his ending.

"Mystery of Mrs. Dickinson, The" (1889)
NICHOLAS CARTER

The wife of a wealthy antiques dealer appears to be afflicted with kleptomania whenever she enters the premises of Ferris & Steele, jewelers. The pretty young woman pays for several items with her husband's checks. In the course of her legal transaction, she pilfers jewels worth more than $40,000, according to the aggrieved proprietors. They call on the famous detective, Nick Carter★. While they know the lady is guilty, she maintains her innocence. They fear offending her husband, who does a brisk business with the jewelers. When Nick confronts Mr. and Mrs. Dickinson with Mr. Ferris, Mr. Steele and Richard Steele, the prominent businessman's nephew, the real mystery begins—Mrs. Dickinson isn't really Mrs. Dickinson.

MYSTERY OF THE DEAD POLICE (1933)
PHILIP MAC DONALD, originally published
under the pseudonym Martin Porlock

The London "Bobby" almost is a symbol of the city. Londoners enjoy a sense of security when these tall constables are seen patrolling their beats. Terror grips the great metropolis when eleven constables are murdered in succession. English title: X. V. Rex

MYSTERY OF 31, NEW INN, THE (1912)
R. AUSTIN FREEMAN

A closed cab rushes Dr. Jervis● on a secret journey to a mysterious patient—Mr. Graves, who has all the symptoms of opium poisoning. The young doctor tells Dr. Thorndyke★ of his suspicions, aroused by the patient's strange attendants. Thorndyke, involved in a case concerning the will of Jeffrey Blackmore, establishes a connection between the two cases that leads to their mutual solution.

NARROW SEARCH, THE (1957)
ANDREW GARVE, pseudonym of Paul Winterton

Arnold Hunter's fashion-model wife has left him for another man. Hunter plots the kidnapping of their daughter. He is arrested, refuses to reveal the child's whereabouts, is convicted and sent to prison. His wife, aided by the man who loves her, sets out on a tortuous trail to find the missing child.

"Newtonian Egg, The" (1951)
PETER GODFREY

A hospital patient is found dead, poisoned after eating a previously unbroken egg. This "sealed egg" case is a mystery reader's mystery, dealing with the works of John Dickinson Carr and Jacques Futrelle. Detective: Rolf Leroux★.

NIGHT AT THE VULCAN (1951)
NGAIO MARSH

A young New Zealand actress joins the company at the Vulcan, said to be a jinxed theater. Backstage, emotions run high; there is constant bickering. Perhaps this is normal for a group of highly strung people before opening night. But murder on opening night is distinctly abnormal. Detective: Roderick Alleyn★.

NIGHT HAS A THOUSAND EYES (1945)
GEORGE HOPLEY, pseudonym of Cornell Woolrich

A recluse with uncanny powers predicts a man's death at the jaws of a lion. The doomed man's daughter and a sympathetic detective attempt to avert a destiny they suspect was conceived by a human power, in a terrifying tale.

NINE MILE WALK, THE (1967)
HARRY KEMELMAN

This is a collection of stories about Nicky Welt★, the perceptive New England professor-detective. The title story, which Welt constructs from a chance phrase, is one of the more compelling mysteries of the purely intellectual variety.

NO ENTRY (1958)
MANNING COLES

George Micklejohn, a young Oxford scholar and the son of the British Foreign Minister, disappears across the border into East Germany. Since the senior Micklejohn is the only Cabinet member who favors the arming of the Western powers with atomic weapons, the student is of great interest to the Russians. English super-intelligence agent Tommy Hambledon★ is sent to retrieve him. The apparently-naive George steals important state documents and wreaks havoc on the East German landscape. Meanwhile, the more experienced Hambledon impersonates a German officer as part of his plan to bring the student back to West Germany.

NO HERO (1935)
JOHN P. MARQUAND

Commander James Driscoll, a young American aviator in the Far East, gets involved with a beautiful Russian, some sinister Chinese, an oil formula and Japanese Secret Serviceman Mr. Moto★, who must be at top form because the balance of power in the Pacific is in his hands.

N OR M? (1941)
AGATHA CHRISTIE

The Battle of Britain is part of daily life in England; the future of the Empire rests on the shoulders of a husband and wife team, Tommy and Tuppence Beresford★. They are staying at a sea-side boarding house where they suspect the presence of German spies, identified only by the titular initials.

NORTHS MEET MURDER, THE (1940)
FRANCES and RICHARD LOCKRIDGE

Pam is not dismayed when a corpse appears in the studio where she has planned a party. She is certain that she can identify the murderer by inviting all the suspects to the party. This mystery is suffused with the atmosphere of Greenwich

Village in the days just before World War II. Detectives: Pamela and Jerry North★.

OBSEQUIES AT OXFORD (1944)
EDMUND CRISPIN

Famous but fading playwright Robert Warner goes to Oxford University to mount his latest experimental drama in the college repertory theater. One of the actresses dies under mysterious circumstances that point to neither accident nor suicide, nor to murder. Detective: Gervase Fen★. English title: The Case of the Gilded Fly

ON HER MAJESTY'S SECRET SERVICE▲ (1963)
IAN FLEMING

A mass murder plot is conceived behind the closely guarded doors of the Institute, high in the Swiss Alps. Ernst Stavro Blofeld, SPECTRE's arch fiend, is the leader of the planned massacre. Ten gorgeous girls, hypnosis, skiing expertise, a Christmas Eve skaters' ball and the marriage of James Bond★ are elements in the adventure.

"Ordeal of Father Crumlish, The" (1963)
ALICE SCANLAN REACH

During his 48 years as a priest, St. Brigid's Annual Field Day Festival has been Father Crumlish's★ private Purgatory. For an entire hot summer day he has to consume vast portions of homemade jellies, pies, etc., judge contests and award prizes. This year, after the day finally ends, Father Crumlish cannot rest. He receives a phone call; a murder has taken place, apparently resulting from the day's festivities.

OVERTURE TO DEATH (1939)
NGAIO MARSH

The peaceful English village of Pen Cuckoo, in the days just before World War II, is an unlikely setting for murder. Violence is even less likely when the people involved include the Rector and his daughter, the squire and his son (who is in love with the Rector's daughter), the local doctor and an assortment of genteel spinsters. A baffling, bizarre murder must be solved by Roderick Alleyn★.

PATRIOTIC MURDERS, THE (1940)
AGATHA CHRISTIE

Hercule Poirot★ exhibits a rare humanity as he visits the dentist: petrified in advance, he is exquisitely relieved when

the ordeal is over. Later, the dentist is murdered. Other deaths
and narrow escapes follow. The Mother Goose nursery rhyme
used in the English title is a recurrent theme in the book.
English title: One, Two, Buckle My Shoe

PAYMENT DEFERRED (1926)
C. S. FORESTER

Mr. Marble was deeply in debt, the victim of black despair,
when chance intervened. He takes the opportunity to murder
a visiting nephew from Australia and helps himself to a well-
filled wallet. Mr. Marble's next killing is in the stock market;
he nets a small fortune. Like many other people who attempt
the perfect crime, Marble had not reckoned with his torment-
ing conscience.

"Perkins Finds $3,400,000" (1931)
PHILIP WYLIE

Former bank clerk (now self-styled detective) Willis Perkins★
is interested to see digging near the Manhattan Commercial
Bank and Trust Co. He warns the police but is, perhaps, too
pedantic when he tells them, ". . . if I were a police officer,
I would give the greatest attention to such items as excavations
that are made in juxtaposition to banks." They ignore his
warning and the large-scale robbery he predicted takes place.
A large reward is offered but Perkins solves the case largely
to satisfy his ego.

PENGUIN POOL MURDER, THE▲ (1931)
STUART PALMER

Elementary school teacher Hildegarde Withers★ takes her
class to visit the New York City Aquarium. A dead man is
discovered in the area reserved for living penguins. Hildegarde
confidently decides to discover the murderer, much to the
consternation of Inspector Oscar Piper. The school teacher and
the Inspector often collaborate to solve a case.

PHANTOM LADY (1942)
WILLIAM IRISH, pseudonym of Cornell Woolrich

An innocent man is convicted of his wife's murder. The girl who
loves him races the clock frantically in search of the vanished
woman he claims can prove his innocence, in a justly-famous
novel of suspense.

"Philo Gubb's Greatest Case" (1918)
ELLIS PARKER BUTLER

The body of Henry Smitz is found sewn into a burlap sack and drowned in the Mississippi River. Emily Smitz comes to Philo Gubb★, the correspondence-school detective, and confesses that she is responsible for her husband's death. They quarrelled about wallpaper, she tells Gubb, so Henry must have committed suicide by sewing himself into a sack and throwing himself into the river. Believing there are easier ways to commit suicide, Gubb suspects foul play. He learns that Herman Wiggins had recently threatened to kill Smitz. On page 17 of lesson 11 of his detection course, it says: "In cases of extreme difficulty of solution it is well for the detective to reenact as nearly as possible the probable action of the crime." Gubb does, and finds himself all wet.

"Philomel Cottage" (1929)
AGATHA CHRISTIE

Alix Martin, at the age of 33, is swept into marriage by a man she scarcely knows. Soon after, she has disquieting dreams about her husband, and events indicate these dreams have a basis in reality. Alix becomes convinced that her husband is a Bluebeard and that she will be his next victim. This story has been adapted for theater and screen as "Love from a Stranger."

"Photographer and the Undertaker, The" (1962)
JAMES HOLDING

Manuel Andradas (The Photographer)● is a professional assassin. He deals in murder but prefers the euphemism, "nullification." Normally he receives a million cruzeiros, Brazilian money, for each killing. His current victim, an undertaker, seems a routine assignment—until Andradas learns that someone wishes to kill the killer.

"Poetical Policeman, The" (1929)
EDGAR WALLACE

Police-Constable Burnett, looking into the window of the Scottish and Midland Bank, finds the night-light off, the door opened, and the night watchman, Arthur Malling, bound and dead from chloroform, with a number of fresh scratches on his palm. Lamberton Green, the bank manager, is found fully dressed with a bag packed. Mr. J. G. Reeder★ is called and recognizes Green as an ex-convict. Green's story is that he had decided to resign, leaving the directors his keys and a letter of explanation—none of which can be found. He had told his plans only to his lady friend, 30 years his junior. Constable Burnett is also attracted to the lady.

POISONED CHOCOLATES CASE, THE (1929)
ANTHONY BERKELEY

The mailman delivers a box of candy to Mrs. Graham Bendix. Shortly afterward, she collapses, her jaws locked and an unmistakable smell of bitter almonds on her lips. After the police have failed, The Crimes Circle, composed of six amateur detectives, takes over. They arrive at no fewer than six perfect solutions to the crime. Detectives: Ambrose Chitterwick★ and Roger Sheringham★.

POSTMAN ALWAYS RINGS TWICE, THE (1934)
JAMES M. CAIN

This popular, naturalistic novel is the story of an ambitious crime and a devouring physical passion. The involvement of Cora Smith Papadakis with Frank Chambers leads to murder, cowardice, drunkenness, a fatal automobile accident and an eventual execution.

John Garfield and Lana Turner played the leads in the 1946 MGM film version.

"Problem of Cell 13, The" (1907)
JACQUES FUTRELLE

On the premise that "the mind is master of all things," The Thinking Machine★, Professor van Dusen, accepts the challenge of two scientific colleagues to escape from a prison cell within a week. Supremely confident, he tells his housekeeper to prepare dinner for himself and guests one week later. At Chisolm Prison, he is to receive the same attention as a prisoner condemned to death—no more, no less. His clothes were minutely checked before he was led into the escape-proof cell and care was taken to ascertain that he could communicate with no one. Van Dusen made three small requests before his incarceration: he wanted a five and two ten dollar bills, toothpaste, and a shoeshine. The guards were vouched for—$25 wouldn't bribe any of them—and the heavy steel door was double-locked by the warden himself. To reach van Dusen's cell, one had to pass through seven doors. One week later, Prof. van Dusen was seated at dinner with his guests, recounting his escape from Cell 13.

"Problem of the Emperor's Mushrooms, The" (1945)
JAMES YAFFE

Impossible crimes are the specialty of young Mr. Paul Dawn★. With his feet firmly in the middle of the 20th century, he attempts to solve the murder of the Emperor Claudius in the year 54 B.C.

"Purloined Letter, The" (1844)
EDGAR ALLAN POE

A document is stolen and the Paris police suspect a particular government official who was seen taking the letter from the royal apartments. The letter questions the honor of a lady of the most exalted station, giving the holder of the document power over her. Despite the efforts of the police, the missing document cannot be found. They bring the problem to C. Auguste Dupin★. Convinced that the police have searched every hiding place in the minister's apartments, he pays a clandestine visit to the official. Upon receipt of a reward, he hands the elusive document to the police.

PUZZLE FOR PUPPETS (1944)
PATRICK QUENTIN

In war-time San Francisco, Peter Duluth★, a U.S. Naval Officer, has come ashore to spend his leave. His wife, Iris★, has traveled from Hollywood to meet him, but murder prevents them from spending time together.

"Puzzle Lock, The" (1925)
R. AUSTIN FREEMAN

Dr. Thorndyke★ and Jervis● are dining at Giamborini's when an unusual pair of gentlemen at a nearby table attracts their attention. Also interested in the pair is another diner, whom Thorndyke recognizes as Inspector Badger in an elaborate disguise. The bungling Badger loses the two gentlemen, but Thorndyke gets the number of their cab and sends it to the unlucky Inspector. Later, Superintendent Miller requests his help in solving a series of unusual robberies. In the course of their investigation, Badger, Thorndyke and Jervis discover a room of treasures protected by a puzzle lock which requires no keys and has 15 alphabets and 40,000 possible combinations. It has contributed to one death and promises to do the same for the three sleuths until Thorndyke deciphers a complicated chronogram.

"Ransom of Angelo, The" (1963)
VICTOR CANNING

The members of London's Minerva Club★ decide to kidnap a child movie star, Angelo Downy, and demand a ransom of about forty thousand pounds. Angelo has the reputation of being a troublesome child.

REBECCA (1938)
DAPHNE DU MAURIER

Maxim de Winter's second wife is a plain, sweet, gentle girl who loves her husband desperately. Though she lives with him in the great Cornwall estate of Manderley, she does not yet seem to be mistress of the house. Rebecca, Max's first wife, a beautiful, graceful, talented woman who had been drowned in a sailing accident eight months ago, dominates the gloomy Gothic mansion. The sinister housekeeper and devoted maid of Rebecca, Mrs. Danvers, Frank Crawley, old Ben and Jack Favell all play a part in the young wife's struggle for Max's affection against his memory of a beautiful woman.

RED HARVEST (1929)
DASHIELL HAMMETT

The Continental Op★ is sent to the mining city of Personville; he learns very quickly why it is more commonly known as "Poisonville." The night The Op arrives, his client is murdered, the first of more than a dozen victims. Nearly everyone connected with the Op, including a girl with whom he drinks bootleg gin, becomes a corpse. The police are as corrupt as the syndicate which controls this ugly city.

This novel, originally a serial in "Black Mask Magazine," was dedicated to Captain Joseph T. Shaw, who did much to promote the hard-boiled mystery while editor of that magazine. It was the first book to feature this anonymous sleuth.

"Red-Headed League, The" (1892)
SIR ARTHUR CONAN DOYLE

Shopkeeper Jabez Wilson comes to Sherlock Holmes★ at Baker Street with a curious story. He has flaming red hair and recently answered an advertisement seeking such persons. A rich, eccentric American had established a fund for red-headed persons. This fund pays red-heads four pounds a week to copy the Encyclopaedia Britannica in a rented office. This day, however, a sign on the office door read: "The Red-Headed

League is dissolved." Wilson is dismayed, Holmes is curious —especially as he notes Wilson's shop is next to a bank.

RED HOUSE MYSTERY, THE (1922)
A. A. MILNE

Apprehensively, Mark Ablett awaits the return to England of his black-sheep brother, Robert, after a 15-year absence in Australia. Shortly after his arrival, Robert is shot to death, and Mark is missing from his home, the Red House. Was it self-defense? If so, why didn't Mark, a man of impeccable reputation, stay to face the consequences of his action? Arriving to help the local police is amateur detective Antony Gillingham★, who performs in a light-hearted manner.

RED THUMB MARK, THE (1907)
R. AUSTIN FREEMAN

Dr. Thorndyke★, the medico-legal detective, attempts to capture the thief who stole the diamonds entrusted to Hornby's of London by a rich South African. The major evidence in the case is a bloody thumb print; the trial features some interesting revelations about finger prints. This is the novel that introduced Dr. Thorndyke to the world of mystery readers.

REPLY PAID (1942)
H. F. HEARD

Following his near-encounter with death, as recorded in A Taste for Honey■, Sidney Silchester takes a job in America as a word-decoder. He becomes involved with the sinister Mr. Intil and Intil's cryptic communication through the efforts of a medium, Miss Brown. Silchester has another narrow escape but Miss Brown and others are not so lucky. Mr. Mycroft★ attempts to solve the code while aiding in a hunt for treasure that makes "the Potasi silver, Inca gold and Eldorado itself, all rolled into one, so much waste product."

RESERVATIONS FOR DEATH (1957)
BAYNARD KENDRICK

Multimillionaire steel tycoon Hugo Breitmeyer craves anonymity and will go to any lengths to preserve it. In fact, there are rumors that he has committed murder to keep his identity secret. Many people have seen his signature on various contracts but no living person had ever seen his face. Blind Captain Duncan Maclain★ wants to find him but Breitmeyer would kill Maclain to preserve his secret.

"Retrieved Reformation, A" (1909)
O. HENRY

Three hours after his release from prison, Jimmy Valentine● walks into Mike Dolan's cafe, finds his superb set of burglar's tools still in perfect order after a 10-month stretch. One week later, a safe is cracked in Richmond, Indiana; then, a burglar-proof safe in Logansport is opened, closely followed by another in Jefferson City. Detective Ben Price knows Jimmy's habits, recognizes the expert cracksman's touch and sets out to find Valentine.

Casing his next job, Jimmy falls in love with the beautiful Annabel Adams, daughter of the bank owner. Love transforms Jimmy into an honest man and, for a year, he lives a quiet, happy life as a shoe salesman. Then Annabel's little sister is locked in the bank's new vault. Price is present when Annabel asks her lover to save her sister.

RETURN OF RAFFLES, THE (1933)
BARRY PEROWNE, pseudonym of Philip Atkey

After two years abroad, living within the law, Raffles● and his friend, Bunny Manders●, return to England. A changed world of crime awaits them. Now, the gangs have the upper hand, the fences are part of the monopoly and the freelance cracksman has been "muscled out." In their first adventure with the Black Bats, Raffles and Bunny prove their wits and resourcefulness have not rusted; they emerge glistening, pockets filled with diamonds and coin of the realm. English title: Raffles After Dark

RIDDLE OF THE AMBER SHIP, THE (1924)
MARY E. & THOMAS W. HANSHEW

Young Ching Loo, the schoolboy son of an important Chinese governor, brings to England his collection of carved gems, including an historic, intricately carved piece of amber in the shape of a junk. Scotland Yard is warned that a plot is afoot to attack the young prince and rob him of the priceless collection of gems. Detective Hamilton Cleek★, entrusted with the task of guarding the boy, takes him to live with the famed Oxford don, Octavius Spender. During the night, a shot rings out, a woman screams and the don is discovered murdered. The prince and the jade ship are gone. English title: The Amber Junk

RIDDLE OF THE NIGHT, THE (1915)
THOMAS W. HANSHEW

As Superintendent Maverick Narkom of Scotland Yard drives home in his limousine late one night, he and his chauffeur hear a shot and a cry. They find a man murdered and nailed to a wall; cabalistic figures are scrawled across his shirt front with axle grease. Hamilton Cleek★ is called to take charge of the case.

RIDDLE OF THE YELLOW ZURI, THE (1930)
HARRY STEPHEN KEELER

Clifford Carson, agent of a new Federal bureau for the investigation of fraudulent mines, strives frantically to keep his missing foster father from being declared legally dead and the family property from being seized by a loanshark. Intermingled with the main plot, and connected by a series of broad coincidences, are a hunt for an Indian tiger snake, a haggle over a helium stock certificate and an embezzler who has invented a burglar-proof safe.

ROGUE RUNNING (1966)
MAURICE PROCTER

The idea of a police constable having his pocket picked and wallet stolen at a soccer game is a laughing matter to neither the constable nor the Granchester Police. It is the first in a series of crimes, including murder. Chief Inspector Harry Martineau★, as soccer fan and policeman, is doubly involved in a police procedural mystery.

ROOT OF HIS EVIL, THE (1957)
WILLIAM ARD

A nightclub singer hires private eye Timothy Dane★ to deliver $100,000 in cash to a vicious Miami gambler. The money is to be used to finance a Latin American revolution and the party in power is determined to prevent the payoff. The Miami gambler is anxious to punish Dane for getting involved with his girlfriend.

ROSEMARY'S BABY (1967)
IRA LEVIN

Hutch warns Rosemary and Guy Wodehouse not to move into the Bramford, one of Manhattan's oldest and most celebrated apartment houses. Some tenants were frightening, but the newly-married couple wasn't superstitious. After Rosemary became pregnant, a nice young girl in the building plunged to her death from a window, and Rosemary came to believe the Bramford was inhabited by devil worshippers who now sought to claim her husband and baby.

SAD SONG SINGING, A (1963)
THOMAS B. DEWEY

This mystery seems ahead of its time. A sympathetic private eye, "Mac"★, acting for humane, not economic, reasons, travels through Illinois to investigate the killing of a young folk singer.

SAINT IN NEW YORK, THE▲ (1935)
LESLIE CHARTERIS

When New York City's Police Commissioner receives a communication warning him to keep an eye on Simon Templar, The Saint★, he takes an amused interest. This changes, however, when a gunman, on trial for shooting a policeman, is acquitted and then shot by a "nun" before leaving the courtroom. Next, a New York Police Commissioner is taken for a "ride"—a first in the city's history. At this point, the police appreciate what it means to host The Saint.

SALT IS LEAVING (1966)
J. B. PRIESTLEY

Salt, an overworked and underpaid doctor, wants to leave his dreary Midland town, but has a problem that first must be solved. One of his patients, Noreen Wilks, a bad lot in precarious health, has vanished. Then the daughter of an elderly bookseller comes to Salt for aid in locating her missing father. Are the two disappearances related?

SCARAB MURDER CASE, THE (1930)
S. S. VAN DINE

Whimsical Philo Vance★, an Egyptologist of renown, is called when art patron Benjamin H. Kyle is found murdered in the museum of the eminent archeologist, Dr. Bliss. A rare blue scarab is found near the body. A sinister Egyptian servant, a string of perfectly planted clues and the blundering inefficiency of District Attorney Markham● and Sergeant Heath● are among the obstacles the nonchalant Vance must overcome.

"Secret Garden, The" (1911)
G. K. CHESTERTON

Aristide Valentin●, Chief of the Paris Police, gives a dinner party, in a house with only one exit. The garden has many doors leading to it, but there was absolutely no exit from the garden itself. Father Brown★, the gentle little Essex priest, finds himself in odd company and an even odder situation—a murder by beheading, with an extra head. Dismissed as a lunatic when he offers his solution, Father Brown is proven correct when the unsuspected murderer is a suicide.

"Secret of Headlam Height, The" (1927)
ERNEST BRAMAH

German spy Karl von Groot● is recognized by Parkinson●, the assistant of blind detective Max Carrados★. Von Groot, masquerading as a Dutchman named Karl Vangoor, is working as an assistant curator in the English coastal town of Castlemouth in August, 1914. With headlines screaming of the imminent war with Germany, Carrados suspects that von Groot's presence can mean no good for England. When he discovers the German agent digging for the golden coffin of Epiovanus on Headlam Height, which has a clear view of the harbor, Carrados risks death with a bold scheme.

SEVEN SUSPECTS (1937)
MICHAEL INNES

The president of St. Anthony's College has been murdered, seven distinguished scholars at the school are suspects. Matters are complicated by the fact that the murder took place in a completely sealed-off area to which no one apparently could have had access. Detective John Appleby★ is in charge. English title: Death at the President's Lodging

"Shot That Waited, The" (1947)
VINCENT CORNIER

A bullet, fired in 1710, wounds a bank cashier in 1933. How can this be possible? Detective: Barnabas Hildreth.★

SILENT BULLET, THE (1912)
ARTHUR B. REEVE

This is a collection of short stories featuring Craig Kennedy★▲. He puts himself under the influence of mescal in "The Artificial Paradise." In "The Steel Door," he is disguised

as a French dandy. He and Jameson, his assistant, take on the
1910 version of the Mafia in the exciting story entitled "The
Black Hand."

SMILER WITH THE KNIFE, THE (1939)
NICHOLAS BLAKE

Georgia Strangeways, cutting her hedge, finds a locket that puts
her life, and the future of England, in peril. This spy story
combines diverse elements such as an amorous cricketer, a
playful scientist, detective Nigel Strangeways★ and his uncle,
who heads the C Branch of Scotland Yard.

SNATCH AN EYE (1967)
HENRY KANE

An elaborate insurance swindle has Jayjay Fargo insured for
two million dollars. He plans to "die" in New York City and
disappear to South America to spend his declining years in
luxury. However, to prove that Jayjay is really dead, his
brother, racket boss Frankie Fargo, needs a corpse. The only
person known to resemble the insured man closely is private
detective Peter Chambers★.

SOME BURIED CAESAR (1939)
REX STOUT

Nero Wolfe's★ prize orchids get him into trouble when he
takes a rare trip out of his stronghold in Manhattan, the brownstone on West 35th Street. Some of the most distinguished
orchid-growers in North America are competing for prizes at
the North Atlantic Exposition in upstate New York. While
winning the medal and all three ribbons, he also solves three
murders—one of which is that of a $45,000 prize bull.

"Spy Who Came to the Brink, The" (1965)
EDWARD D. HOCH

A Foreign Office typist reports to Jeffrey Rand★ that she has
just seen a famous TV actor trying to break into the restricted
wing where the Message Center is located. The Department
of Concealed Communications is concerned because the security of Britain's diplomatic code may be jeopardized. The
situation becomes even more complicated when spies have the
actor killed.

"S.S., The" (1895)
M. P. SHIEL

A suicide epidemic hits the capitals of Europe—Berlin, London, Paris—accounting for 8,000 deaths in three weeks. Shiel visits Prince Zaleski★ to enlist his help in finding a cause for the rash of deaths. Curious strips of ancient papyrus, on which grotesque figures are traced, are discovered under the tongues of several victims. A strong smell of honey surrounds their mouths. Employing his powers of concentration, Zaleski establishes a motive for the deaths and sets out to solve the cipher, employing his mastery of Greek, Latin, and Spartan rituals. He finally uncovers a secret brotherhood, The Society of Sparta, which seeks to end pampering the weak.

STILL NO ANSWER (1958)
LEE THAYER

Peter Clancy★ and his butler, Wiggar, investigate the strangling of a Canadian poetess on an island off the coast of British Columbia.

"Stock Market Detective, The" (1962)
JAMES M. ULLMAN

John Trakker is president, board chairman and founder of Trakker Trucking Corporation. He tells Michael Dane James★ that he is unhappy and perplexed because the common stock in his company is rising in value. It isn't that he is unhappy about added profits; he has reason to fear it is a prelude to the takeover of his company.

"Stolen Romney, The" (1928)
EDGAR WALLACE

A splendid art collection, which includes an invaluable painting by Romney, is exhibited at the mansion of John Tresser, a millionaire whose fortune was amassed by rather dubious means. Chief Superintendent Peter Dawes of Scotland Yard visits the premises and, after a detailed inspection, is satisfied that if the notorious criminal, Four Square Jane●, attempts to steal the priceless work of art, her job would be cut out for her. That very afternoon, Jane leaves her calling card on the empty frame. The only clue is a long, white pin, similar to those used by bankers to fasten notes together.

STRANGE CASE
OF DR. JEKYLL AND MR. HYDE, THE (1886)
ROBERT LOUIS STEVENSON

Dr. Henry Jekyll, a brilliant doctor and chemist, had led a double life since he was very young. Publicly, he appeared genteel and circumspect; privately, he indulged strange vices without restraint. He became obsessed with the idea that people possessed dual personalities and were, therefore, capable of having two physical beings. Experimenting with drugs, he achieved his objective, committing the vilest acts as Mr. Hyde without fear of recognition. Lusting for evil, Hyde murdered Sir Danvers Carew and was responsible for the death of Dr. Lanyon.

It has been said that this celebrated novel is the only detective-crime story in which the solution is more terrifying than the problem.

"Stone of the Edmundsbury Monks, The" (1895)
M. P. SHIEL

After a close examination of a missing baronet's diary, Prince Zaleski★ discovers the reason for his disappearance. He also predicts the nobleman's death at a specified time and place. Attempts to recover a valuable gem play a part in this bizarre tale.

STOPOVER: TOKYO▲ (1957)
JOHN P. MARQUAND

Japanese Secret Service agent Mr. Moto★, Jack Rhyce of American Intelligence and his beautiful associate, Ruth Bogart, posing as his secretary, get involved in a struggle for political supremacy in postwar Japan. Rhyce's mission is to break up a communist espionage and terrorist ring known to be planning anti-American riots and political assassination. Working with an apparently harmless organization called The Asia Friendship League, Rhyce must locate and silence Skirov, a Russian believed to be master-minding the communist secret apparatus. He must also eliminate an unidentified American presumed to be Skirov's next in command.

"Sunday Fishing Club, The" (1962)
VICTOR CANNING

Young Renoblier, new to the Department of Patterns★, has discovered a pattern in the murder of eight former members of an association of Sunday fishermen. If form is followed, the ninth member will be shot to death.

"Tahitian Powder Box Mystery, The" (1964)
JAMES HOLDING

Mystery writers King Danforth and Martin LeRoy, who use the pseudonym "LeRoy King"★, are in the South Seas on a world wide tour. Anchored off Papeete on the island of Tahiti, they spot a box, apparently of Chanel powder, being dumped overboard. Strangely, the powder's appearance is similar to heroin, chalky white.

TASTE FOR HONEY, A (1941)
H. F. HEARD

Sidney Silchester, who prefers his own company to that of others, has one great passion: honey. He obtains it from the village beekeepers, Mr. and Mrs. Heregrove. Shortly after one of his visits to replenish his empty honey jars, Mrs. Heregrove's body is found, black and swollen from bee stings. The coroner orders the bees destroyed; Mr. Heregrove readily agrees. Silchester, seeking another source for his beloved honey, locates Mr. Mycroft★, whose knowledge of science and detection are equal to his knowledge of bees. Mycroft tells a fantastic story about Heregrove's killer bees and Silchester returns home, not quite sure whether to believe the wild, fanciful tale. Silchester quickly learns the truth of Mycroft's tale, escaping a horrible death in a bee attack.

TEETH OF THE TIGER, THE (1914)
MAURICE LEBLANC

Cosmo Mornington is murdered; Arsène Lupin● is immediately suspect because he was remembered in the will. When the heirs to Mornington's wealth are killed, one by one, the police narrow their choice of suspects to two people: Lupin and Mme. Fauville. Because the Paris police muddle along with little success, Lupin—the chief suspect—must play detective to exonerate himself.

"Theft of the Meager Beavers, The" (1969)
EDWARD D. HOCH

The baseball-mad dictator of a small Caribbean country, "Jabali," wants his personally-trained local team to play a major league team from the United States. When he cannot get an opponent, he decides to hijack a National League team, and offers the job to Nick Velvet●.

"Thing Invisible, The" (1913)
WILLIAM HOPE HODGSON

An old chapel attached to Sir Alfred Jarrock's castle has a long history of being haunted. It becomes the scene of a brutal attack on the family butler, who is nearly stabbed to death by the dagger which is popularly supposed to haunt the chapel. The myth has it that an enemy who dares enter the chapel after night-fall will be struck down by the sinister weapon. Carnacki★, the Ghost-Finder, proves no human being could have entered the chapel and perpetrated the deed. Fortunately, he has the foresight to wear a suit of armour on his night-time investigation.

THIN MAN, THE▲ (1934)
DASHIELL HAMMETT

Nick and Nora Charles★ arrive in New York for the Christmas holidays and immediately become involved in a murder case. The dead woman, Julia Wolf, had been the secretary of Nick's former client, Clyde Wynant, an eccentric inventor reported to be working out of the city on a new project. Suspicion rests on virtually everyone connected with the case: Mimi Jorgensen, Wynant's former wife, who returned from Europe in time to have Julia die in her arms; Christian Jorgensen, who already had a wife but married Mimi to get the Wynant money; Shep Morelli, a gangster who had once been fond of Julia; Wynant himself; as well as Arthur Nunheim, an ex-convict who was later murdered, and Gilbert Wynant, an 18-year-old boy who asks Nick about incest and cannibalism. Nick gets shot by Morelli. Nora decides the detective business isn't such a great idea.

THOSE WHO PREY TOGETHER SLAY TOGETHER (1961)
DON VON ELSNER

The board of directors of a packaging empire hires business troubleshooter David Danning★ to protect subsidiary companies from a status-hungry gangster-turned-corporate-raider. The trail leads from Chicago to Honolulu, from stock-market deals to murders. Danning must solve the killings on the run from mobsters and police.

TIGER IN THE SMOKE, THE (1952)
MARGERY ALLINGHAM

Albert Campion★ is confronted with undiluted evil in the person of Jack Havoc, sometimes called The Tiger. He operates in metropolitan London which, in the argot of the underworld, is called the Smoke; much of the action takes place while London is enshrouded by fog. The Tiger has escaped from prison and is looking for a priceless hidden treasure. He does not care how many he has to kill to get what he wants.

TOO MANY COOKS (1938)
REX STOUT

Every five years, the Fifteen Masters—the world's greatest chefs—and one guest each, meet on the home ground of their eldest member. Nero Wolfe★ is the guest of Louis Servan and has persuaded Marko Vukcic, another Master, to invite Archie Goodwin●. When Wolfe makes one of his rare forays out of his New York City brownstone, he is shot in the cheek trying to solve the murder of a Master. At the conclusion of the case, Wolfe receives a most treasured fee—one Master's carefully guarded recipe for saucisse minuit.

"Too Many Detectives" (1956)
REX STOUT

Forty-eight detectives, including six women operatives, are involved in this case which centers on an investigation into the activities of private investigators in New York City. Nero Wolfe★ is summoned to Albany with Miss "Dol" Bonner● and they work together on the solution to a murder. At the conclusion, the woman-hating Wolfe invites Miss Bonner to dinner at his West 35th Street brownstone home.

TOO SOON TO DIE (1953)
HENRY WADE

Colonel Jerrod is told by his doctor that he has only six months to live. His estate faces financial ruin through exorbitant inheritance taxes—unless the Colonel can prolong his life for an extra six months. The Colonel and his son (who has a great deal to lose) evolve a fool-proof scheme to conceal the Colonel's death for six months but suspicion is aroused by the discovery of a body. Detective: Inspector John Poole★.

TOUR DE FORCE (1955)
CHRISTIANNA BRAND

Inspector Cockrill's★ conducted tour of the Mediterranean is plagued by excessive heat, unpalatable food and language barriers. The doughty policeman wishes he had stayed home in Kent. Cockrill's troubles are multiplied by the murder of a lady guest. His own existence is imperilled when he becomes the number one suspect of the local police—and finds himself imprisoned in a medieval dungeon.

"Tragedy at Brookbend Cottage, The" (1914)
ERNEST BRAMAH

Lieutenant Hollyer visits Max Carrados★, the blind detective, to relate suspicious circumstances surrounding the unhappy marriage of his sister, Millicent, to philandering Austin Creake. Hollyer had visited his sister, when she confided that Creake had made an attempt to poison her. Hollyer urges her to run away from him but, although she despises her husband, she refuses to leave. Carrados discovers that a passionate typist, an inheritance, gardening, kites, and electricity are involved in Creake's next attempt to do away with his long-suffering wife.

TRAGEDY AT LAW (1942)
CYRIL HARE

A judge in a British circuit court is forced to the wrong side of the law through an unexpected auto accident. There are further complications when one of the judge's colleagues collapses outside the Central Criminal Court Building and the verdict is murder. Detective: Francis Pettigrew★.

TRAGEDY ON THE LINE (1931)
JOHN RHODE

Gervase Wickenden's hobby is the study of crime. One day a railway laborer finds Wickenden's smashed body lying by the railroad tracks near a small-town station. Is it accident, suicide, or has someone tried to commit the "perfect crime"? Detective: Dr. Lancelot Priestley★.

TRENT'S LAST CASE (1913)
E. C. BENTLEY

An important London newspaper sends Philip Trent★ to cover the murder of millionaire financier Sigsbee Manderson. Trent matches wits with Scotland Yard Inspector Murch until he finds himself falling in love with the chief suspect. Trent deduces a brilliant solution to this baffling crime. Then, another solution presents itself.

TRENT'S OWN CASE (1936)
E. C. BENTLEY and H. WARNER ALLEN

James Randolph, an elderly philanthropist, is shot in the back. Chief Inspector Gideon Bligh investigates and immediately finds a clue that points the finger of guilt directly at amateur detective Philip Trent★.

TRIAL AND ERROR (1937)
ANTHONY BERKELEY

When Lawrence Todhunter learns he has only six months to live, he decides to commit the perfect crime against the most obnoxious person he knows. An innocent man is accused of the crime, and Mr. Todhunter has to prove the innocence of the unjustly accused. Detective: Ambrose Chitterwick★.

TROJAN HEARSE, THE (1964)
RICHARD S. PRATHER

Although published in 1964, this book is set in 1968, immediately preceding the Presidential election. Shell Scott★, hired to investigate an "accidental" death in the entourage of a pop-music superstar, is framed for a murder, chased by the Mafia and the police and is in a position to swing the Presidential election single-handed.

TURN OF THE TABLE (1940)
JONATHAN STAGGE

Dr. Hugh Westlake★, looking forward to a quiet summer in Grovestown, fills in for an old friend, Dr. Hammond. He sends his daughter to camp because she is getting too interested in the activities of their temporary neighbors, the wealthy Bannister family. Westlake then gets more involved with the Bannisters, even participating in a seance at which a death occurs. Further, it appears that Hugh gave the victim a fatal dose of "medicine." With these happenings to whet her interest, Dawn rushes home from camp.

"Tut, Tut! Mr. Tutt" (1923)
ARTHUR TRAIN

Edna Pumpelly, a wealthy woman and an insufferable snob, carries a grudge against her husband's valet, a respectable young Englishman named Beaton. Beaton does his best to treat her with respect, but when her husband leaves for Europe, Mrs. Pumpelly calls the police to arrest Beaton, claiming he had stolen valuables. Beaton, taken to jail, engages Mr. Tutt★. When the venerable lawyer learns of the injustice of the charge he promises the woman will pay for her flagrant abuse of the law and of Beaton.

UNHOLY TRIO (1967)
HENRY KANE

Private eye and man-about-town Peter Chambers★ is invited to a weekend party at a luxurious mansion in South Hampton. Chambers is to be paid an astronomical sum to get married for a short time—part of a political campaign to elect Huntington Arlington Bradley to the Senate. Chambers does **not** realize that his "honeymoon" idyll will be interrupted by murder and by a group of dangerous neo-Fascists.

UNICORN MURDERS, THE (1935)
CARTER DICKSON

Sir Henry Merrivale★ is marooned in a decaying chateau on the river Loire with the passengers of a forced-down airliner. Among them are the chief of the French police (in disguise) and France's master criminal (also in disguise), who has committed an "impossible" murder with a weapon comparable only to the horn of a unicorn.

VALLEY OF FEAR, THE▲ (1915)
SIR ARTHUR CONAN DOYLE

A coded message from an underworld informant alerts Sherlock Holmes★ that a plot is afoot against "Douglas" of "Birlstone." The detective learns that Jack Douglas, residing at Birlstone Manor, Sussex, was horribly murdered that very morning, his head shot away. Arriving in Sussex, Holmes notes the absence of the murdered man's wedding ring, a strange tattoo on the man's arm, and his curiously unruffled wife. Before the crime is solved, we learn that Douglas has long feared for his life. Years ago, in the Pennsylvania coal fields known as the Valley of Fear, he was a Pinkerton agent. He had infiltrated the secret society working against the mine owners and exposed it.

John Dickson Carr, among other experts, has singled out this Sherlock Holmes novel as one of the best classical mysteries ever written; certainly, its surprise solution is the model on which several outstanding mystery authors have based their best work.

"Vanishing Diamonds, The" (1898)
M. MC DONNELL BODKIN

The famous Harcourt diamonds are removed from the vault for the wedding of Sydney Harcourt to Lilian Ray. The family gems are sent to the jewelers, the setting to be checked. A new case is ordered to set off the stones to their best advantage. When a well-sealed package returns from the jewelers, it is opened carefully, to reveal a handsome brown morocco case —which is empty. The Harcourt family sends a note to the jeweler, informing him the jewels are missing, and suggesting a detective be hired. Shortly thereafter, a man arrives, identifies himself as Paul Beck, puts the case in one pocket, the wrapping material in another, and leaves. Five minutes later, a hansom cab pulls up to the door, and stepping out of it briskly, is a man who identifies himself as Paul Beck★.

VANISHING GOLD TRUCK, THE (1941)
HARRY STEPHEN KEELER

Angus MacWhorter★ and his crazy circus become ensnared in the enigma of bankrobbers and a truckful of stolen gold that vanished in the middle of a mountain tunnel. Light at the end of that tunnel is finally provided by shambling country sheriff Bucyrus Duckhouse in this parody of the locked-room novel.

VERDICT OF 12 (1940)
RAYMOND POSTGATE

Rosalie van Beer, a pudgy, middle-aged widow with a fondness for wine, is on trial for murder by poisoning. However, this is less her story than that of her jury—twelve people who hold, in their hands, the power of life or death. The book probes the lives and characters of the ten men and two women selected to judge Rosalie van Beer, and tells how their pasts will affect the verdict they are to render.

"Wally and the Three-Dollar Bill" (1960)
PAUL W. FAIRMAN

Eighteen-year-old grocery clerk Wally Watts★ attempts to apply the lessons he has received through the mail from the Watchful Eye Detective School. Wally is involved in a case with Sherlockian overtones; the most important clue is a dog that did not bark. One of Lettyville's wealthiest citizens has been stabbed to death. Watts arrives at the scene of the crime employing transportation unique in American detective history: a bicycle filled with groceries in the delivery basket. He reasons that his nemesis, Sheriff Smiley Keenan, would not otherwise let him near the scene. Wally's mentor at Watchful Eye, John Hayden, like the Sheriff, is skeptical of his pupil's talents. Wally has the last laugh.

WARRANT FOR X (1938)
PHILIP MAC DONALD

American playwright Sheldon Garrett, wandering through the damp fog of a typical London day, stops at a small tea shop for a warm drink. He overhears two whisperers plotting a crime. He knows neither the plotters nor their victim, only that a horrible crime will take place unless he can prevent it. He goes to Scotland Yard, but the police do not take him seriously. Fortunately, Colonel Anthony Gethryn★ hears his story and believes him. The monumental problem is finding the potential murderers. English title: The Nursemaid Who Disappeared.

WAS IT MURDER? (1931)
JAMES HILTON

Young Colin Revell, an aspiring writer of modest means, is summoned to his old school by its new headmaster. There is curiosity about the accidental death of a student named Marshall—the victim of a falling gas pipe. Revell's efforts seem to confirm the accident theory and the matter is dropped. Six months later, Marshall's older brother meets his end by diving into an empty, unlighted swimming pool. Revell immediately returns to the school to investigate. There are numerous complications; then, Detective Guthrie of Scotland Yard arrives. English title: Murder At School under pseudonym Glen Trevor.

WHOSE BODY? (1923)
DOROTHY L. SAYERS

The body in the bathtub wore gold pince-nez, nothing else. Lord Peter Wimsey★ was going to a rare book auction when he received a call for help from the architect who discovered the body. Wimsey, that man of many interests, cannot resist the summons. He is off to investigate the first in a long series of corpses.

WILFUL AND PREMEDITATED (1934)
FREEMAN WILLS CROFTS

Charles Swinburn suffers equally from financial difficulties and blind love for a worthless woman. He feels the only solution to his problems is to murder his rich, unpopular uncle and inherit a fortune. He meticulously plans his crime to evade detection. When the uncle's body is discovered in an airplane that has just landed in France, the police investigate. Swinburn must wait patiently to see if his effort will be successful. Detective: Inspector Joseph French★. English title: The 12:30 from Croydon.

WIND BLOWS DEATH, THE (1949)
CYRIL HARE

The amateur musical society's most ambitious performance has been rehearsed and is ready to begin. England's foremost violinist, who had agreed to perform as guest artist, has not appeared. An announcement is made that the violinist will not perform, and the audience is stunned by a request for a doctor. Someone had arranged for a death by strangulation. Detective: Francis Pettigrew★. English title: When the Wind Blows

"Winter's Tale, A" (1961)
FRANCES and RICHARD LOCKRIDGE

Captain Merton Heimrich's★ concern for people is in evidence in this story in which weather plays a major role. It is an unusually cold winter; an old barn and an old man feel the chill —especially since murder is in the air.

WOMAN IN WHITE, THE (1860)
WILKIE COLLINS

Walter Hartright, new drawing master for Frederick Fairlie's nieces, Laura and her half-sister, Marian Halcome, is on the way to his new residence. He encounters a strange woman dressed all in white; he later learns she is Anne Catherick, a patient escaped from a nearby lunatic asylum. When he meets the beautiful Laura, Hartright falls in love with her, despite her betrothal to the wicked Sir Percival Glyde. Walter leaves for Central America. After the marriage of Laura and Glyde, Marian moves in with her unhappy sister, much to Sir Percival's annoyance. The sinister Count Fosco and his wife (Laura's aunt) arrive from Italy and Marian learns that Fosco and Glyde have financial involvements. When Glyde tries to force Laura to sign papers, Marian realizes the evil men are trying to take Laura's fortune from her. Laura is drugged, falsely declared insane and brought to the asylum in place of Anne, who dies and is buried under Laura's name. Marian helps her sister escape and they meet Walter Hartright, who has returned to England to pay his respects at Laura's grave. They set out to avenge these injustices foisted upon them by the evil-doers.

"Yellow Slugs, The" (1935)
H. C. BAILEY

Nothing enrages Reggie Fortune★ as much as a crime committed against a child. When a little boy is accused of an attempt to drown his younger sister, Reggie is sure both children are victims of a third person. A killing occurs; on the body of the dead woman, a slug leaves a mysterious trail.

MOVIES

A brief selected survey of detective, crime and mystery fiction as seen in motion pictures from Archer, Lew to Wong, Mr.

ARCHER, LEW

Ross Macdonald's acclaimed private eye has had a difficult transition to the screen. His initial appearance was in a lavish, superior adaptation of THE MOVING TARGET with Archer well played by Paul Newman but renamed HARPER, the title of the film (1966). Newman returned as Harper in a screen version of THE DROWNING POOL (1975), but this movie fared less well. The California settings of the latter book were transformed to Louisiana.

On television Archer was first portrayed by Peter Graves in a TV feature made from THE UNDERGROUND MAN (1974), which many critics thought flat and without the depth of its source. That same year a television series starred Brian Keith as a weathered Archer often involved in the same complex family problems as the books, but the show was not well received.

BATMAN

Bob Kane's comic-book costumed crime-fighter first was brought to the screen by Columbia in a 1943 serial. Lewis Wilson, who has something of a Boston accent, made a properly aristocratic Bruce Wayne, the rich young idler who in secret is the bat figure, at war with gangsters. Wilson's speaking voice did little to conceal the shabby look of the serial, the rundown sets and props.

Despite its low budget, the chapterplay did manage to retain some of the verve and excitement of the original, especially in the characterization of its villain. J. Carroll Naish, as the fiendish Japanese espionage agent Dr. Daka, has his headquarters in an amusement park. Next to his office there is an alligator pit into which he drops unwanted visitors. Daka also can command zombies.

Forced by low budgets to use existing locales, Batman frequently indulges in rooftop fights, extremely exciting, especially when young assistant Robin (Douglas Croft) gazes horrified as his beloved mentor tumbles off a ledge. Happily, there are always telephone wires strung below.

Six years later, Columbia brought out a sequal, BATMAN AND ROBIN, with the caped crusader (this time portrayed by Robert Lowery) struggling against The Wizard, who had an apparatus on his secret submarine with the power to stop all electric motors everywhere. In this serial, the Wizard devoted himself to insane attempts to destroy Gotham City.

In 1965, BATMAN became a television series with Adam West in the title role. Burt Ward was Robin. In lavish color, this half-hour twice-a-week program, a "camp" reprise in which Gotham City, Wayne Manor, the futuristic Batmobile and other familiar settings were most expensively mounted. Batman struggled against some of his favorite opponents, including the umbrella-wielding penguin (played by Burgess Meredith) and the Joker (Cesar Romero).

The following year West and Ward starred in BATMAN, the first theatrical feature devoted to the crimefighter, inspired by the TV series and using most of its sets and major villians.

BLACKIE, BOSTON

Jack Boyle's light-hearted reformed criminal first was portrayed on the silent screen in 1918 by Bert Lytell, a year after the actor had starred as the Lone Wolf. In the 1920's, several actors, including Lionel Barrymore, performed Blackie. Perhaps a trifle more serious than most films in this decade was the BOSTON BLACKIE of 1923, with William Russell in the lead. Russell's Blackie was a convict so cruelly used by a vicious prison warden that, upon release, he vows to go straight and expose prison conditions. A reviewer of the day called the film depressing, making one "an unwilling witness to the misfortune of others."

Blackie faded into obscurity during the 30's, but in 1941 Chester Morris revived him for a series of more than a dozen films which outlined the character as a glib, often light-fingered adventurer, happy to bend or skirt the law in order to help an innocent caught in its machinery. Blackie is always at odds with Inspector Faraday, who is never ready to believe Blackie truly is rehabilitated. Blackie is footloose; there is never a continuing heroine. His closest chum is an eccentric art dealer, Arthur Manleder (Lloyd Corrigan). The city of Boston has nothing to do with the stories.

Among the better films in the series in the first, MEET BOSTON BLACKIE (1941), in which Blackie comes to the rescue of a girl being stalked by an unknown man, in a Coney Island setting. CONFESSIONS OF BOSTON BLACKIE (1942), like many of the entries in the series, deals with stolen art treasures. In THE CHANCE OF A LIFETIME (1943), Blackie convinces the Governor to ease the wartime manpower shortage by using prison labor in war plants; despite Blackie's good intentions, he is accused of the murder of a convict. Blackie often gives inspirational talks and magic shows to prison assemblies; one such show unwittingly helps a woman convict to escape, in BOSTON BLACKIE AND THE LAW (1946). The final film in the series, BOSTON BLACKIE'S CHINESE VENTURE (1949), is an unremarkable but solid Chinatown pursuit of jewel thieves.

A successful radio show developed from the film character, radio programs in which Blackie was "friend to those who need a friend; enemy of those who made him an enemy." As Blackie, Kent Taylor foiled a blustery Inspector Faraday in an early television version.

BLAKE OF SCOTLAND YARD

Largely forgotten today, Scotland Yard's Angus Blake probed his way through three very exciting serials. In BLAKE OF SCOTLAND YARD (1927), Hayden Stevenson in the title role is called out of retirement by the pleas of Lady Diana Blanton, whose father's formula for making gold out of lesser metals has been stolen by "The Spider."

The locales are in London and Canada; much of the serial is set in a grim, dark castle. Two years later, a sequel was made, ACE OF SCOTLAND YARD, with Blake (this time Crauford Kent) again recalled out of retirement to investigate the disappearance of a priceless Egyptian relic, "The Love Ring." The trail takes Blake to Limehouse.

The next serial, seven years later, finds BLAKE OF SCOTLAND YARD (now played by Herbert Rawlinson) no longer retired, but active at his desk at the Yard. His brilliant young friend Jerry Sheehan, an American scientist, has invented a ray with power to destroy over vast distances. ("Munition stocks will be worthless!") The Scorpion, "the most dangerous menace for peace in Europe," seeks the ray machine. His agents are everywhere, at all levels: some are delegates to a Peace Conference; others are munitions kings, servants, beggars, apache dancers; many come from gangs in both the Limehouse and the Left Bank of Paris. The serial flits back and forth with dizzying frequency along the corridors of the Peace Conference, and through secret passageways. The 1936 serial was based on a story by Rouk Hawkey.

Finally, Blake unmasks one of the delegates as the Scorpion, and he looks on proudly as Jerry presents his invention to the League of Nations at a special ceremony.

BOND★, JAMES

Ian Fleming's suave, virile secret agent, numbered 007 and licensed to kill, has enjoyed the most fantastic cinematic career of modern times, has inspired countless imitators and, single-handedly, has brought the pure screen thriller back into vogue.

Played with muscular grace by the previously little-known Sean Connery, Bond's lush high living, roving eye, non-stop violence and sexual encounters, all treated with high style, have made his adventures earn millions at the world's box offices.

Commander James Bond first came to the screen in DOCTOR NO (1963). A British secret agent and his secretary have vanished from a listening post in Jamaica; Bond is sent to investigate. Attempts on his life all seem to emanate from a mysterious island, where Eurasian scientist Dr. No (Joseph Wiseman) has barricaded himself against intruders. Making his perilous way to the island, Bond discovers another trespasser, beautiful Honey Wilder (Ursula Andress). Together they end No's evil enterprise: the deflection of American moon missiles sent up from nearby Cape Kennedy.

In FROM RUSSIA WITH LOVE (1964), the international conspiracy known as SPECTRE sends agent Lotte Lenya and assassin Robert Shaw to Istanbul after Bond, who has gone to meet a beautiful, and supposedly defecting, Russian decoder, Daniela Bianchi. The film proceeds through a wild tangle of flesh and mayhem, and ends with a fantastic chase over land and sea.

In 1965, Bond sets out after the villainous GOLDFINGER● ■ (played by stout, aggressive Gert Frobe), who has cornered most of the gold in the world, and now plans an invasion of Fort Knox. Bond's motives are personal as well as professional: Goldfinger has killed one of Bond's compliant girls (Shirley Eaton) by painting her body gold. Man-hating Pussy Galore (Honor Blackman), one of the gang leaders Goldfinger has assembled for his Fort Knox raid, becomes Bond's ally after one session in a hay loft, and in a climactic encounter in the bowels of Fort Knox, they win out against Goldfinger and his murderous Korean servant (whose deadly weapon is a steel-rimmed hat thrown with an executioner's fatal accuracy).

THUNDERBALL (1966) opens with SPECTRE stealing two atomic bombs by hijacking a NATO plane during a training mission, and threatening to blow up American cities unless a million pound ransom is met. The action is in the Bahamas, most of it underwater, climaxing in a battle of massed swimmers wearing aqualungs.

In 1967, CASINO ROYALE was filmed as a spoof, with David Niven as an aging, retired Bond rescuing his illegitimate daughter Joanna Pettet—her mother was Mata Hari—from the secret head of SMERSH, who turns out to be his nephew, Woody Allen. Orson Welles and Deborah Kerr are other spies.

Aso in 1967, YOU ONLY LIVE TWICE sought to outdo its predecessors in action and in the deadly gadgetry which is a staple of each film. Bond, in a hand-assembled helicopter, manages to down four fighter planes and spots a SPECTRE missile-launching pad beneath the false lake on a volcanic island in the Sea of Japan.

Upon completing YOU ONLY LIVE TWICE, Connery declined to associate himself further with the Bond role. After a worldwide search, male model George Lazenby was selected as 007, and teamed with Diana Rigg. In ON HER MAJESTY'S SECRET SERVICE■ (1970), Bond rescues, tames and weds the temperamental daughter of a Corsican bandit chief. Lazenby did not settle well into the part, and Sean Connery was persuaded to return as James Bond for DIAMONDS ARE FOREVER (1971).

After dispatching SPECTRE chief Blofeld, who had taken up residence in Las Vegas, Connery made his final exit. Roger Moore, who had previously portrayed a very winning Saint on television, was selected as 007. A dashing and popular Bond, he tackled villains and voodoo in LIVE AND LET DIE (1971), and went to the Far East to stop THE MAN WITH THE GOLDEN GUN (1974), with Christopher Lee in the title role. Moore is next scheduled to play Bond in THE SPY WHO LOVED ME.

CAT AND THE CANARY, THE

Made in 1927, this film was an early model for the genre of creaking-house melodramas, imitated for decades thereafter. Based on the stage thriller by John Willard, the story was transcended by the camera of Paul Leni, the great German director who made every billowing curtain fraught with terror. The sliding panels, clutching hands and black-cloaked mystery killers which he introduced have become hallowed traditions of the film melodrama, as has the heroine (Laura La Plante), caught in claustrophobic terror.

The house itself is the film's most important prop, and is introduced first: a wildly haunted pile whose eccentric millionaire owner dies under suspicious circumstances. The relatives gather one sinister night to hear the will, the dead man's lawyer reads a clause saying that Laura, the ostensible heiress, must be examined by a doctor of his choosing to prove she is sane. After midnight strange things happen. An escaped lunatic is said to be hiding in the house. A hairy, evil arm reaches out from a wall panel above the heroine's bed and snatches at her necklace; when she—with more than ordinary courage—pries open the panel, the lawyer's corpse topples out, a knife in its back!

Doubt builds as to the girl's sanity, and she herself begins to lose control, especially when battered by the fake doctor who has arrived to examine her mind—his wild-eyed, deranged face borrowed straight from the mad psychiatrist of the German "The Cabinet of Dr. Caligari." At the end, Laura and the witless, comedy-relief hero prove it is all a relative's plot to filch the inheritance, and daylight sweeps away the evil shadows.

A 1939 Paramount remake, with Bob Hope and Paulette Goddard, set the old mansion in the Louisiana bayous, and had more than its share of paintings with rolling eyes, sliding walls, bodies and chills.

CHAN★, CHARLIE

Aside from Sherlock Holmes★ ■, the most durable and popular detective in films is the affable, middle-aged Charlie Chan of the Honolulu Police. It is notable that he has never been portrayed on the screen by a Chinese. Indeed, early films based on Earl Derr Biggers' Chan books underplayed the Oriental detective or even eliminated him, perhaps in concession to the prejudices of the time. In the character's film debut, a Pathé serial HOUSE WITHOUT A KEY■ (1926), made from the book, Chan was listed twelfth in the cast, and played by the Japanese actor George Kuwa. The great German director Paul Leni gave Chan more footage in his stylized THE CHINESE PARROT■ of 1928, assigning the role to the noted Japanese villain Sojin, but in 1929 the Fox Studio, in BEHIND THAT CURTAIN■ changed the detective to a Scotland Yard Inspector, with Chan (played by English actor E. L. Park) relegated to two brief appearances, and listed last in the credits.

In 1931, when Fox decided to film CHARLIE CHAN CARRIES ON with a Chan more closely patterned on the wise, philosophic Chinese policeman Biggers had created, they gave the role to Swedish-born Warner Oland. He had appeared in silent serials as an Oriental villain menacing Pearl White. The role of mild-mannered Charlie was an abrupt change, but not too large a risk on the studio's part; the plot is so structured Chan does not appear until fairly close to the end of the film. Oland was a sensation and Chan was in full charge of investigations in dozens of films over the next two decades.

The story of CHARLIE CHAN CARRIES ON concerns a group of wealthy people on a round-the-world tour. In London, one of their number is found murdered, but Scotland Yard can find no clues, and cannot keep the group from continuing its journey. In Paris, two new murders are again unsolved, and the tour, now accompanied by a police officer, continues to Honolulu where the policeman becomes the target. His friend, Charlie Chan, of the Honolulu Police, is engaged to join the cruise on its last lap, to San Francisco, and solves the case.

Much of Chan's popularity was based on common elements running through the films. Almost always they end with Chan gathering his suspects and pointing a finger: "You are murderer!" In all the films one or more of his Americanized off-spring try to help "Pop" solve the case; they fail and paternal wisdom wins out. Also characteristic are the quasi-Confucian aphorisms Chan offers during his investigations: "Clue like treasure buried in snow. Sooner or later it come to surface."

CHARLIE CHAN AT THE OPERA (1936) featured Boris Karloff as a deranged opera singer—with dubbed voice he sings Mephistopheles in an operatic interlude composed for the film by Oscar Levant. It is during that performance that the singer's faithless wife and her lover are murdered, but Chan orders the opera to be restaged, and proves Karloff committed neither killing.

The golden age of the Chan films lasted through the thirties. Chan traveled around the world, giving the series interesting locations such as CHARLIE CHAN IN LONDON (1934), IN PARIS (1935), IN EGYPT (1935)—notable for the early appearance of Rita Hayworth, then known as Rita Cansino—CHARLIE CHAN AT THE OLYMPICS (Berlin, 1937), CHARLIE CHAN ON BROADWAY (1937).

Warner Oland died in 1938, but the series lost no ground with Sidney Toler replacing him. Indeed, CHARLIE CHAN ON TREASURE ISLAND (1939) is considered by many critics to be the best of all. While it follows the familiar rituals and devices of the series, the film is original in plot with a well-concealed murderer and a surprise climax. Investigating the death of a young writer, Chan encounters a sinister, bearded psychic named Dr. Zodiac, many of whose "clients" have committed suicide. Chan joins forces with a magician, "The Great Rhandini," to expose Zodiac as a blackmailer. Zodiac apparently is killed, but Rhandini's assistant, in a trance, warns the detective his life is in danger, and in a dramatic climax Chan and his son expose Zodiac during Rhandini's stage magic show.

In 1944, Monogram picked up the series. When Sidney Toler died in 1947 the role went to Roland Winters. The last Chan film, in 1949, was SKY DRAGON, about murder on board a plane in flight, a locked-room problem in the clouds.

J. Carroll Naish played Chan in a brief television series made in England The first Chan film in color, made for television, has a non-Chinese, Ross Martin, playing the Chinese detective.

CHARLES★, NICK and NORA

The light-hearted film series based on Dashiell Hammett's sophisticated New York couple began with THE THIN MAN■ made by MGM in 1934. Nick was played by William Powell and Myrna Loy was switch-cast as Nora Charles after years of playing sultry Oriental villainesses. Directed by W.S. Van

Dyke, it was an instant success, arising, perhaps, not just from its mystery and adventure, but from the portrayal of the carefree, alcoholic good life of the Charles' and their terrier, Asta. The title of the film was then retained for the series, although "The Thin Man" is not Nick Charles but the first victim.

The story starts as the daughter (Maureen O'Sullivan) of a missing inventor pleads with Nick Charles to find him. The inventor's secretary is found murdered; he had been her lover and it is assumed he killed her, but Nick is suspicious. A charred body which Asta finds in the ruins of the inventor's wrecked laboratory turns out to be the scientist's, and the story builds to a zany party where Nick closes in on the killer.

The film's popularity assured a sequel two years later, although, in the interim, the Charles' winning ways were duplicated in dozens of other mystery thrillers. AFTER THE THIN MAN finds Nora's cousin (Elissa Landi) accused of shooting her errant husband. Nick casually throws her gun into the river and sets about trying to clear her name. James Stewart appears as the cousin's former sweetheart, too easygoing and nice to be suspected of being an insane, jealous killer. The film ends with Nora announcing that she is about to have a baby.

The child, Nick, Jr., makes his appearance in ANOTHER THIN MAN (1939), in which Nora's old guardian (C. Aubrey Smith) is threatened and then murdered, and his daughter (Virginia Grey) is involved with a gangster. The next film, SHADOW OF THE THIN MAN (1941), has Nick at the races investigating the death of a jockey, while at home he sets a good example for his growing son by drinking milk instead of martinis. In THE THIN MAN GOES HOME (1944) he is visiting his elderly parents in their peaceful hamlet when a local youth is killed. Nick connects the boy's amateur paintings to an espionage ring and stolen plans for a new propeller.

The final film in the series, SONG OF THE THIN MAN (1947), takes Nick and Nora, investigating the shooting of a shipboard band leader, on a tour of jazz haunts, and thus offers some choice swing music of the 40's. Gloria Grahame, a sizzling band singer, also is killed. Nick gives a shipboard party designed, as are most of the Charles' parties, to corner the murderer.

Ten years later, Peter Lawford and Phyllis Kirk starred in a television reprise of the "Thin Man" characters.

A recent attempt (1974) to bring the Charles' charms to late-night television, with Craig Stevens and Jo Ann Pflug in the leads, and with the late hour permitting the couple freer rein on their drinking habits and sexual innuendos, was not a success.

CRANE★, BILL

Bill Crane, based on the Jonathan Latimer novels and delineated by Preston Foster in three Universal Studios "Crime Club" features, lives in a Depression world of greys and blacks, of lengthening shadows and growing desperation. It is a world of city prisons and lawyers' offices, of small businesses on the edge of bankruptcy and criminality, of bars upon bars. Through it moves Bill Crane, too glib and often too drunk to be defeated by this world, and too clever not to snatch some personal victories.

The films are realistic stories of crime and people. Bill is a product of his hard times, tough and resilient. A private detective, Crane has a devotion to alcohol rivalling Holmes' study of the varieties of cigar ash. When we first meet him in THE WESTLAND CASE (1937), unsteady, heavy-lidded Bill successfully determines the type of whiskey a stranger has imbibed merely by sniffing his breath! In this film, Bill saves a convicted man from the electric chair at almost the last minute.

LADY IN THE MORGUE (1938) is the story of a girl found hanged in a hotel bathroom; Bill believes she is a missing society girl, but finds this identification difficult to prove when the body vanishes from the morgue. Bill's final case, THE LAST WARNING (1938), takes him to Los Angeles, where he tangles with a rich, troubled family threatened with kidnapping and murder.

CRIME DOCTOR, THE

Medical detectives are rare on the screen. Doctor Robert Ordway was such a specialist; most of his cases involved the mentally aberrant, and his solutions were psychiatric. Based on a long-running radio program, at a time when psychiatry was entering its first big vogue as a dramatic device, the Crime Doctor was ready to answer any problems with glib Freudian generalities. The character was created by Max Marcin first on radio.

In the first of a series of nine films, CRIME DOCTOR (1943) Ordway (Warner Baxter) is a noted criminal psychiatrist and head of a parole board, whose past is obscured by amnesia. A convict whose parole is denied reveals that Ordway once was the leader of a criminal gang, but Ordway's many subsequent good works exonerate him. In SHADOWS IN THE NIGHT (1944), a young heiress tells the Crime Doctor of a recurrent dream about a ghost persuading her to jump into the ocean; Ordway discovers the ghost is real. CRIME DOCTOR'S WARNING (1945) is about the murder of three girls who have modeled for an artist afflicted by spells; Ordway proves that the suspected artist is not guilty. The last in the series, THE CRIME DOCTOR'S DIARY (1949), deals with the efforts of a convict whom Ordway has paroled, to vindicate himself in a juke-box syndicate frame.

DRACULA●

Bram Stoker's Transylvanian vampire count first was made the subject of a film by the Germans in 1922. More substantial in its terror was the 1931 Universal Studios film, directed by Tod Browning and based on a 1927 hit Broadway stage version. Browning chose as his screen Dracula the play's star, Hungarian actor Bela Lugosi.

DRACULA begins in the Count's ancestral castle in the Carpathians. Officially dead for hundreds of years, he lives by drinking the blood of humans. Dracula sails for England inside his coffin; when the ship docks, every one else on board is dead or has vanished. Among Dracula's many English victims is a girl whose worried fiancé consults Dr. Van Helsing (Edward Von Sloan), an exorcist who has made his life's work a study of vampires. Van Helsing uses deductive reasoning and whatever clues are at hand to run Dracula down. Ultimately, he and the fiancé (David Manners) drive a stake through the vampire's heart.

Dracula has reappeared on screen many times since. DRACULA'S DAUGHTER (1936) starts immediately after the death of the Count in the previous film, and chronicles the exploits of his offspring, flitting through London society under the name of Countess Marya Zaleska (played by Gloria Holden) and victimizing girls of the street. Ultimately a servant kills her, piercing her heart with an arrow shaft.

In SON OF DRACULA (1943), the mysterious Count Alucard (played by Lon Chaney, Jr.) travels to the American South for fresh sources of blood. Notable among the many other screen Draculas is the English series, in color, launched by Hammer Studios in 1958 with HORROR OF DRACULA. Christopher Lee plays the title role.

Since then the vampiric count has had a multitude of adventures on the screen, and many interpreters, including black actor William Marshall (BLACKULA, 1972, actually a disciple). Even David Niven tried his hand at a spoof (OLD DRACULA, 1976) of the tradition. In 1971 Christopher Lee attempted a serious version of the Bram Stoker book, sticking closely to its events, but the resultant COUNT DRACULA was uninspired.

DRUMMOND,★ BULLDOG

H. C. McNeile's dashing adventurous young ex-officer Captain Hugh "Bulldog" Drummond, has had a long, varied screen career. In the 20's, Carlyle Blackwell and Jack Buchanan portrayed him in Britain, where Ralph Richardson and John Lodge were to follow in the next decade. In 1929, United Artists and Ronald Colman brought to the screen the basic Bulldog situation as outlined in the famed "Sapper" novel and stageplay: Drummond comes to the rescue of terrified, beautiful Phyllis Benton, whose uncle is being held prisoner by the magnificently evil Carl Peterson. In a plot which moves like a serial thriller, Colman jumps through skylights, scales walls, speeds about in motor cars, outwits evil-doers, and finally, cheerfully chokes Peterson's chief aide, a manic doctor skilled in torture. Joan Bennett played Phyllis, whose family name in later films is changed to Clavering.

The next year, Kenneth McKenna was Bulldog in TEMPLE TOWER, an adventure involving murder and robbery at a locked, guarded estate with a secret passageway. In 1934, Ronald Colman returned in BULLDOG DRUMMOND STRIKES BACK: villainous prince Warner Oland (who by then had been playing Charlie Chan for several years) has kidnapped heroine Loretta Young.

Three years later, Paramount cast Ray Milland as "young Hughie Drummond" in BULLDOG DRUMMOND ESCAPES, a retelling of the Phyllis Clavering-Carl Peterson situation. In England, also in 1937, John Lodge as BULLDOG DRUMMOND AT BAY escaped from a poison-gas room and married a secret service agent. Later in the same year, Paramount turned the property into a series, with John Howard as Hugh Drummond. Heather Angel played Phyllis in most of the films, and Colonel Nielson of Scotland Yard was portrayed first by John Barrymore, and then by H. B. Warner. A recurring theme in the films is Hugh's ever-impending marriage to Phyllis, which events always prevent. In BULLDOG DRUMMOND COMES BACK (1937), Peterson's insane widow plots to kidnap Phyllis; giving Barrymore the opportunity to lurk through Limehouse in a variety of disguises. BULLDOG DRUMMOND'S REVENGE (1937) has the hero tracking down a missing explosives formula, and BULLDOG DRUMMOND'S PERIL (1938), a formula for manufactured diamonds. In BULLDOG DRUMMOND IN AFRICA (1938) master spy J. Carroll Naish ties Colonel Nielson to a post facing a flimsily-chained hungry lion. ARREST BULLDOG DRUMMOND (1938) follows Hugh in pursuit of a villain with a death ray aboard a boat carrying Phyllis as a passenger. In BULLDOG DRUMMOND'S SECRET POLICE (1939), Hugh and Phyllis are about to be married in an old family residence, whose foundations are discovered to conceal underground passages, an underground river, torture rooms, a hidden treasure, and a corpse. BULLDOG DRUMMOND'S BRIDE (1939) takes Hugh on a foot-race through a traffic snarl on High Regent Street after a bank robbery, and a chase across rooftops of a French town. At the end of the film Hugh and Phyllis actually marry.

In 1947, Coumbia revived the character with Ron Randell as a less flamboyant, unmarried Drummond. In BULLDOG DRUMMOND AT BAY, Hugh sees two men carry off a supposed drunk; this leads him to discover a fortune in gems, hidden in a doll. BULLDOG DRUMMOND STRIKES BACK (1947) requires him to determine which of two girls is heiress to a large estate. The following year, 20th Century Fox picked up the character with Tom Conway (he had played his last Falcon the year before) as a drier, more mature Hugh, again unmarried, with teenager Terry Kilburn as a live-in boy assistant. THE CHALLENGE (1948) is a hunt for the hidden gold of a murdered sea captain; the secret is a code stitched into the sails of a ship model. THIRTEEN LEAD SOLDIERS (1948) is the search for the key to a treasure hidden in a secret compartment behind an old fireplace.

In 1951, MGM conceived a middle-aged Hugh Dummond (Walter Pidgeon) called from retirement by an anxious Scotland Yard powerless to cope with a series of large-scale robberies committed by a gang using radar, walkie-talkies, and commando tactics.

For over a decade Captain Drummond seemed too much of an old-fashioned Establishment hero for popular appeal. But in 1967, in the wake of the James Bond series, Richard Johnson was selected as a new, virile, mod Hugh Drummond. Muscular, though urbane, polished, and distinctly upper-class, Hugh is an insurance investigator in DEADLIER THAN THE MALE, tackling a band of assassins delivering international oil properties worth millions into the hands of Carl Peterson (played by Nigel Green). Hugh is a bachelor with a boy assistant, though he has an eye for the ladies. Elke Sommer and Sylva Koscina are cool, spirited killers with an amazing arsenal of murder devices. The film ends with a memorable battle between Hugh and Peterson among the towering pieces on a gigantic death-trap chessboard. A sequel, SOME GIRLS DO (1971), has Peterson (now played by James Villiers) pulling down Britain's supersonic airliner, with the aid of another team of deadly girls (Daliah Lavi and Bebe Loncar), who are programmed with "artificial brains."

FALCON★, THE

Michael Arlen's insouciant Gay Stanhope Falcon was advanced from his earlier decade to the 40's by RKO Pictures to replace their series on "The Saint." Both are debonair, jovial scoundrels, often living by their wits, almost always tangling with the police. Both are irresistible to women; nearly every pretty girl they meet has a problem—missing jewels, vanished uncle, unjust accusations—for the adventurer to solve. Both were played most often by George Sanders.

Gay Lawrence is introduced in THE GAY FALCON■ (1941) as a bored young upperclass type who promises to enter the family brokerage house and abandon his amateur sleuthing but changes his mind when Wendy Barrie asks him to uncover a gang of jewel thieves. The third film in the series, THE FALCON TAKES OVER (1942), is a loose adaptation of Raymond Chandler's "Farewell My Lovely," with the plot altered to suit the Lawrence characterization. The next, THE FALCON'S BROTHER (1942), marked Sanders' last appearance in the series; Gay is joined by his brother Tom in exposing a Nazi spy ring; at the finish Gay heroically gives his life to capture the spies. With George Sanders' career heading towards more important roles, RKO turned the Falcon series over to his real-life brother, Tom Conway.

Nine Falcon films featured Tom Lawrence; considered the best of the lot is 1943's THE FALCON AND THE CO-EDS, in which Tom investigates several grim murders at a girls' school. In THE FALCON STRIKES BACK (1943), Tom, trying to clear himself of a murder charge, follows clues to a lush country hotel, where several more deaths take place, involving puppeteer Edgar Kennedy and an automated puppet show. The final film in the series, THE FALCON'S ADVENTURE (1946), has a familiar plot: a girl begs Tom to take a formula for artificial diamond-making to her uncle in Miami; Tom does undertake the errand. When he reaches the man, he finds the uncle murdered and is himself accused of the deed.

FU MANCHU●, DR.

Sax Rohmer's incredibly popular Chinese mastermind made his first cinema appearance in a series of British short films. Harry Agar Lyons was an aristocratic, reserved Fu Manchu in these silents, released in 1923 and 1924. Lasting about twenty minutes each, they were episodes from early Rohmer novels, such as "The Fungi Cellars" and "The Coughing Horrors."

In 1929, Warner Oland, Swedish-born, assumed for Paramount the mandarin cap of THE MYSTERIOUS DR. FU MANCHU; "bloodcurdling" was the critics' comment. In the story, Fu Manchu's wife is killed during the Boxer Rebellion, and he swears revenge on all the foreign devils who suppressed the uprising. Soon he is in London eliminating half the British Foreign Office with ingenious murder devices. O. P. Heggie as Nayland Smith of Scotland Yard is the only effective defense against the doctor, who, at the climax, drinks poisoned tea rather than be captured.

A year later, THE RETURN OF FU MANCHU revealed

that actually the tea contained a suspended animation potion, and the same cast faced Fu once again. In this sequel, after much action over trapdoors and in secret riverside dens, the doctor is torn to pieces by a bomb in the Thames. But we are never quite sure—especially as in 1931, in DAUGHTER OF THE DRAGON, a dying Fu Manchu (again Oland, but with no reference to the bomb) makes his daughter Anna May Wong swear she will continue their vengeance against a certain Petrie family by eliminating the last of the line. Fu Manchu's daughter is just about to achieve her mission when she is shot down by Sessue Hayakawa who loves her.

In 1932, Boris Karloff, for MGM, took over the character, as a sinisterly civilized Fu Manchu, doctor of medicine, doctor of science, doctor of philosophy. In THE MASK OF FU MANCHU■, Sir Nayland Smith (Lewis Stone) must stop the Oriental from finding the lost tomb of Genghis Khan. "Once Fu Manchu puts the mask of Genghis Khan across his yellow face and takes that scimitar into his hands, all Asia rises!" At the climax, Fu Manchu, holding aloft the sword of Khan, is electrocuted by one of his own devices, commandeered by Nayland Smith.

After eight years of silence, the doctor returned in a 15-chapter Republic serial, DRUMS OF FU MANCHU, one of the truest representations of the Rohmerian netherworld. Again Fu Manchu (Henry Brandon) searches for the tomb of Khan and its secret scepter, possession of which would make him master of all Asia.

In the eary 50's, Republic released to television a series of thirteen Fu Manchu half-hour programs featuring a chubby, less vigorous doctor, Glen Gordon. Economies are evident—throughout the series, Fu scarcely stirs from his drab throneroom—but the shows borrow generous stock-footage chunks from Republic's earlier productions. The doctor attempts some rather sophisticated schemes, in one episode moving behind the scenes to gain management control of large industrial companies.

Changes in attitude towards the Chinese lessened the popularity of Fu Manchu until, in 1965, an elaborate new version appeared on the screen, THE FACE OF FU MANCHU. It was the first in color, and set for the first time in period, the city of Dublin passing creditably for 1920's London. Sir Denis Nayland Smith was played by Nigel Green, the late Howard Marion Crawford was Petrie, and Christopher Lee was tall and sinister as Fu Manchu. Experimenting with a poisonous gas with which he intends to make himself master of the world, Dr. Fu wipes out all life in a small English village. Sir Denis finally tracks him to a Tibetan monastery, which blows up—but over the noise of the explosion we hear the snarling challenge: "The world has not heard the last of Fu Manchu!"

The following year, in THE BRIDES OF FU MANCHU, Sir Denis (this time played by Douglas Wilmer) resists the advances of Fu's evil daughter, portrayed by Tsai Chin, while the doctor holds captive twelve beautiful girls, each a member of a powerful political or industrial family. In the 1967 VENGEANCE OF FU MANCHU, the doctor uses a look-alike to have Sir Denis accused of murder, and plots to replace with look-alikes all the police chiefs of the world, gathered at an Interpol convention. Finally, in the 1970 KISS AND KILL, in which Richard Greene plays Nayland Smith, Fu Manchu sends out infected girls to give kisses of death to unsuspecting victims.

GANGBUSTERS

Unlike the radio programs of the same name, which gave factual accounts of the apprehension of real criminals, the 1942 Universal film serial was fictional and flamboyant. The mysterious Professor Mortius threatens the entire city government: either all officials are thrown from office, or they will be killed. Mortius heads the League of Murdered Men, executed criminals who have been put into suspended animation through drugs, and then revived. From his headquarters beneath the subway system, Mortius plots such acts as the burning of the city hall and the harbor. Finally he is traced to his lair by a gangbusting special police force.

The serial is adapted from the radio series created by Phillips H. Lord.

GHOUL, THE

An otherwise unremarkable mystery melodrama, this 1933 Gaumont-British feature is significant as one of the few "lost" films Karloff made after achieving stardom in "Frankenstein." A print of this feature was rescued from oblivion largely through the work of film historian William K. Everson. The story is from the novel by Dr. Frank King and Leonard Hines.

Professor Morlant (Karloff) has stolen a fabled diamond, "The Eternal Light." His dying instructions are that he be buried in a special crypt, the gem beside him, threatening to return from the grave if his wishes are violated. The diamond is stolen, and soon Morlant is limping through the house, killing servants. Ultimately he recovers his diamond and offers it to the statue of an Egyptian god he worships. When the statue takes the diamond, the shock is too much for Morlant and he falls over, this time really dead.

HAMMER★, MIKE

Six years after Mickey Spillane's first rugged mystery burst on the literary scene, it exploded on the screen—in three-dimension process. Because of the physical restrictions of the 3-D cameras, I, THE JURY ■ (1953) seemed somewhat static and talky, but remained true to the best-seller, though the sex and the fistfights were softened. Biff Elliott was private detective Mike Hammer, with Preston Foster as the hard, compassionate New York City police captain. As in the book, Hammer vows vengeance on the murderer of the army buddy who saved his life. Suspects abound, most of them seamy, and Mike involves himself in a number of brawls, not all of which he wins. He falls in love with a beautiful psychiatrist, only to learn one cannot always trust one's doctor.

Mike Hammer's next screen portrayal, in the weird, sadistic KISS ME DEADLY (1955), featured Ralph Meeker. We see him first giving a lift on a highway to a distraught, half-nude blonde—she claims to have escaped from a mental institution, incarcerated there because she knew too much. Almost immediately a gang of toughs takes over the car, viciously beats Mike and the girl, and pushes them over a cliff. Only Mike survives; after several more beatings, he discovers a stolen lead box containing a radioactive element as the root of the problem. At a beachhouse where Mike and his faithful secretary Velda are held prisoner, the villain opens the box, an instant later the house is an inferno; we are not sure whether Mike and Velda escape.

Robert Bray then portrayed Hammer in MY GUN IS QUICK (1957), which opens traditionally with the murder of a B-girl whom Mike had befriended for the night. He learns her death is connected with precious gems stolen years before, and the trail leads to a deaf-mute.

Ultimately, author Spillane himself undertook to portray Hammer on the screen. THE GIRL HUNTERS (1963) features newspaper columnist Hy Gardner, and is concerned with communist penetration in the United States. Mike, gone to pieces over the disappearance and probable death of his secretary Velda at the hands of a political assassination group, is picked out of the gutter because the police need help in solving the murder of a Senator. Mike falls in love with the Senator's widow (Shirley Eaton), only to meet eventual betrayal.

Darren McGavin created an intelligent as well as belligerent character in the television series, MICKEY SPILLANE'S MIKE HAMMER, which ran for two years, starting in 1957.

HOLMES ★, SHERLOCK

Through more than six decades and more than one hundred feature films, Sherlock Holmes has been the cinema detective without equal; Holmes is the most popular and enduring motion picture detective of all.

Holmes' cases, and short film parodies like SURELUCK

JONES, were filmed in the earliest movie years. Their inspiration was William Gillette's popular stage dramatization of the great detective; in 1916 the elderly Gillette became the first important screen Holmes. Another important stage star, John Barrymore, attempted a definitive film version in 1922. Titled SHERLOCK HOLMES, it was a flamboyant portrayal. The English Eille Norwood was a more subdued Holmes, embarking in the 1920's on a lengthy series of short films carefully adapting the Canon; a stolid interpretation which exhibited a flair for disguise that included female impersonation.

In the 30's there were many Holmes interpretations. In 1931, Raymond Massey appeared in a version of THE SPECKLED BAND, and Clive Brook offered a stiff, British portrayal in two feature portraits of the super sleuth. The Watson● of the second of these films, Reginald Owen, then played an outsized Holmes in A STUDY IN SCARLET (1933), tangling with Anna May Wong in what is actually an old house mystery. Germany's Hans Albers played a private detective pretending to be Sherlock in DER MANN DER SHERLOCK HOLMES WAR (1937).

Considered by many the best Holmes of this period was England's Arthur Wontner. Quiet and meditative, almost shy, Wontner starred in five English Sherlock Holmes films; the best of them, THE TRIUMPH OF SHERLOCK HOLMES (1935), was an adaptation of "The Valley of Fear." Ian Fleming is the Watson of this production, and Lyn Harding plays a hearty, white-maned Moriarty. Other Wontner portrayals of Holmes include MURDER AT THE BASKERVILLES (actually an American retitling of "The Silver Blaze"), THE MISSING REMBRANDT, THE SIGN OF THE FOUR, and THE SLEEPING CARDINAL. All were released in the early thirties.

The decade ended with Basil Rathbone as the great detective in THE HOUND OF THE BASKERVILLES■ (1939). Holmes was the role for which Rathbone had been born, and he was associated with it so closely in the 1940's that he found it impossible to shed. Basil Rathbone had previously enjoyed a varied acting career in a wide spectrum of roles. Legend has it that at a cocktail party Darryl Zanuck pounced on him in sudden inspiration; "You'd make a perfect Sherlock Holmes!" There and then plans were evolved for a super production of THE HOUND, sparing no expense—a vast moor was built on the Fox stages, with $93,000 alone allocated for rolling ground fog. Holmes' London and Baker Street were painstakingly reproduced with the accurate trappings of the Victorian period. The film was a faithful and successful screen translation. Rathbone made another Holmes film for Fox, then—accompanied by his faithful Watson, Nigel Bruce, moved to Universal Studios for a series of twelve Sherlockian adventures involving secret agents and creeper murders. None of these films dramatized complete stories from the Canon; most used bits and pieces.

THE SCARLET CLAW (1944) was completely original. It brings Holmes and Watson to a meeting of a Canadian occult society, where supernatural forces are suspected in the murder of a woman. Holmes thinks otherwise, despite an encounter with a glowing creature in a marsh-fog. He turns up a vengeful former lover of the dead woman, an escaped murderer, so skilled at disguise that he has impersonated several villagers.

Others in the 1940's series were THE HOUSE OF FEAR, a reworking of "The Five Orange Pips," and SHERLOCK HOLMES FACES DEATH, based on "The Musgrave Ritual," but brought forward from Victorian times into the London of World War II.

For some years, Rathbone had no successor as Sherlock Holmes. Then, as England's horror star, Peter Cushing attempted a dwarfed and neurotic Holmes in a large-scale, color remake of THE HOUND (1959). Christopher Lee, another name associated with horror films, also has played an interpretation of the detective in Germany.

In 1965, young Shakespearean John Neville put on the deerstalker for A STUDY IN TERROR, an interesting attempt to bring a young, mod Sherlock Holmes to the screen. As Holmes, Neville is pitted against perhaps the ultimate British criminal, Jack the Ripper. Robert Morley is a portly brother Mycroft, and Donald Huston is Watson. The film is highly atmospheric, indeed, originally it was to have been called "Fog." (A novelization of the film by Ellery Queen takes the story into a new dimension by having Ellery attempt to solve the mystery from fragments of a newly discovered Watson manuscript.)

The Sherlockian cinema shows little sign of slowing. Billy Wilder's slightly irreverent THE PRIVATE LIFE OF SHERLOCK HOLMES offered some pointed hints about the detective's sexual makeup, but provided a romance to soften his heart. The more recent THERE MIGHT BE GIANTS, although not about Holmes himself, presented George C. Scott as a lunatic with the delusion he was the detective, and a lady doctor named Watson. Both of these films were released in 1971.

In 1972 Stewart Granger appeared as the master sleuth in a not very well regarded telefeature based on THE HOUND OF THE BASKERVILLES. Since then, however, the enormous success of the revival in 1974 of the William Gillette melodrama by Britain's Royal Shakespeare Company has made interest in the detective even stronger. Comic Gene Wilder contributed an affectionate spoof in THE ADVENTURE OF SHERLOCK HOLMES' SMARTER BROTHER (1975), in which young Sigerson Holmes, obsessively jealous of his brother's skills, tries to save England on his own, even crossing swords with Professor Moriarty. 1976 saw the release of a lavish screen version of Nicholas Meyer's SEVEN-PER-CENT SOLUTION, in which Holmes travels to Vienna to be cured of his cocaine addiction by none other than Freud himself—and becomes involved in a convalescent mystery of terrifying international complications—and of the television film SHERLOCK HOLMES IN NEW YORK, in which the detective (portrayed by 007 Roger Moore) comes to America in desperate search for his illegitimate son, kidnapped by Moriarty (John Huston).

I LOVE A MYSTERY!

Radio writer Carleton E. Morse, creator of "One Man's Family," also wrote the radio adventure series "I Love A Mystery." In 1945, Columbia produced the first of three films based on the program. I LOVE A MYSTERY was based on one of the most successful sequences in the radio serial, "The Head of Jonathan Monk." An eerie plot with several gruesome twists, it involves a millionaire whose resemblance to the long-dead leader of a secret Oriental cult nearly costs him his head. The following year's sequel also was grotesque: in THE DEVIL'S MASK, Jack Packard, hero of the radio and film series, discovers that a shrunken head donated to a museum really is that of a famous explorer, and a coded message is entwined in the braided hair! THE UNKNOWN (1946) is placed in a crumbling Southern mansion, some of whose occupants have been driven mad by the wailing of a phantom baby. In all three films, Jim Bannon is a rugged Jack Packard. Barton Yarborough was carried over from the radio series as his friend, Doc Long.

After some years in retirement, Jack Packard (now played by Les Crane) made a brief comeback in a television feature made from I LOVE A MYSTERY, this time joined not only by Doc (David Hartman) but also by a third pal from the original radio show, Englishman Reggie York (Hagen Beggs). Made after the Batman TV craze—and released after some delay in 1973—its attitude was outrageously camp and the adventure was not well received.

KENNEDY ★, CRAIG

Arthur B. Reeve's scientific detective made his appearance in the 1915 Pathé serial, THE EXPLOITS OF ELAINE. Professor Craig Kennedy (Arnold Daly) is a criminologist with a well-equipped laboratory, who pursues the new science of detection. He wages war against The Clutching Hand, a mystery figure who seeks to destroy Craig's girl, Elaine. Wild battles occur between the two opponents. In one episode, The Clutching Hand threatens to death-ray passersby on the hour;

in another, the Hand unleashes a poisoned gas epidemic. Kennedy's friend, newspaper reporter Jameison is the Watson who records the exploits.

In 1919, in THE CARTER CASE, also called THE CRAIG KENNEDY SERIAL, Craig (this time played by Herbert Rawlinson), faced such menaces as phosgene bullets and a vacuum room. In THE RADIO DETECTIVE, made in 1926, Craig comes to the assistance of a boy scout leader who had invented a radio-wave element wanted by the syndicate.

For ten years, Kennedy retired; then, in 1936, Craig (Jack Mulhall) returned to battle THE CLUTCHING HAND in a new 15-chapter serial, featuring a formula for making synthetic gold, and futuristic television with multi-screen monitors.

The early scientific detective was somewhat smoothed down, broadened and redressed to become the Philo Vance-style detective of the 30's. Neither type survived. Craig Kennedy's last known case was a short-lived early television series with Donald Woods.

LONE WOLF★, THE

The cultured jewel thief Michael Lanyard, whose alias added a new expression to our language, has been in films almost since the first Lone Wolf story was published in 1914. Silent screen star Bert Lytell played THE LONE WOLF first in 1917, followed by Henry B. Walthall and Jack Holt, among others. In 1926, Lytell re-appeared in THE LONE WOLF RETURNS —a melodrama in which a society thief is redeemed through his love for a girl met on the job at a masked ball. Lytell starred in three further films, finishing with THE LAST OF THE LONE WOLF (1930), a pure Graustarkian adventure involving a sinister Prime Minister and a Queen's missing jewels.

In 1936, THE LONE WOLF RETURNS returned again, with Melvyn Douglas crashing another masked ball and foiling a team of international jewel thieves. Next, we find THE LONE WOLF IN PARIS (1938), (Francis Lederer), mixing with Queen's Regent, Grand Dukes and crown jewels, and managing to avert a revolution.

Warren William assumed the role in 1939, for nine features. In the first, THE LONE WOLF'S SPY HUNT (1939), enemy agents try to make Lanyard open a safe where government plans for a new anti-aircraft gun are hidden. Beautiful spy Rita Hayworth attempts to entice him, but Lanyard resists her wiles. In this film, the obligatory masked ball sequence is strikingly surrealistic.

Lone Wolves in the following decade included radio actor Gerald Mohr and Australian Ron Randell, who made Lanyard's final screen appearance with THE LONE WOLF AND HIS

LADY (1949). Louis Hayward played The Lone Wolf in a brief, dapper television series revival.

MARLOWE★, PHILIP

Raymond Chandler's greatest detective at first was approached by Hollywood with hesitation: the studio seemed more interested in his cases than in the intelligent, introspective Philip Marlowe himself. "Farewell My Lovely" was considerably flattened and altered for a Falcon adventure, THE FALCON TAKES OVER, in 1942; ex-convict Ward Bond's search for a former girl friend only echoed the source. In the same year, Lloyd Nolan as Mike Shayne took over "The High Window" —the film was retitled TIME TO KILL—in which the search for a missing rare coin leads to a bizarre blackmail plot.

In 1944, Dick Powell took on the Philip Marlowe role in MURDER MY SWEET, a faithful version of "Farewell My Lovely." The film deals with the efforts of herculean ex-convict Mike Mazurki, to find his vanished girl. He hires Marlowe, who follows a trail that leads to a wealthy, self-destructive family and to murder. The motion picture won the first Edgar Award given by the Mystery Writers of America for the best mystery film of the year.

Two years later, Humphrey Bogart played Marlowe in THE BIG SLEEP■, an adaptation written in part by William Faulkner and directed by Howard Hawks. A rich, elderly retired colonel hires Marlowe to get his daughter out of trouble; drug-ridden, unbalanced Martha Vickers has fallen into the clutches of a pornographer and has posed for his pictures. Another daughter, Lauren Bacall, tries to keep Marlowe out of the case for fear her gambling losses will be exposed. A series of murders and beatings bring her over to the detective's side, and in a wild climax, both triumph in a shoot-out against the villains.

A few months later, MGM released LADY IN THE LAKE, which was directed by Robert Montgomery, and in which he portrayed Marlowe. It employed a subjective technique. The camera became the eyes of the detective, seeing only what he sees. Montgomery's face is almost never seen on the screen, except as a reflection at the very end of the film. The camera itself is talked to, kissed, assaulted. The subjective camera pokes its way through a complicated case that starts with a missing wife, uncovers a corpse at the bottom of a mountain lake, and tangles with a crooked detective, played by Lloyd Nolan. When the camera kisses scheming Audrey Trotter, it closes its eye.

In early 1947, George Montgomery was a muscular Marlowe in THE BRASHER DOUBLOON, a straightforward version of "The High Window." Marlowe is hired by a rich widow (Florence Bates) to find a missing valuable coin. Nancy Guild, the widow's secretary, is terrified lest somebody learn she had pushed the woman's husband out of a high window some years before, when he tried to molest her. That incident had been photographed, and the coin is being traded for the film in a round of blackmail and murder.

Two decades later, in 1968, MGM released a color version of "The Little Sister," titled MARLOWE, with James Garner in the title role. Gayle Hunnicut is a blackmailed starlet in a complex case of the innocent Ozark girl who hires Marlowe to find her wandering brother, and without a qualm, sets up the detective to be killed.

Director Robert Altman experimented with a bewildered, unsure Marlowe, coping badly with the changing values of the seventies, when he cast a scruffy Elliott Gould in an irreverent updating of THE LONG GOODBYE (1973). Many critics thought it unsuccessful. In a happier casting, Robert Mitchum portrayed a world-weary, aging Marlowe in a version of FARE-WELL, MY LOVELY (1975) very close to the spirit of its source and deliberately set back in the 1940's.

Philip Marlowe first came to television in the mid-50's on "Climax!" in an adaptation of THE LONG GOODBYE■. A 1959 TV series, with Philip Carey as Marlowe, was restricted by its half-hour format from exploring the complications of true Chandler plots.

MASON★, PERRY

Erle Stanley Gardner's famed Perry Mason is the only major cinematic detective who is a practicing criminal lawyer. This provides rich opportunities for dramatic courtroom confrontations.

The first four Perry Mason films starred Warren William. In THE CASE OF THE HOWLING DOG■ (1934), he tries his best to save Mary Astor from a murder charge, even though he thinks she killed her husband in circumstances no jury would believe, involving a maddened watchdog. Helen Trenholme is Della Street●. In the next year's THE CASE OF THE CURIOUS BRIDE, newlywed Margaret Lindsay is horrified to learn her first husband, whom she thought dead, is alive and a blackmailer, and she is his target. Mason calls on the man and finds him murdered. Della is now Claire Dodd, to whom Mason proposes! Marriage is forgotten, however, when some months later, in THE CASE OF THE LUCKY LEGS, Mason investigates the killing of a crooked beauty contest promoter who had skipped town with the prize money. In 1936, THE CASE OF THE VELVET CLAWS opens with Mason and Della (Claire Dodd) just married. Their honeymoon is interrupted by gun-wielding Wini Shaw, who is certain she has killed her husband. Mason proves another member of the family fired the fatal shot; he speeds off on his wedding journey.

That same year, Ricardo Cortez became Mason, in THE CASE OF THE BLACK CAT, with June Travis as a yet unmarried Della. The complex murder plot is taken from "The Case of the Caretaker's Cat." In 1937, Donald Woods took the Mason role in THE CASE OF THE STUTTERING BISHOP, in which an Australian churchman stammeringly asks Mason to clear the name of a woman who has been framed by her ruthless millionaire father-in-law. In the complicated plot, a substitute granddaughter is being presented as heiress to a fortune, the father-in-law is killed, and Mason's suspicions are aroused when he reflects that a stuttering man never could have become bishop. This was the last Perry Mason film.

It was in the courtrooms of television that Perry Mason made his greatest impact. Raymond Burr, who for years had played middle-aged heavies, was transformed into the perfect young American lawyer. For ten years, this hour series has stayed close to the Gardner model, surrounding Perry with a familiar group of associates: Barbara Hale as a warm, efficient Della, the late William Hopper as investigator Paul Drake●, Ray Collins as Police Lieutenant Tragg, and the late William Tallman as combative District Attorney Hamilton Burger●.

An attempt in 1973 to duplicate the fantastic success of the original series with a newer television version, this time with slim, brash Monte Marham playing Mason, had only a brief run.

MOTO★, MR.

John P. Marquand's diminutive and unobtrusive Japanese secret agent, Mr. Moto, was brought to the screen in 1937 by Peter Lorre. With very little makeup beyond eye-glasses and an individual hair-style, Lorre deftly created the Oriental sleuth. In THINK FAST, MR. MOTO and seven other films shot in a two-year span, Lorre personified Moto, even to the obligatory display of judo in each case.

The Moto stories ran the gamut from foiling spies and villains to adventure yarns in jungle ruins. The first few films were adaptations of Marquand books. MR. MOTO ON DANGER ISLAND (1939), set in Puerto Rico and featuring some highly culpable government officials, was based on a mystery written by commentator John W. Vandercook. The eighth and last film in the series, MR. MOTO TAKES A VACATION (1939), concerned a secret criminal genius seeking to steal the fabulous crown of the Queen of Sheba. The growing popular-feeling against Japan brought Mr. Moto's American career to a close.

In 1957, Marquand wrote a best-selling thriller, STOPOVER TOKYO■, in which an older, more communicative Moto returned; during the war he had been involved with the Japanese secret police. When this book was filmed, Mr. Moto vanished.

In the 60's, Henry Silva starred as a muscular, mod secret agent in THE RETURN OF MR. MOTO.

MYSTERIOUS DOCTOR SATAN

Eduardo Cianelli portrayed a super criminal in this classic film crime serial, made by Republic in 1940. He is the mysterious Doctor Satan, a madman who wishes to take over the State by means of minions whose minds he controls, and a militia of robots. The Governor is murdered, and his muscular young ward—son of "The Copperhead," a masked Westerner who righted frontier wrongs—assumes his dead father's disguise, a copper hood. Ultimately The Copperhead turns one of the robots against his master.

PERILS OF PAULINE, THE

The most popular of the early thrillers, this 15-chapter 1914 serial did much to lay the foundation for the genre. Its heroine, Pearl White, became the personification of the "girl in danger." The original story was by Charles Goddard.

Pauline Marvin is an heiress adopted by a millionaire, whose son, Harry, is desperately in love with her. Raymond Owen, the millionaire's secretary, is a morphine addict. When the old man dies, Owen becomes Pauline's guardian; he has designs on her inheritance. Owen knows every tout, gypsy, criminal, and animal trainer in the vicinity, and Pauline is put through a rapid succession of hair-breadth escapades. Ultimately, Harry is convinced of Owen's treachery, and Owen dies from an overdose of drugs.

Another PERILS OF PAULINE serial in 1934 had a different story. Pauline Hargraves and her scientist father have come to wartorn China to search for an ancient disk on which is written in Sanscrit the formula for an invisible poison gas. Also in search of the disk is the evil Dr. Dashar.

A 1947 Paramount feature titled PERILS OF PAULINE starred Betty Hutton in a fictionalized biography of Pearl White's serial career. In 1967, Universal Studios issued a camp comedy feature called THE PERILS OF PAULINE, with Pamela Austin as Pauline and Pat Boone as her swain. The perils are as wild as ever—the heroine is aloft in a space capsule, carried off by a gorilla, nearly frozen in a block of ice—but the film is a spoof rather than a mystery.

PSYCHO!

Alfred Hitchcock's 1960 adaptation of Robert Bloch's novel was a cinema milestone, the inspiration for dozens of psychiatric thrillers to follow. It was the all-time top-earning mystery film.

To give away the core of PSYCHO's secret would be to violate a surprise ending that has become almost legendary. The story concerns a secretary who has stolen $40,000 and is driving to meet her lover. She drives over lonely roads, through heavy rain, stopping at last at an isolated, decaying motel run by a sensitive young man whose hobby is stuffing birds. The motel's only customer, she talks with the boy, who tells her of his invalid mother, with whom he lives in an eerie Victorian house behind the motel. Later the girl hears the old woman shriek at the son for having neglected her. Then, as the secretary is showering, a gray-haired old woman with a long knife is seen through the curtain; she rushes in and stabs the girl repeatedly. Later the boy finds the body and sinks girl, car and money in a swamp.

The secretary's sister, lover, and a private detective converge upon the motel, looking for the dead girl. Each in turn confronts the terrifying old woman and her murderous knife—even though the sheriff of the town tells them the motel owner's mother has been dead for years!

POIROT★, HERCULE

The dapper little Belgian detective was portrayed by an almost unrecognizable Tony Randall in an adaptation of THE A.B.C. MURDERS called THE ALPHABET MURDERS (1966), made in England. Then, in 1974, Albert Finney in heavy make-up was an inquisitive Poirot in an extremely successful screen version of MURDER ON THE ORIENT EXPRESS; Richard Widmark is killed on a snowbound train, and all the suspects are played by well-known stars (Sean Connery, Lauren Bacall, Ingrid Bergman, Tony Perkins and Michael York among them).

QUEEN★, ELLERY

The great American detective first came to the screen in 1935; Donald Cook portrayed him in an adaptation of THE SPANISH CAPE MYSTERY, a tricky case in which a man is found dead on a beach, wearing only a cape. The next to play Ellery was brash comic Eddie Quillan; his THE MANDARIN MYSTERY (1936) retained only part of the plot and solution of "The Chinese Orange Mystery."

In 1940, Columbia Pictures cast Ralph Bellamy as an urbane,

scholarly Ellery Queen. Little more than low budget, formula melodrama, the series did give Ellery some of his familiar friends from the then very popular radio show: Sergeant Velie, old Inspector Queen, and Nikki Porter, a character introduced on the radio show.

ELLERY QUEEN, MASTER DETECTIVE (1940) restaged the first meeting between Ellery and Nikki, a girl determined to become a mystery writer, who, after she is rescued by Ellery, took a job typing his manuscripts. The relationship continued through all the films, though Ellery's constant complaint is that Nikki is more interested in sleuthing than typing. ELLERY QUEEN'S PENTHOUSE MYSTERY (1941) involved Anna May Wong, a murdered ventriloquist, and missing Chinese jewels.

Feuding stockbrokers brought together ELLERY QUEEN AND THE PERFECT CRIME (1941); ELLERY QUEEN AND THE MURDER RING (1941) was an adaptation of the "Dutch Shoe Mystery."

William Gargan then replaced Bellamy in the role. A CLOSE CALL FOR ELLERY QUEEN (1942) and A DESPERATE CHANCE FOR ELLERY QUEEN (1942) were investigations of blackmail, theft and murder, and the final film in the series, ENEMY AGENTS MEET ELLERY QUEEN (1942), offered a train carrying diamonds smuggled out of Occupied Holland.

Lee Bowman and George Nader are among those who have portrayed Ellery in television series. In 1971's ELLERY QUEEN: DON'T LOOK BEHIND YOU, featuring Peter Lawford in an updating of "Cat O' Many Tails," the family tree is shaken somewhat: Inspector Richard Queen (Harry Morgan) becomes the detective's uncle. The change was not well received. Four years later Jim Hutton was a young, clumsy, very sincere Ellery forsaking his typewriter to help his police inspector father (well played by David Wayne) in solving puzzle mysteries; just before the solution the audience is warned it is in possession of all the clues. The series, set vaguely in the year 1946, after an uncertain first season gathered a good deal of strength on TV.

RADIO PATROL

This 1947 Universal serial was based on a comic strip by Edward F. Sullivan and Charles Schmidt, and which heralded the introduction of two-way radios in police cars as an innovation certain to paralyze big-city crime. "Signal boxes are old-fashioned! Quick contact needed to combat motorized crime!" The heroes, uniformed cops Pat O'Hara and his partner Sam, seek to recover a stolen formula for flexible steel (. . . "it will revolutionize modern warfare!"), as they prowl in their patrol car through a sort of Casbah where most of the villains lurk.

RED BARRY

Starring swimming champion Buster Crabbe, this 1938 Universal serial was based on a comic strip of the 1930's. It follows a young police detective "Red" Barry as he searches for stolen Russian war bonds through the dens and wharves of a sinister Chinatown. One of the most effective of the Chinatown melodramas, the serial abounds in intrigue and in colorful characters, such as Hong Kong Charlie, singsong and simple in his contacts with the white world, but actually a skilled agent buying munitions for his wartorn homeland. Although the standard, traditional portrayal of sinister Chinatown is still much in evidence, there is considerable sympathy for the Chinese; even menacing Tong leader Wing Fu is clothed with nobility, and the ultimate villain turns out to be a white man.

The original comic strip was by Will Gould.

SAINT★, THE

Simon Templar, Leslie Charteris' dashing "Robin Hood of modern crime" known as "The Saint," made his cinema debut in 1938 with THE SAINT IN NEW YORK■. Louis Hayward, in the title role, is brought to New York by a citizens' committee, and is given *carte blanche* to rid the city of six vicious gangsters. Simon tracks them down, exposes corruption in the city government.

RKO then placed George Sanders in the lead for a brief series of Saint films. In THE SAINT STRIKES BACK (1939) he is again meshed in big city corruption, helping Wendy Barrie clear the name of her dead father, a police captain who had been convicted of graft. THE SAINT IN LONDON (1939) finds Simon unable to save the life of an ambassador he himself had hidden in a boarding-house. In THE SAINT'S DOUBLE TROUBLE (1940), Bela Lugosi does mischief with a substitute Simon Templar. New York police corruption again is the topic of THE SAINT TAKES OVER (1940). George Sanders' final portrayal of the role was in THE SAINT IN PALM SPRINGS (1941), guarding a very valuable stamp.

RKO produced another Saint film, THE SAINT MEETS THE TIGER, in 1941. Made in England, it starred Hugh Sinclair, who played The Saint with schoolboyish charm, unearthing a criminal mastermind at a British seacoast resort. For over a decade, there were no more Saint films. Then, again in Britain, Louis Hayward played an older, more serious Simon Templar in THE SAINT'S GIRL FRIDAY (1953). His investigation of a suspicious auto accident takes The Saint to a gambling boat; among those he encounters is gangleader's girl friend Diana Dors.

In 1963 Britain's ITC launched a weekly hour-long "Saint" television series starring Roger Moore, which lasted for several years.

SHADOW, THE

"The Shadow" started as an anonymous voice introducing a series of radio mysteries. Almost immediately he became a pulp magazine figure as well, evolving into the familiar black-coated crime-stalker of many identities, including that of millionaire explorer Lamont Cranston. Later, The Shadow's other roles were reduced to the single Cranston alter ego; still later, on radio, he was given hypnotic capabilities so powerful he could render himself invisible to all onlookers. Maxwell Grant was the author.

The only Shadow serial in films was a fast-moving 1940 chapterplay, in which Victor Jory played three roles: Lamont Cranston, The Shadow, and a Chinese named Lin Chang. All fought against a villainous mystery figure called The Black Tiger, in what chapter one called "The Doomed City." Earlier, in 1937, Rod LaRoque appeared as crusading newspaperman Cranston in THE SHADOW STRIKES—a mystery-mansion melodrama with the traditional suspected butler, and in 1938 he played The Shadow as a radio crime reporter, without cape or black hat, exposing bungling foreign spies in INTERNATIONAL CRIME.

In 1946, Monogram cast Kane Richmond as an athletic, darkly handsome Shadow-Cranston, in a series of three films. THE SHADOW RETURNS eerily opens in a graveyard; smuggled jewels are found in a newly-opened grave. Industrialist Michael Hasdon, who has claimed ownership of the gems, is killed in a fall from the balcony of his suburban mansion. Before the case is over, two more men fall to their deaths from that balcony, and The Shadow is suspected of their murders. He discovers that the purported gems are really capsules containing a formula for a new plastic; also he finds the killer's weapon, and proves his case.

In BEHIND THE MASK, Cranston interrupts his marriage because someone disguised in The Shadow's cloak has killed a blackmailing newspaper columnist. THE MISSING LADY has The Shadow investigating the murder of an art dealer and the theft of a valuable jade statuette.

The (1962) BOURBON STREET SHADOWS, a gangster film laid in New Orleans in which Cranston was played by Richard Derr, was notable mainly as the only screen version in which The Shadow makes himself invisible, clouding men's minds.

SHAYNE★, MICHAEL

Brett Halliday's brash Mike Shayne was the prototypal screen detective of the 40's. Less dour, more flip and self-assured than his 1930's counterpart, he and his colleagues enjoyed decidedly improved fringe benefits: more liquor, friendlier girls, and fewer beatings. Lloyd Nolan perhaps best personified him.

His first case set the stage. MICHAEL SHAYNE, PRIVATE DETECTIVE (1941), is hired by a wealthy sportsman to look after his daughter (Marjorie Weaver) while the father is away on a business trip. The story involves a lush gambling club which the girl frequents, where a murdered caretaker's body is found in a parked car.

Three more Shayne mysteries were released in 1941. SLEEPERS WEST finds Shayne on a San Francisco-bound train guarding Mary Beth Hughes, witness to an important murder trial. Attempts are made on her life, and the closed universe of the express forces an interesting clash of characters. In the following two films, Mary Beth Hughes is Shayne's fiancée, unhappy with his line of work. He is headed for the marriage bureau in DRESSED TO KILL when he stumbles on a double murder, and must discover how two people could be killed at the same time, with different pistols, yet with only one shot heard. BLUE, WHITE AND PERFECT refers to diamonds, used in defense production, which are stolen by enemy agents. Shayne books passage on a Honolulu-bound liner in pursuit of the spies; Mary Beth fumes on shore.

Three more Shayne films were released in 1942. THE MAN WHO COULD NOT DIE is a melodrama featuring a haunted mansion, a missing millionaire, a slashing thunderstorm, and a midnight burial. In JUST OFF BROADWAY, Shayne as a member of the jury sees a witness while testifying on the stand, killed by a thrown knife. He sneaks out of the rooms where the jury has been locked for the night to search for the killer, and then, in a dazzling courtroom session, points out the murderer from the jury box. TIME TO KILL, the last Shayne with Lloyd Nolan, was a reworking of Raymond Chandler's "The High Window."

In 1946, three Mike Shayne thrillers were made by PRC Studios, starring Hugh Beaumont. MURDER IS MY BUSINESS requires Mike to solve the killing of a playboy, to clear his own name. In LARCENY IN HER HEART, Mike sets out to find the missing stepdaughter of a politician. A girl answering her description is being held prisoner in a sanatorium—to which Mike promptly has himself committed. A crusading newspaperman is shot in BLONDE FOR A DAY, and Mike runs into a few very dangerous ladies in the course of his investigations.

Mike Shayne (still played by Beaumont) made his last two screen appearances in 1947. THREE ON A TICKET opens with a fellow private eye falling dead in Mike's office. A baggage check found on his body provides a trail leading either to stolen bank loot or to plans for a top secret weapon. The final film, TOO MANY WINNERS, is set at a racetrack where a gang is counterfeiting parimutuel tickets; the gang leader commits suicide before Mike can expose him.

SPADE★, SAM

The quintessential private eye of the 1930's, Dashiell Hammett's Sam Spade has had a curious cinematic history. THE MALTESE FALCON has been filmed three times. Only the last is remembered, yet the first version, made in 1931 (a year after the book was published) won excellent reviews. Ricardo Cortez made a dark, serious Sam Spade—finding his partner murdered, setting out in pursuit of the jewel-encrusted falcon statuette, and bringing the girl he loves, Brigid O'Shaughnessy● (Bebe Daniels) to trial, with a surprise eyewitness to pin the crime on her.

There were changes in more than the title in the 1936 version, SATAN MET A LADY. Instead of a falcon, the prize is a horn supposedly filled with diamonds. In Spade's place, debonair Ted Shayne (Warren William) is a private eye who tries to double-cross everybody to get the horn for himself. After much comedy banter with Bette Davis, he makes love to her to get a confession that she killed his partner, planning to turn her in for a $10,000 reward. She gives herself up, and the horn turns out to be filled with ordinary stones. The "Fat Man" part later to be played by Sidney Greenstreet was portrayed in this version by Allison Skipworth.

John Huston's 1941 version of THE MALTESE FALCON is, for many, the definitive private eye motion picture. Much of its success is due, undoubtedly, to Humphrey Bogart's dour, haunted Sam Spade, tight-lipped as he investigates his partner's murder, very much in love with Mary Astor, wary in his dealings with the eccentric, neurotic criminals portrayed memorably by Peter Lorre, Elisha Cook, Jr., and Sidney Greenstreet. So definitive are both the film and the performances that there has not yet been another Sam Spade screen case.

Spade was, however, the hero of a long-lived popular radio series. As played by Howard Duff, he was considerably less dour as he started each program with a telephone call to his secretary, Effie, and ended every show with, "Period. End of report."

In 1975 George Segal portrayed the detective's offspring, Sam Spade Jr., still after the falcon statue in the comedy, THE BLACK BIRD. Secretary Effie and the gunsel turn up once more as well. At the movie's finish the statue is being carried off by a shark along the botton of the ocean.

SPIDER★, THE

R. T. M. Scott's pulp magazine creation, The Spider ("Master of Men") was translated to the screen in 1936 by Columbia, in the 15 chapter serial THE SPIDER'S WEB. An aggressive, enthusiastic Warren Hull played the role of the blackclad mystery figure, alter ego of criminologist Richard Wentworth.

The Spider's antagonist is The Octopus, a white-hooded, crippled, four-armed figure ruling a criminal empire from a large desk in a secret Gothic meeting room, who seeks "supreme power" through an orgy of destruction. In a second secret identity as petty criminal Blinky McQuade, Wentworth gains information on the plans of The Octopus, then drills his team for a counter-attack, led by The Spider with guns blazing.

The Spider blasted his way through a second serial, THE SPIDER RETURNS (1941), this time battling a mystery menace known as The Gargoyle, "backed by millions from a foreign power to wreck our national defense!"

THIRTEENTH GUEST, THE

Typical of the mystery-house melodramas of its day, this 1943 Monogram production harked back to THE CAT AND THE CANARY▲, with its frightened heiress and the stock will which goads a minor relative into eliminating the rest of the family in wholesale lots. On her twenty-first birthday, Marie Morgan is to open and read the will of her late grandfather, in his unused old house, alone at a table set for thirteen guests. Assaulted by a mysterious intruder, she is saved when another relative enters the house. Later, a girl exactly resembling Marie is found murdered at the table. A young private detective hired to protect the girl cannot prevent the murder of three members of the family; he and Marie fall in love, and finally he unmasks the murderer who has been killing off the competition for the million dollar inheritance.

TRACY★, DICK

Four serials have been made from Chester Gould's comic strip police hero, although none of these borrowed much from the strip, besides Dick himself. Even he is changed from a plainclothes cop to an FBI operative. Ralph Byrd played Tracy in all four Republic productions.

The first, DICK TRACY (1937), has him pitted against a mystery villain called variously The Spider and The Lame One. By the end of episode one, this criminal has altered Tracy's brother, through brain surgery, into a gruesome degenerate, and has perfected a sound vibration machine with which to collapse the Golden Gate bridge. Eventually, Tracy saves the bridge by driving a fleet of trucks onto it, their weight countering the effects of the vibration. In the last serial, DICK TRACY VERSUS CRIME INCORPORATED (1941), an invisible criminal called The Ghost is about to cause a gigantic tidal wave to sweep over Manhattan. Tracy manages to divert the wave, but it takes him until the end of the serial to short-circuit The Ghost's electronic invisibility device and unmask him.

Four feature films based on the Tracy character were made by RKO Pictures, the first two (1945 and 1946) starred Morgan Conway, and the last two (1947) brought Ralph Byrd back to the character. These "B" melodramas remained close to the comic strip, featuring heroine Tess Trueheart, such familiar secondary characters as Shakespearean actor Vitamin Flintheart (patterned, apparently, upon John Barrymore), and such bizarre, sinister villains as Scarface and Cueball. The last of these features, DICK TRACY MEETS GRUESOME (1947), has Boris Karloff as an escaped convict who kills to obtain a paralyzing gas with which to rob banks.

Ralph Byrd also starred as Dick Tracy in a series of early television half-hour programs.

VANCE★, PHILO

S. S. Van Dine's scholar and dabbler in mystery has had a wide range of screen interpretations, and many interpreters, over nearly two decades. Two years after a great success in book form, THE CANARY MURDER CASE■ became a Paramount film (1929) with William Powell as Vance, investigating the murder of a Broadway musical star known as "The Canary." This film was made during the screen's transitional year from silent to sound, and much rests on the dead girl's voice being heard through a locked door. In the same year, Powell again played Vance in THE GREENE MURDER CASE■, the story of a crazed, hate-filled, and apparently doomed family. Early the following year, Powell portrayed Vance in THE BENSON MURDER CASE■, in which a nasty stockbroker is killed. It is a trick murder: a shot rings out, and a body tumbles down the stairs, but Vance reveals that the two events are not necessarily related.

A few months before BENSON, MGM released THE BISHOP MURDER CASE■, with Basil Rathbone (nine years before the English actor was cast as Sherlock Holmes) as a crisp, scholastic Vance. This is the most grotesque of Van Dine's tales, in which an executioner who signs himself "The Bishop" eliminates a group of people in the manner of nursery rhymes:

an arrow shot into the air, Humpty Dumpty falling from a wall, etc.

In the same year, William Powell made a spoof guest appearance as Vance—with Clive Brook as Sherlock Holmes and Warner Oland as Fu Manchu—in one of the skits in PARAMOUNT ON PARADE. Three years later Warner Brothers cast Powell as Vance. The KENNEL MURDER CASE (1933), directed by Michael Curtiz, was a classic screen whodunit: Archer Coe, hated by everyone, is found locked inside a bedroom of his townhouse; he has been shot, stabbed, and his skull is fractured. His missing brother, the chief suspect, is discovered dead in a closet. Vance solves the crimes by careful reconstructions using floor plans and scale models, as camera flashbacks show the murderer's movements.

The next Philo Vance was Warren William, in Warner Brothers' THE DRAGON MURDER CASE (1934), where at a house party a guest dives into the dark Dragon Pool and is never seen again. The following year, MGM renewed its Vance series with European import Paul Lukas as the detective in THE CASINO MURDER CASE. Here, again, an aristocratic family is threatened with extinction as its members are struck down one by one; a particularly cold-blooded murder device is the eye-wash which seeps poison into the brain of a beautiful young girl. In 1936, MGM gave the role to Edmund Lowe, to investigate the weird deaths in THE GARDEN MURDER CASE, where victims seemed to kill themselves deliberately. An especially gruesome moment occurs when a woman hurls herself from the top of a double-decker bus into the traffic below. Clever Philo suspects hypnosis.

Grant Richards was a less cerebral, heartier Vance in a 1937 version of "The Greene Murder Case," remade as NIGHT OF MYSTERY. Warren William played Vance again in 1939, considerably softened by contact with the bewildering comedienne in THE GRACIE ALLEN MURDER CASE, as both try to solve a death at a factory picnic. CALLING PHILO VANCE (1940) had the detective (British-born actor James Stephenson) a member of the United States Secret Service; the plot is an adaptation of "The Kennel Murder Case."

The next film, PHILO VANCE RETURNS (1947) offered a changed Vance, more along the lines of a tough private eye. The mystery, however, was along S. S. Van Dine lines—a playboy and his six ex-wives being eliminated one by one by interesting methods, including a poisoned bubble bath. Alan Curtis played the detective twice more in the same year. In PHILO VANCE'S GAMBLE, he traps a jewel-stealing killer who uses as his weapon a lipstick coated with phosphorus. PHILO VANCE'S SECRET MISSION, in which the detective served as technical advisor to a true-crime pulp magazine and solves a seven-year-old murder problem, was Philo Vance's last screen case. However, attempts are now being made to convert Vance into a television detective.

WHISTLER, THE

A series of mysteries produced in the 1940's by Columbia Pictures had as its unifying theme an unnamed, unseen narrator, who, before introducing his stories, whistled a somber little tune. This secret observer of strange events was borrowed from an extremely successful radio series, which lasted more than a decade. The Whistler delighted in suspense stories about men who turned to crime and came to sticky ends.

In THE POWER OF THE WHISTLER (1945), Richard Dix is a homicidal maniac seeking to present a poisoned birthday cake to the judge who committed him. In THE MARK OF THE WHISTLER (1944)—a story by Cornell Woolrich— a plot to take over a dormant bank account is foiled by a chance sidewalk photograph. In the first film of the series, THE WHISTLER (1944), Dix, depressed by the news of his wife's death, hires someone to kill him, and then learns his wife is still alive.

WITHERS★, HILDEGARDE

Stuart Palmer's spinster schoolteacher sleuth made an extremely successful transfer to the screen in an RKO Pictures series which began in 1932. A great deal of its success lay in the casting of Edna May Oliver as Hildegarde Withers and James Gleason as Inspector Oscar Piper.

The film adventures of Withers and Piper began with THE PENGUIN POOL MURDER■ (1932), when teacher Hildegarde, taking her class on a trip to the Aquarium, found a corpse floating in the penguin tank. In MURDER ON THE BLACKBOARD (1934), a killer roams through Hildegarde's school, a dark, eerie institution, whose cellar had been used by a Prohibition gangster to store quantities of liquor. In MURDER ON A HONEYMOON (1935) several strange deaths on a Catalina honeymoon resort appear to be related to a gangster trial in New York. Considered among the best in the series, this was the last Hildegarde Withers film to feature Miss Oliver; illness forced her to retire.

Helen Broderick created a tougher Hildegarde in MURDER ON A BRIDLE PATH (1936), which found menace in New York's Central Park. In the same year, Zasu Pitts did a scatterbrained Hildegarde Withers in THE PLOT THICKENS, which begins with a fairly routine murder and then moves to a museum from which the priceless Cellini Cup has been stolen. The last Withers and Piper case for the screen was the 1937 FORTY NAUGHTY GIRLS; the title refers to a chorus line.

However, after more than 30 years in retirement, Hildegarde appeared in a television feature, A VERY MISSING PERSON (1971), played by a younger, less spinsterish, but just as crusty Eve Arden.

WONG, MR.

Chinese sleuth James Lee Wong was brought to the screen in 1938 from a series of Hugh Wiley stories in Collier's magazine. The films featured Boris Karloff as the tall, unruffled Mr. Wong, dressed in a black suit or in Oriental robes, reflecting on a case over a pot of scented tea in the study of his Chinatown home.

In MR. WONG, DETECTIVE (1938), the first in the series, a number of industrialists are killed by poisoned gas; a parrot's screech is one of the clues Mr. Wong finds to the murderer's identity. THE MYSTERY OF MR. WONG (1939) takes place at a houseparty whose host, possessor of a historic, stolen sapphire, is murdered, after which the jewel disappears. A Chinese princess is killed at the start of MR. WONG IN CHINATOWN (1939). Rival ship owners and missing Chinese bonds are the subject of DOOMED TO DIE (1940), and in THE FATAL HOUR (1940), the instrument of murder is a complicated hookup between a remote control radio and a standard type of telephone.

Boris Karloff made no more Wong films after 1940, but in the same year the character was revamped so that Keye Luke (who had gained fame as a son of Chan) could play him. Young "Jimmie" Wong in PHANTOM OF CHINATOWN (1940) investigates the deaths of the returned members of an expedition to the Mongolian desert, involved with a scroll showing a large oil deposit there.

INDEX

Listing of categories
alphabetically, by authors,
from Abbot, Anthony
to Yaffe, James.

ABBOT, ANTHONY
Detective:
  Thatcher Colt
Titles:
  About the Murder of the Clergyman's Mistress, 1931
  About the Murder of Geraldine Foster, 1930
  About the Murder of the Night-Club Lady, 1931
ADAMS, CLEVE F.
Detective:
  Rex McBride
Title:
  Sabotage, 1939
ADAMS, SAMUEL HOPKINS
Detective:
  Average Jones
Titles:
  Average Jones, 1911, includes "Man Who Spoke Latin"■
AIRD, CATHERINE
Detective:
  Detective Inspector C. D. Sloan
Titles:
  Henrietta Who?, 1968
  Late Phoenix, 1970
  Religious Body, 1966
  Stately Home Murder, 1969
ALEXANDER, DAVID
Detective:
  Bart Hardin
Titles:
  Dead Man, Dead, 1959
  Die, Little Goose, 1956
  Terror on Broadway, 1954
ALLEN, GRANT
Rogues & Helpers:
  Colonel Clay
Titles:
  African Millionaire, 1897, includes "Diamond Links"■

ALLINGHAM, MARGERY
  Detective:
    Albert Campion
  Titles:
    Allingham Casebook, 1969
    Allingham Minibus, 1973
    Beckoning Lady, 1955
    Cargo of Eagles, 1968
    Case of the Late Pig, 1937
    Casebook of Mr. Campion, 1947
    China Governess, 1962
    Coroner's Pidgin, 1945
    Crime at Black Dudley, 1929
    Dancers in the Mourning, 1937
    Death of a Ghost■, 1934
    Fashion in Shrouds, 1938
    Flowers for the Judge, 1936
    Hide My Eyes, 1958
    Look to the Lady, 1931
    Mind Readers, 1965
    Mr. Campion and Others, 1939
    Mr. Campion, Criminologist, 1937
    Mr. Campion's Falcon, 1970
    Mr. Campion's Farthing, 1969
    More Work for the Undertaker, 1948
    Mystery Mile, 1929
    Police at the Funeral, 1931
    Sweet Danger, 1933
    Tiger in the Smoke■, 1952
    Traitor's Purse, 1941
AMBLER, ERIC
  Detective:
    Dr. Czissar
  Titles:
    "Bird in the Trees"■, 1942
    "Case of the Landlady's Brother," 1949
AMES, DELANO
  Detectives:
    Jane and Dagobert Brown
  Titles:
    For Old Crime's Sake, 1959
    Landscape with Corpse, 1955
    Murder Begins at Home, 1949
    Nobody Wore Black, 1950
    She Shall Have Murder, 1949
ANDERSON, FREDERICK IRVING
  Detectives:
    Deputy Parr & Oliver Armiston

BAILEY, H. C.
  Detectives:
    Joshua Clunk
    Reggie Fortune
  Titles: Joshua Clunk
  Titles: Reggie Fortune

Titles:
  Dear Reckoning, 1943
  King Is Dead on Queen Street, 1945
  "Loaded House," 1950
BOUCHER, ANTHONY
  Detectives:
  Nick Noble
  Fergus O'Breen
  Titles: Nick Noble
  "Black Murder," 1945
  "Crime Must Have a Stop," 1951
  "Girl Who Married a Monster"■, 1954
  Titles: Fergus O'Breen
  Case of the Crumpled Knave, 1939
  Case of the Seven Sneezes■, 1942
BOX, EDGAR
  Detective:
  Peter Sargeant
  Title:
  Death in the Fifth Position■, 1952
BRAMAH, ERNEST
  Detective:
  Max Carrados
  Rogues & Helpers:
  Parkinson
  Karl Von Groot
  Titles:
  Eyes of Max Carrados, 1923
  Max Carrados, 1914, includes
     "Tragedy at Brookbend Cottage"■
  Max Carrados Mysteries, 1927,
     includes "Secret of Headlam Height"■
BRAND, CHRISTIANNA
  Detective:
  Inspector Cockrill
  Titles:
  Green for Danger■, 1944
  Heads You Lose■, 1941
  "Poison in the Cup," 1969
  Tour de Force■, 1955
  "Twist for Twist," 1967
BRANSON, H. C.
  Detective:
  John Bent
  Titles:
  Beggar's Choice■, 1953
  Case of the Giant Killer, 1944
  Fearful Passage■, 1945
  I'll Eat You Last■, 1941

BUSH, CHRISTOPHER
Detective:
Ludovic Travers
Titles:
BUTLER, ELLIS PARKER
Detective:
Philo Gubb
Titles:
CAIN, JAMES M.
Titles:

Mignon, 1962
Mildred Pierce, 1941
Moth, 1948
Past All Dishonor, 1946
Postman Always Rings Twice■, 1934
Rainbow's End, 1975
Root of His Evil, 1951
Serenade, 1937

CANNING, VICTOR
  Detectives:
    Department of Patterns
    The Minerva Club
  Rogues & Helpers:
    Doctor Lin Kang
  Title: Department of Patterns
    "Sunday Fishing Club"■, 1962
  Title: The Minerva Club
    "Ransom of Angelo"■, 1963
  Title: Doctor Lin Kang
    "Death in Australia"■, 1957

CARNAC, CAROL
  Detective:
    Chief Inspector Julian Rivers
  Titles:
    Affair at Helen's Court, 1958
    Copy for Crime, 1951
    Late Miss Trimming, 1956
    Over the Garden Wall, 1949

CARR, JOHN DICKSON
  Detectives:
    Henri Bencolin
    Dr. Gideon Fell
  Titles: Henri Bencolin
    Castle Skull, 1931
    Corpse in the Waxworks, 1932
    Four False Weapons, 1937
    It Walks by Night, 1930
    Lost Gallows■, 1931
  Titles: Dr. Gideon Fell
    Arabian Nights Murder, 1936
    Below Suspicion, 1949
    Black Spectacles, 1939
    Blind Barber, 1934
    Case of the Constant Suicides, 1941
    Crooked Hinge, 1938
    Dark of the Moon, 1967
    Dead Man's Knock, 1958
    Death Turns the Tables, 1941
    Death Watch, 1935

"CARTER, NICHOLAS"
Detective:
CARVIC, HERON
Detective:
CASPERY, VERA
Detective:
CHANDLER, RAYMOND
Detective:

Simple Art of Murder, 1950
Smell of Fear, 1965
CHARTERIS, LESLIE
Detective:
The Saint (Simon Templar)
Titles:
Ace of Knaves, 1937
Alias the Saint, 1931
Angels of Doom, 1931
Avenging Saint■, 1930
Brighter Buccaneer, 1933
Call for the Saint, 1948
Catch the Saint, 1975
Enter the Saint, 1930
Featuring the Saint, 1931
Follow the Saint, 1938
Getaway, 1932
Happy Highwayman, 1939
Last Hero■, 1930
Meet the Tiger■, 1928
Misfortunes of Mr. Teal, 1934
Prelude for War, 1938
Saint Abroad, 1969
Saint and Mr. Teal, 1933
Saint and the Fiction Makers, 1968
Saint and the People Importers, 1970
Saint Around the World, 1956
Saint Errant, 1948
Saint Goes On, 1934
Saint Goes West, 1942
Saint in Europe, 1953
Saint in Miami, 1940
Saint in New York■, 1935
Saint in Pursuit, 1970
Saint Intervenes, 1934
Saint in the Sun, 1963
Saint on Guard, 1944
Saint on the Spanish Main, 1955
Saint on TV, 1967
Saint Overboard, 1936
Saint Returns, 1968
Saint Sees it Through, 1946
Saint Steps in, 1943
Saint to the Rescue, 1959
Saint vs. Scotland Yard, 1932
Senor Saint, 1958
Thanks to the Saint, 1957
Thieves' Picnic, 1937
Trust the Saint, 1962

Titles: The Toff (Richard Rollison)

CRISPIN, EDMOND
  Detective:
    Gervase Fen
  Titles:
CROFTS, FREEMAN WILLS
  Detective:
    Inspector Joseph French
  Titles:

CUMBERLAND, MARTEN
  Detective:
    Saturnin Dax
  Titles:
CUNNINGHAM, A. B.
  Detective:
    Jess Roden
  Titles:
DALY, ELIZABETH
  Detective:
    Henry Gamadge

My Late Wives, 1946
Men Who Explained Miracles, 1963
Night at the Mocking Widow, 1950
Nine—and Death Makes Ten, 1940
Peacock Feather Murders, 1937
Plague Court Murders, 1934
Punch and Judy Murders, 1936
Reader Is Warned, 1939
Red Widow Murders, 1935
Seeing Is Believing, 1941
She Died a Lady, 1943
Skeleton in the Closet, 1948
Third Bullet and Other Stories, 1954
Unicorn Murders■, 1935
White Priory Murders, 1934

DISNEY, DORIS MILES
Detectives:
Jefferson DiMarco
David Madden
Title: Jefferson DiMarco
Method in Madness■, 1957
Titles: David Madden
Mrs. Meeker's Money■, 1961
Unappointed Rounds, 1956

DOYLE, SIR ARTHUR CONAN
Detective:
Sherlock Holmes
Rogues & Helpers:
Irene Adler
Professor James Moriarty
Mycroft Holmes
Mrs. Martha Hudson
Inspector Lestrade
Dr. John H. Watson
Titles:
Adventures of Sherlock Holmes, 1892
Adventure of the Bruce-Partington Plans, 1908
Case Book of Sherlock Holmes, 1927
"Final Problem," 1893
"Greek Interpreter," 1893
His Last Bow, 1917
Hound of the Baskervilles■, 1902
Memoirs of Sherlock Holmes, 1894
Return of Sherlock Holmes, 1905
"Scandal in Bohemia," 1891
Sign of Four, 1890
Study in Scarlet, 1887
Valley of Fear■, 1915

DUBOIS, THEODORA
  Detectives:
    Anne and Jeffrey McNeill
  Titles:
    Death Dines Out, 1939
    Death Is Late to Lunch, 1941
    Death Tears a Comic Strip, 1939
    Death Wears a White Coat, 1938
    Seeing Red, 1954
DU MAURIER, DAPHNE
  Title:
    Rebecca ■, 1938
DURHAM, DAVID
  Rogues & Helpers:
    Fidelity Dove
  Titles:
    Exploits of Fidelity Dove, 1924, includes
      "Meanest Man in Europe" ■
EBERHARDT, MIGNON G.
  Detectives:
    Susan Dare
    Nurse Sarah Keate
  Title: Susan Dare
    Cases of Susan Dare, 1934
  Titles: Nurse Sarah Keate
    Man Missing, 1954
    Murder by an Aristocrat, 1932
    While the Patient Slept, 1930
    Wolf in Man's Clothing, 1942
EGAN, LESLEY
  Detectives:
    Jesse Falkenstein
    Vic Varallo
  Titles: Jesse Falkenstein
    Against the Evidence, 1962
    My Name Is Death, 1964
  Titles: Vic Varallo
    Borrowed Alibi, 1962
    Detective's Due, 1965
    Run to Evil, 1963
EHRLICH, JACK
  Detective:
    Robert W. Flick
  Titles:
    Girl Cage, 1967
    Parole, 1960
    Slow Burn, 1961

FREEMAN, R. AUSTIN
Detective:
Rogues & Helpers:
Titles:
FROME, DAVID
Detective:
Titles:

HAMILTON, DONALD

Detective:

Matt Helm

Titles:

IRISH, WILLIAM
  Titles:
    Deadline at Dawn■, 1944
    I Married a Dead Man■, 1948
    Phantom Lady■, 1942
KANE, HENRY
  Detective:
    Peter Chambers
  Titles:
    Armchair in Hell, 1948
    Death Is the Last Lover■, 1959
    Fistful of Death■, 1958
    Snatch an Eye■, 1967
    Too French and Too Deadly, 1955
    Unholy Trio■, 1967
KEATING, H. R. F.
  Detective:
    Inspector Ganesh Ghote
  Titles:
    Bats Fly Up for Inspector Ghote, 1974
    Inspector Ghote Breaks an Egg, 1970
    Inspector Ghote Caught in Meshes, 1967
    Inspector Ghote Goes by Train, 1971
    Inspector Ghote Hunts the Peacock, 1968
    Inspector Ghote Plays a Joker, 1969
    Inspector Ghote Trusts the Heart, 1972
    Inspector Ghote's Good Crusade, 1966
    Perfect Murder, 1964
KEELER, HARRY STEPHEN
  Detectives:
    Angus MacWhorter
    Tuddleton Trotter
  Titles:
    Case of the Barking Clock■, 1947
    Matilda Hunter Murder, 1932
    Riddle of the Yellow Zuri■, 1930
    Vanishing Gold Truck■, 1941
KEITH, CARLTON
  Detective:
    Jeff Green
  Titles:
    Rich Uncle, 1963
    Taste of Sangria, 1968
KEMELMAN, HARRY
  Detectives:
    Rabbi David Small
    Nicky Welt
  Titles: Rabbi David Small
    Friday the Rabbi Slept Late■, 1964

Saturday the Rabbi Went Hungry, 1966
Sunday the Rabbi Stayed Home, 1969
Wednesday the Rabbi Got Wet, 1976
Title: Nicky Welt
Nine Mile Walk■, 1967
KENDRICK, BAYNARD
Detectives:
Cliff Chandler
Captain Duncan Maclain
Stan Rice
Rogues & Helpers:
Rena Savage
Samuel "Spud" Savage
Title: Cliff Chandler
"Death at the Porthole"■, 1938
Titles: Captain Duncan Maclain
Blind Man's Buff, 1943
Death Knell■, 1945
Odor of Violets, 1941
Out of Control, 1945
Reservations for Death■, 1957
Titles: Stan Rice
Death Beyond the Go-Thru, 1938
Iron Spiders■, 1936
KERSH, GERALD
Rogues & Helpers:
Karmesin
Title:
"Impossible Crime"■, 1954
KING, RUFUS
Detectives:
Reginald De Puyster
Doctor Colin Starr
Lieutenant Valcour
Titles: Reginald De Puyster
"Man Who Didn't Exist," 1925
"Weapon that Didn't Exist," 1926
Title: Doctor Colin Starr
Diagnosis: Murder, 1941
Titles: Lieutenant Valcour
Crime of Violence■, 1937
Murder by the Clock, 1929
KLINGER, HENRY
Detective:
Lieutenant Shomri Shomar
Titles:
Essence of Murder, 1963
Lust for Murder, 1966

MOYES, PATRICIA
  Detective:
    Chief Inspector Henry Tibbett
  Titles:

NOLAN, WILLIAM F.
  Detective:
    Bart Challis
  Title:

OFFORD, LENORE GLEN
  Detective:
    Todd McKinnon
  Titles:

QUENTIN, PATRICK
Detectives:
Titles:
RAWSON, CLAYTON
Detective:
Titles:

REACH, ALICE SCANLON
  Detective:
    Father Crumlish
  Title:
    "Ordeal of Father Crumlish"■, 1963
REEVE, ARTHUR B.
  Detective:
    Craig Kennedy
  Titles:
    Adventuress, 1917
    Atavar, 1924
    Boy Scouts' Craig Kennedy, 1925
    Clutching Hand, 1934
    Craig Kennedy Listens In, 1923
    Craig Kennedy on the Farm, 1925
    Dream Doctor, 1914
    Ear in the Wall, 1916
    Enter Craig Kennedy, 1935
    Exploits of Elaine, 1915
    Film Mystery, 1921
    Fourteen Points, 1925
    Gold of the Gods, 1915
    Kidnap Club, 1932
    Panama Plot, 1918
    Pandora, 1926
    Poisoned Pen, 1912
    Radio Detective, 1926
    Romance of Elaine, 1916
    Silent Bullet■, 1912
    Social Gangster, 1916
    Soul Scar, 1919
    Stars Scream Murder, 1936
    Treasure Train, 1917
    Triumph of Elaine, 1916
    War Terror, 1915
REILLY, HELEN
  Detective:
    Inspector Christopher McKee
  Titles:
    Compartment K, 1961
    Dead for a Ducat, 1939
    Death Demands an Audience, 1940
    Farmhouse■, 1947
    McKee of Centre Street, 1934
    Not Me, Inspector, 1959
RHODE, JOHN
  Detectives:
    Doctor Lancelot Priestley
    Inspector James Waghorn

Rogues & Helpers:
  Superintendent Hanslet
  Harold Merefield
Titles:

RICE, CRAIG
Detectives:
John J. Malone
Bingo Riggs
RINEHART, MARY ROBERTS
Detective:
"Miss Pinkerton" (Nurse Adams)
Title:
ROBESON, KENNETH
Detective:
The Avenger (Richard Henry Benson)

Titles:
  Cargo of Doom, 1943
  Justice, Inc., 1939
  "To Find a Dead Man," 1944
ROEBURT, JOHN
  Detectives:
    Johnny Devereaux
    Jigger Moran
  Titles: Johnny Devereaux
    Hollow Man, 1954
    Tough Cop, 1949
  Title: Jigger Moran
    There Are Dead Men in Manhattan, 1946
ROHMER, SAX
  Detectives:
    Moris Klaw
    Sir Dennis Nayland Smith
  Rogues & Helpers:
    Doctor Fu Manchu
    Doctor Petrie
  Titles: Moris Klaw
    Dream Detective, 1920, includes "Case of
      the Tragedies in the Greek Room" ■
  Titles: Doctor Fu Manchu
    Daughter of Fu Manchu, 1931
    Devil Doctor, 1916
    Drums of Fu Manchu, 1939
    Emperor Fu Manchu ■, 1959
    Fu Manchu's Bride, 1933
    Golden Scorpion, 1919
    Island of Fu Manchu, 1941
    Mask of Fu Manchu ■, 1932
    Mystery of Fu Manchu, 1913
    President Fu Manchu, 1936
    Re-Enter Fu Manchu, 1957
    Secret of Holm Peel and Other Strange Stories, 1970
    Shadow of Fu Manchu, 1948
    Si-Fan Mysteries, 1917
    Trail of Fu Manchu, 1934
    Wrath of Fu Manchu, 1973
ROME, ANTHONY
  Detective:
    Tony Rome
  Title:
    Miami Mayhem, 1960
ROOS, KELLEY
  Detectives:
    Jeff and Haila Troy

SYMONS, JULIAN
  Detective:
    Francis Quarles
  Titles:
    Francis Quarles Investigates, 1960
    Murder! Murder! 1961
    "Pearl among Women," 1968
    "Santa Claus Club," 1967
TAYLOR, PHOEBE ATWOOD
  Detective:
    Asey Mayo
  Titles:
    Amulet of Guilt, 1938
    Asey Mayo Trio, 1946
    Banbury Bog, 1938
    Cape Cod Mystery■, 1931
    Criminal C.O.D., 1940
    Crimson Patch, 1936
    Deadly Sunshade, 1940
    Death Lights a Candle, 1932
    Deathblow Hill, 1935
    Diplomatic Corpse, 1951
    Figure Away, 1937
    Going, Going, Gone, 1943
    Mystery of the Cape Cod Players, 1933
    Mystery of the Cape Cod Tavern, 1934
    Octagon House, 1937
    Out of Order, 1936
    Perennial Boarder, 1941
    Proof of the Pudding, 1945
    Punch with Care, 1946
    Sandbar Sinister, 1934
    Six Iron Spiders, 1942
    Spring Harrowing, 1939
    Three Plots for Asey Mayo, 1942
    Tinkling Symbol, 1935
TEY, JOSEPHINE
  Detective:
    Inspector Alan Grant
  Titles:
    Daughter of Time■, 1951
    Man in the Queue, 1929
    Shilling for Candles, 1936
    Singing Sands, 1953
    To Love and Be Wise, 1950
THAYER, LEE
  Detective:
    Peter Clancy

Titles:
Accessory after the Fact, 1943
Dead Man's Shoes, 1929
Dead Storage, 1935
Doctor S.O.S., 1925
Still No Answer■, 1958

TILTON, ALICE
Detective:
Leonidas Witherall
Titles:
Cut Direct, 1938
Dead Ernest■, 1944
Hollow Chest, 1941

TRAIN, ARTHUR
Detective:
Ephraim Tutt
Titles:
Adventures of Ephraim Tutt, 1930
By Advice of Counsel, 1921
Hermit of Turkey Hollow, 1921
Mr. Tutt Comes Home, 1941
Mr. Tutt Finds a Way, 1945
Mr. Tutt Takes the Stand, 1936
Mr. Tutt's Case Book, 1937
Old Man Tutt, 1938
Page Mr. Tutt, 1926
Tutt and Mr. Tutt, 1920
Tutt for Tutt, 1934
Tut, Tut, Mr. Tutt■, 1923
When Tutt Meets Tutt, 1927
Yankee Lawyer: The Autobiography of
Ephraim Tutt, 1943

TREAT, LAWRENCE
Detective:
Mitch Taylor
Title:
"H as in Homicide"■, 1964

TUCKER, WILSON
Detective:
Charles Horne
Titles:
Chinese Doll, 1946
Red Herring, 1951
Stalking Man, 1949

UHNAK, DOROTHY
Detective:
Christie Opara

WILLIAMS, VALENTINE
  Detective:
    Trevor Dene
  Titles:
    Clue of the Rising Moon, 1924
    Masks Off at Midnight, 1934
WOODS, SARA
  Detective:
    Anthony Maitland
  Titles:
    And Shame the Devil, 1967
    Bloody Instructions, 1962
    Case Is Altered, 1967
    Done to Death, 1974
    Enter Certain Murders, 1966
    Enter the Corpse, 1973
    Error of the Moon, 1963
    Improbable Fiction, 1970
    Knavish Crows, 1971
    Knives Have Edges, 1968
    Let's Choose Executors, 1966
    Malice Domestic, 1962
    Past Praying For, 1968
    Serpent's Tooth, 1971
    Tarry and Be Hanged, 1969
    They Love Not Poison, 1972
    Third Encounter, 1963
    This Little Measure, 1964
    Though I Know She Lies, 1965
    Trusted Like the Fox, 1964
    Windy Side of the Law, 1965
    Yet She Must Die, 1973
WOOLRICH, CORNELL
  Titles:
    "Beyond the Night," 1959
    Black Alibi, 1942
    Black Angel, 1943
    Black Curtain, 1941
    Black Path of Fear, 1944
    Bride Wore Black■, 1940
    "Dark Side of Love," 1965
    Death Is My Dancing Partner, 1959
    "Hotel Room," 1958
    "Nightmare," 1956
    "Nightwebs," 1971
    Rendezvous in Black, 1948
    Savage Bride, 1950
    "Ten Faces of Cornell Woolrich", 1965
    "Violence," 1958

WYLIE, PHILIP
  Detective:
    Willis Perkins
  Title:
    "Perkins Finds $3,400,000"■, 1931
YAFFE, JAMES
  Detectives:
    Paul Dawn
    Mom
  Title: Paul Dawn
    "Problem of the Emperor's Mushrooms"■, 1945
  Titles: Mom
    "Mom in the Spring," 1954
    "Mom Sings an Aria"■, 1966